IMAGES
of America

JEFFERSONVILLE
INDIANA

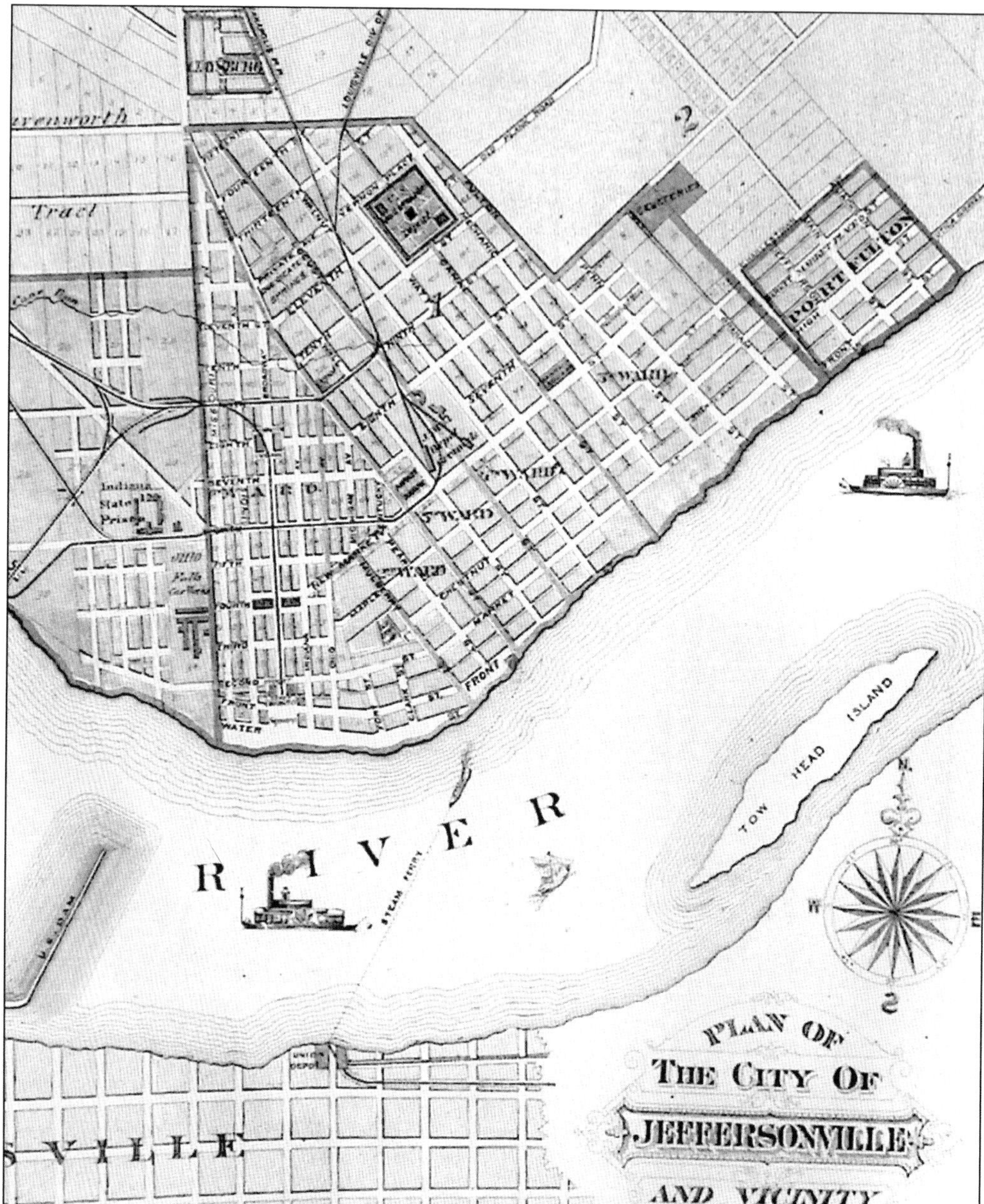

THE CITY OF JEFFERSONVILLE AND VICINITY IN 1876. (Photo: Author's collection)

ABOUT THE COVER. The Schimpff family, inside their confectionery on Spring Street in 1913, have placed their goods on high shelves in anticipation of the Ohio River's rising floodwaters, a measure familiar to Jeffersonville's residents throughout the city's history. Pictured from left to right, starting from the back cover, are Charles (brother of Gustav Sr.), Gustav Sr., Catherine (held by her father), Gustav Jr., Weber, Louisa, and Christine Schimpff. The March/April 1913 swell crept only 60 feet up Spring Street, but the Great Flood of 1937 would rise 22 feet over it, as a mark on Schimpff's attests today. (Photo: Schimpff's Confectionery)

IMAGES
of America

JEFFERSONVILLE INDIANA

Garry J. Nokes

ARCADIA
PUBLISHING

Copyright © 2002 by Garry J. Nokes
ISBN 978-0-7385-2041-4

Published by Arcadia Publishing
Charleston, South Carolina

Printed in the United States of America

Library of Congress Catalog Card Number: 2002112076

For all general information contact Arcadia Publishing at:
Telephone 843-853-2070
Fax 843-853-0044
E-mail sales@arcadiapublishing.com
For customer service and orders:
Toll-Free 1-888-313-2665

Visit us on the Internet at www.arcadiapublishing.com

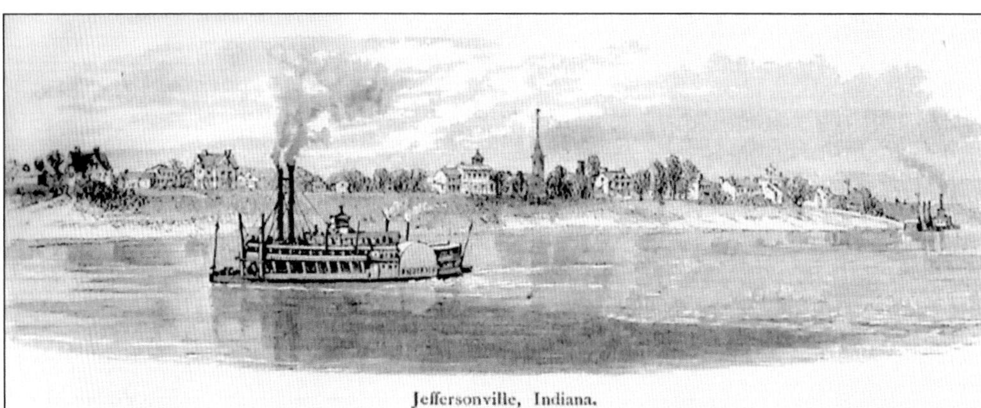

THE CITY OF JEFFERSONVILLE IN 1872. Prominent artist Alfred R. Waud, famous for his Civil War illustrations, engraved this image of Jeffersonville's riverfront for the very popular travelogue *Picturesque America; or, the Land We Live In*, published in 1872. (Photo: Author's collection)

Contents

ACKNOWLEDGMENTS

Jeffersonville has a solid base of those who believe firmly in the value of local history. I owe a debt of thanks to all those individuals and organizations who assisted me in my research for this book and who shared their photographs, expertise, and assistance. Their contributions added immeasurably to this project and their kindness made this book a pleasure to write.

I appreciate the tremendous help of the following individuals: Martha Beatty, Edwin "Huck" Coots, Dennis and Debbie Duffy, Doddie Ellis, Debbie Hannon, Charles and Mimi Heuser, John and Katherine Huddle, Matt Jacobs, William Keeney, Sandy Knott, Charles R. Leap, Tom McCartin, Troy McCormick, Naomi Mitchell, Charles Money, Melody Money, Peggy Nokes, Ned Pfau, Violet Rogers, Bruce "Corky" Scales, Warren and Jill Schimpff, Bill Scott, Terry Stackhouse, Conrad and Judy Storz, Gus Vissing, Jack Vissing, Bob and Jeannie Weber, and Bill Whittaker.

I also thank the following organizations who offered their collections and assistance: Skip Schipper and American Legion Post 35; the Clarksville Historical Society; Bryan Bear and Clark Memorial Hospital; Pat Hoehn and the Cornerstone Group; Sharon Bidwell and the *Courier-Journal*; Thomas Lindley and the *Evening News*; Becky Rice and the Filson Historical Society; Yvonne Knight and the Howard Steamboat Museum; Susan Sutton and the Indiana Historical Society; Jill Costill and the Indiana State Library; Gabriel Swift and Indiana University—Bloomington; Donna Schmink and the Indiana War Memorials Commission; Ron Grimes and the Jefferson County Historical Society; Chief Mike Smith and the Jeffersonville Fire Department; Jay Ellis and Jeffersonville Main Street Inc.; Head of Reference Ilona Franck, volunteer Donna Foster, and the other reference librarians at the Jeffersonville Township Public Library; Jerry Herndon and the Kentucky Board of Architects; the Library of Congress; the National Archives and Records Administration; Sellersburg Public Library; James C. Anderson, Susan Knoer, and the University of Louisville Photographic Archives; and Vicksburg National Military Park.

I appreciate the kindness extended to me on behalf of the following individuals and churches: Rev. Billy Paul Branham and William Branham Ministries; Betty Posey and the First Baptist Church; Rev. Joel Duffield and the First Christian Church; Marleen Hall and the First Presbyterian Church; Rev. Dismas Veeneman, Pat Bullerdick, and St. Anthony of Padua Church; John Thompson and St. Augustine Church; Dee Simpson and St. Luke's United Church of Christ; Sonny McCullough and St. Paul's Episcopal Church; and Miriam Abbott and Wall Street United Methodist Church.

I want to recognize the work of local historians Carl Kramer, Jane Sarles, and Jeanne Burke, whose writings and other work have provided this young historian with information and inspiration. Their examples demonstrate that local history is a worthwhile and important pursuit. I want to thank my editor, Samantha Gleisten, and the rest of the staff at Arcadia Publishing for sponsoring this project and for providing their great assistance along the way.

I offer great thanks to my aunt, Susan O'Neal, whose knowledge of the community and contacts in it greatly improved this book. I offer the deepest thanks to my father, Garry Jack Nokes, who accompanied me through much of my research. I depended on his photographic expertise and other assistance and enjoyed his companionship. In a special way, I thank my wife, Joanne, for her support through this project, and my "junior research assistants," Mary and Matthew, for their patience and understanding.

Introduction

We love our stories in Jeffersonville. We live in a Yankee state, according to our southern friends, but Jeffersonville has much in common with the South. Many who live in Jeffersonville today can trace their ancestry back in a line that extends through Kentucky, Tennessee, and Virginia, on account of the settlement patterns at work here. Jeffersonville's location and commercial history may place us firmly in the North, but we have the South to thank for our slower-paced lifestyle that allows us time to appreciate a good story. We also live in a river community perched on that great artery winding from the eastern part of the nation into the heartland. The Ohio River itself—with its floods, ice gorges, and barriers to navigation (like the Falls of the Ohio just downstream)—provides fodder enough for countless tales. Add to that the accumulated experience of the many river veterans who have passed or dwelled on these shores and our love of a good story makes even more sense.

Jeffersonville has so many stories to tell. The city's illegal but nevertheless wide-open gambling parlors shocked the upright and attracted nearly everyone else during the 1930s and 40s. Meanwhile, Jeffersonville's "marrying squires" drew young couples eager to get an uncomplicated start in life and angered couples' folks back home—often in rural Kentucky—who cursed the marriage parlors. The city's military contributions have aided the nation's war efforts, such as caring for the injured and dying at the Civil War-era Jefferson General Hospital, sewing uniforms at the Quartermaster Depot, and even serving and dying in the ultimate act of patriotism. Always weaving its way through the city's history is the Ohio River and Jeffersonville's attempts to profit from it, get across it, have fun on it, and, sometimes, get away from it.

Readers of *Images of America: Jeffersonville, Indiana* may approach this book in any number of ways. Genealogists will look for familiar names and places. They may find their ancestors, but more likely will discover new details to flesh out the total story of their family tree beyond the names. Where did their ancestors worship? How did they get around the city? What faces did they see across the counter when they went to market? Anyone with even a casual interest in local history will look for information that will add to their understanding of the city. Jeffersonville is known for its manufacturing of steamboats and railcars, but did the city really manufacture locomotives? Everyone has heard of Arthur Loomis, the Jeffersonville architect who designed several of the city's most prominent buildings, but what did he look like? Those interested in military history will appreciate this book's extensive coverage of Jeffersonville's military significance. Why was there a fort at the future site of Jeffersonville? How did the nation's supreme conflict, the Civil War, affect Jeffersonville? Why was the Quartermaster Depot here and what did it do? Preservationists will approach this book with both pride and sadness. What are Jeffersonville's oldest or most unique structures and why are they significant to the history of the city? What has Jeffersonville lost and why?

The first seven topical chapters in this book tell the stories of Jeffersonville though images and captions from the earliest days of settlement through to about 1937. Captions themselves cannot address each subject comprehensively in what is primarily a pictorial work. Rather, the observant reader will approach these photographs with an imaginative eye. One reader may almost smell the fresh pine scent of the knotty boards visible in newly constructed army installations throughout Jeffersonville in the chapter on the military. Another may hear the calliope whistling its tune over the blaring voices of those cheering the steamer *America* as acrid smoke billows from its stacks in the famous 1928 race depicted in the last chapter. Readers should approach this book as a stimulant and let the photographs carry their thoughts to a different world.

The book's primary subject matter ends with the Great Flood of 1937, for it changed Jeffersonville in so many ways. "I think for a long time afterwards," remembered Francis Beard, quoted in *Mud, Sweat and Tears*, an oral history of the disaster, "people would date things—this happened before the flood or after the flood. . . . Your whole life, everything you did was built around that flood—starting all over again." So many of Jeffersonville's families lost their most precious possessions, not money or goods but photographs, heirlooms, and papers. This book may stand in as a kind of partial replacement, substituting the kindness of those who could share what survived from their own collections for the cruelty of the ravaging Ohio.

The content in this book has been driven, obviously, by which photographs are still available, but the author has ranged far and wide to collect the over 200 images included here, many of which have never been published before. The author has compensated for the ravages of time and its many ways of damaging photographs by enhancing the images by computer. A number of photographs, including some preserved by the Indiana Historical Society, have suffered great damage. In no case did the author alter any historical details.

The last chapter in this book looks at some of the ways that elements from pre-flood Jeffersonville either changed or disappeared entirely in the following years. Some of this chapter's subjects address cultural changes, such as the end of gambling and the removal of the toll on the Municipal Bridge, but most deal with the loss of the city's historic fabric. Natural disasters, commercial disinterest, and a genuine but misguided desire for "renewal" conspired to deprive Jeffersonville of many historic structures. First, Mother Nature's capricious cruelty has done much damage in the form of floods and fires. Structures stricken by natural forces often endure damage beyond repair, but owners and community leaders can sometimes restore buildings to their finery, as in the case of the Howard mansion and the Grisamore house. Second, businesses seeking to expand have sometimes found it easier to tear down and build anew, rather than incorporate historic structures into their plans. Success stories include the Cornerstone Group's reuse of the old car works and the many businesspeople on Spring Street who have adapted old storefronts or rebuilt empty lots to match the historic feel of a block. Third, the urban renewal era beginning in the 1960s spirited away much of historic Jeffersonville. Adherents of the philosophy did not seek wholesale destruction, per se, but rather sought genuinely to improve the city. "[S]parkling new dwellings, stores and factories go up in Jeffersonville every day," crowed the *Courier-Journal* in the 1960s, echoing the prevailing attitude that newer is better. Granted, community leaders faced a difficult task; witness the great obstacles recently to the redevelopment of one of the city's most historic structures, the old Quartermaster Depot.

More people today agree that historic buildings merit preservation than perhaps ever before. We understand that historic structures are more than just their constituent bricks and mortar, but rather the physical symbol of the accumulated stories of everyone who has lived, worked, or visited them. Rather than spend time wringing our hands over the losses of the past, we must look forward to safeguarding and showcasing what is left. Those who learn and appreciate the stories of local history will feel the most invested in its preservation.

One

Living

People and Places

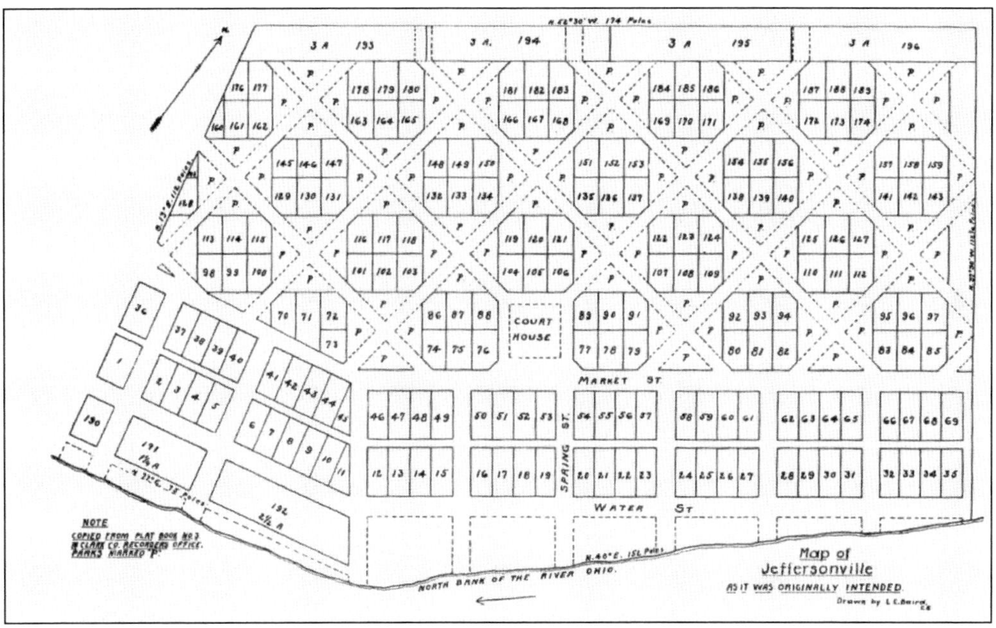

Jefferson's Plan for the City. President Thomas Jefferson designed a unique plan for Jeffersonville consisting of a checkerboard with alternating vacant and developed squares. He envisioned that the open squares, planted with "trees and turf," would create an aesthetically pleasing layout and cleanse the air from "the miasmata which produces yellow fever." Attorney John Gwathmey, however, drew up the actual plan and substituted a diagonal arrangement of streets over Jefferson's plan, resulting in the scheme depicted here in historian Lewis Baird's reconstruction. Gwathmey's changes made the plan unworkable and Jeffersonville replatted its streets in 1817. (Photo: *Baird's History of Clark County*)

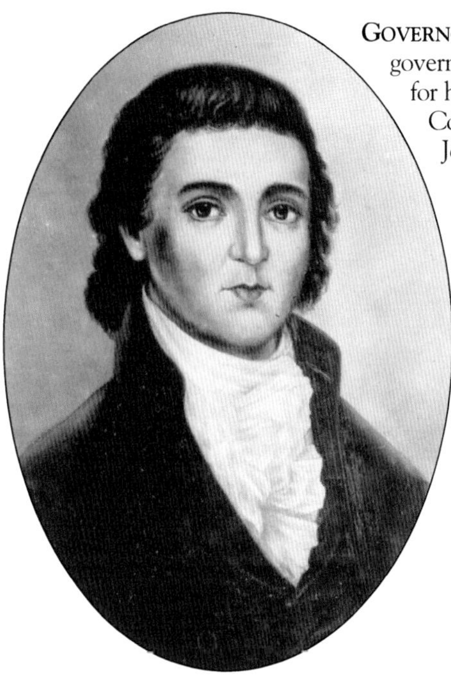

GOVERNOR THOMAS POSEY. Indiana's third and last territorial governor, Thomas Posey, chose Jeffersonville as his home for his term from 1813 to 1816. He is said to have disliked Corydon, the territory's official capital, preferring instead Jeffersonville, for its proximity to his personal physician in Louisville. Posey's mansion occupied the west corner of Front (now Riverside Drive) and Fort Streets. The home hosted one of Jeffersonville's most famous guests, the Marquis de Lafayette, who visited in 1825. Fire destroyed the mansion in 1845. (Photo: Indiana Historical Society)

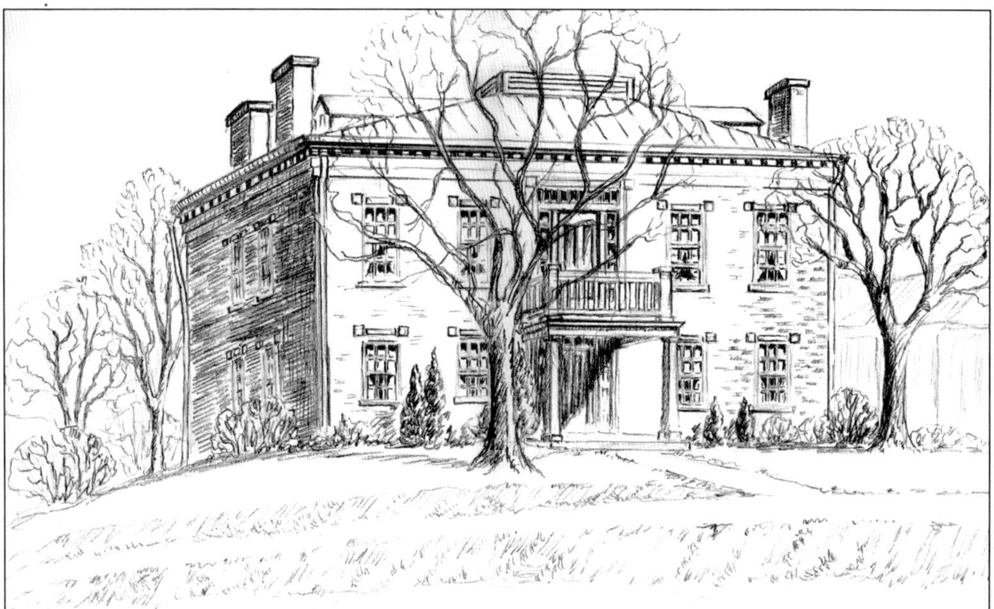

CHALYBEATE SPRINGS. Northwest of today's Eleventh Street and alongside namesake Spring Street, flowed the mineral waters of Jeffersonville's chalybeate (iron-containing) springs. John Fischli, a Swiss immigrant who owned the land, discovered the water's properties, which were described by one source as "very serviceable in many complaints." Fischli built the 13-acre spot into a major summer resort, complete with gambling and other recreation. The drawing above by commercial artist and local historian Walter Kiser depicts a building associated with the site. The Big Four Railroad destroyed the springs property in 1907 when it expanded its facilities in the area. (Photo: Indiana Historical Society)

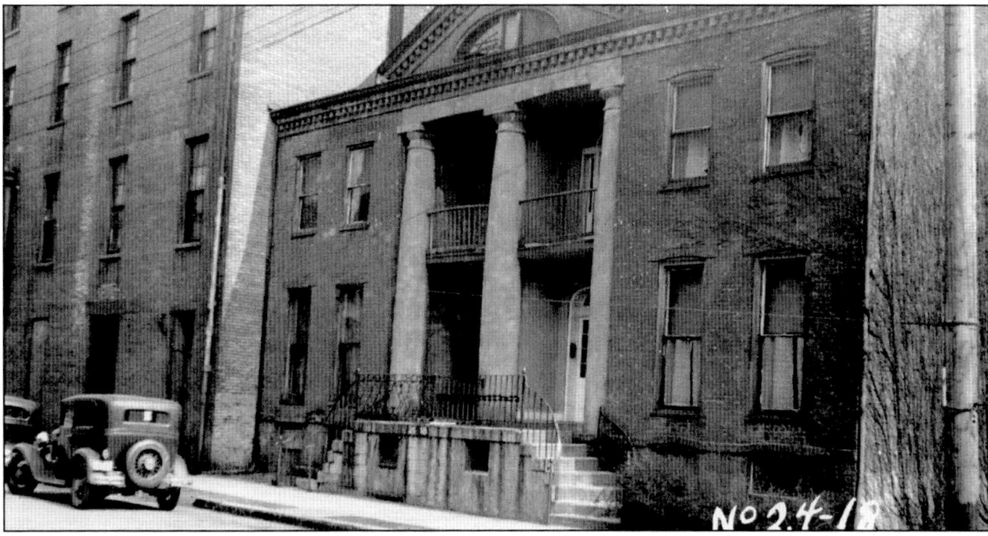

GRISAMORE HOUSE. David and Wilson Grisamore, brothers from Philadelphia, built this double home in 1837 on Chestnut Street just west of Spring Street. In the 1930s, the Historic American Buildings Survey captured this photograph, which shows how the building once adjoined a larger structure, where a garden stands today. A fire nearly destroyed the right half of the home in 1981, but local citizens restored the building, which was placed on the National Register of Historic Places in 1983. (Photo: Library of Congress)

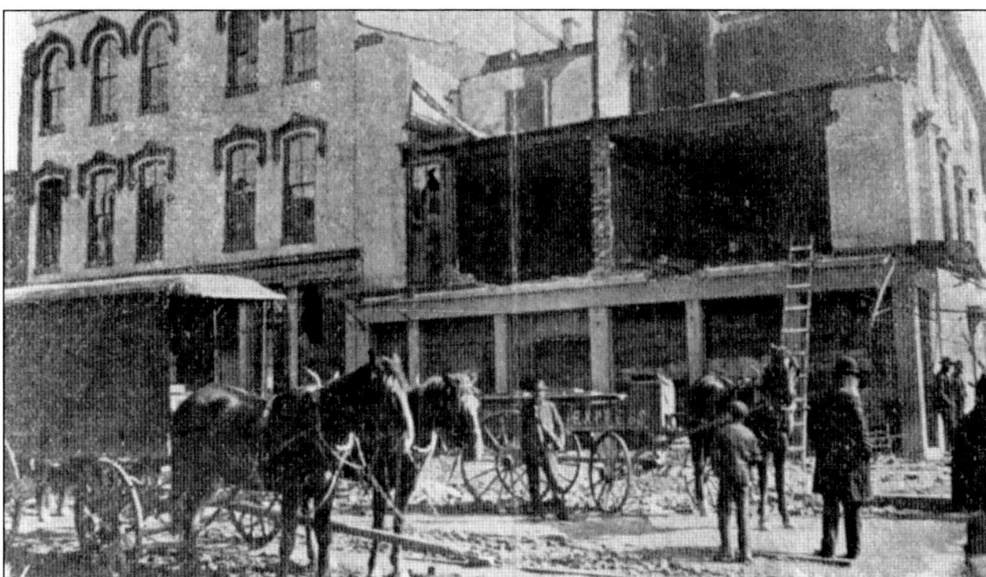

STAUSS HOTEL. The Stauss Hotel, built in the Italianate style in 1867, profited from the river traffic and its prominent spot on the east corner of Spring and Front (now Riverside Drive) Streets. German immigrant William Stauss operated this hotel, and the business remained in his family for 80 years. This image shows the devastation wrought by the cyclone that struck Jeffersonville on March 27, 1890. The cyclone damaged about 200 houses in the city. The hotel survived this storm and a number of floods, but it could not face down the wrecking ball (see page 116). (Photo: Terry Stackhouse)

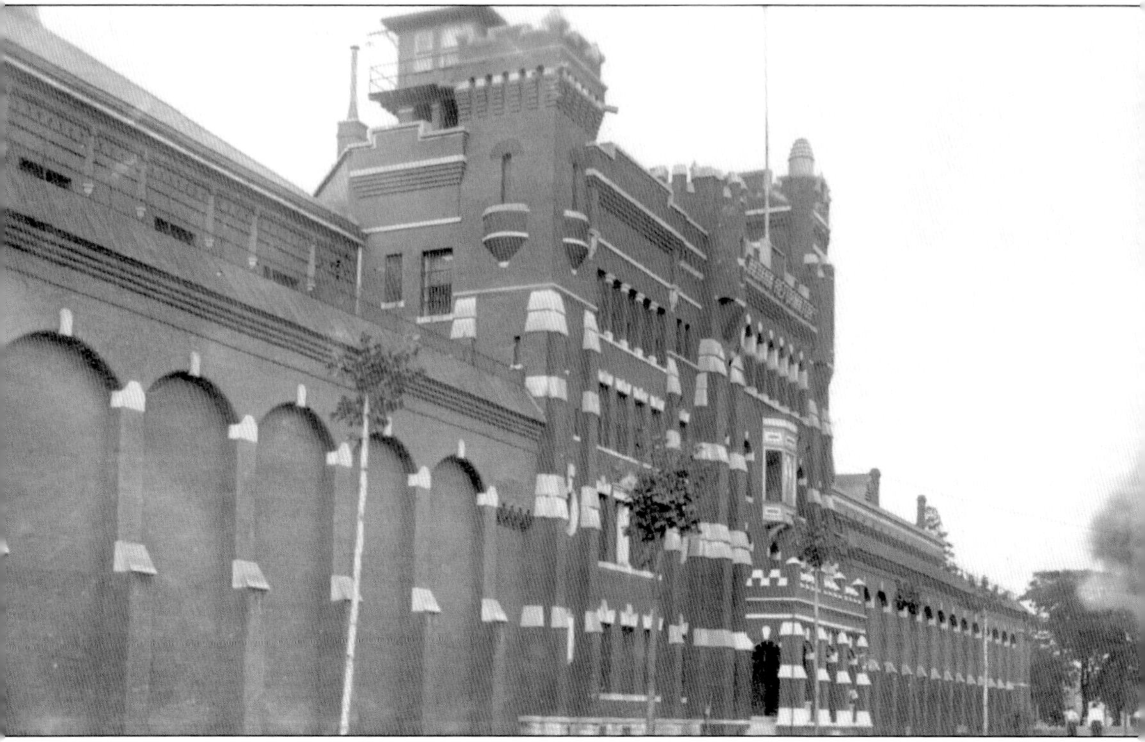

Indiana State Prison. Indiana established its first state prison in Jeffersonville in 1821 at the northeast corner of Market Street and Ohio Avenue. A log cell-house of 15 cells surrounded by a wooden stockade comprised the first structure, later replaced by a brick structure at the same location. In 1847, the state relocated the prison to a new facility in Clarksville, shown above. This Clarksville facility has officially, but erroneously, been described as located in Jeffersonville. The Colgate-Palmolive-Peet Company bought the building and opened a soap manufacturing plant there (see page 78), adding a large clock that can be seen today. (Photo: Howard Steamboat Museum)

Opposite: **City Leaders in the Rauth Administration.** The citizens of Jeffersonville elected Ernest W. Rauth as mayor in 1913. City leaders who took office on January 1, 1914, from left to right, were as follows: (front row) Councilmen E.W. Hydron and H.E. Heaton, Mayor Rauth, and Councilman Luther Childs; (second row, standing) Councilmen John Kipper and Samuel Isler (the only Republican), City Clerk John Snyder, and Councilmen Rudolph Deibel, Thomas Marra, and August Happel (in front of Marra); (rear, behind wreath) City Surveyor Victor Lyons and city hall employee John Chandler. (Photo: Conrad and Judy Storz)

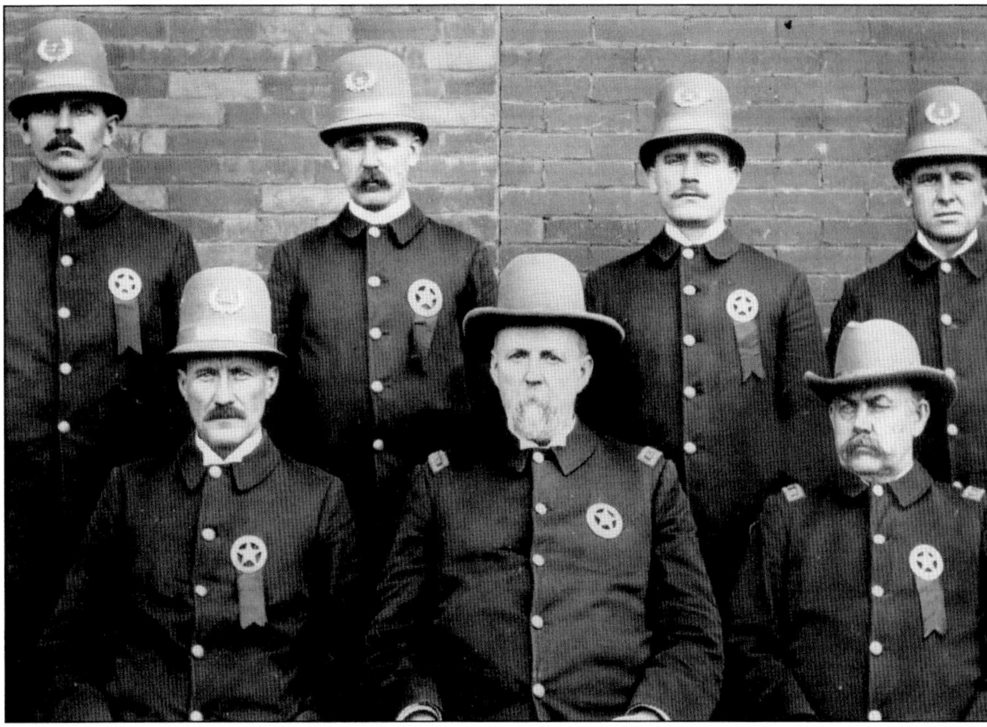

JEFFERSONVILLE POLICE DEPARTMENT. The Jeffersonville Police Department dates to the city's founding in 1802. Pictured from left to right are members of the force in 1899: (front row) Dennis Dunovon, Bill Kendall, Chief Aaron Applegate; (back row) Ed Clegg, Sam Summers, Bill Bruner, and Mike Wall. (Photo: Jeffersonville Township Public Library)

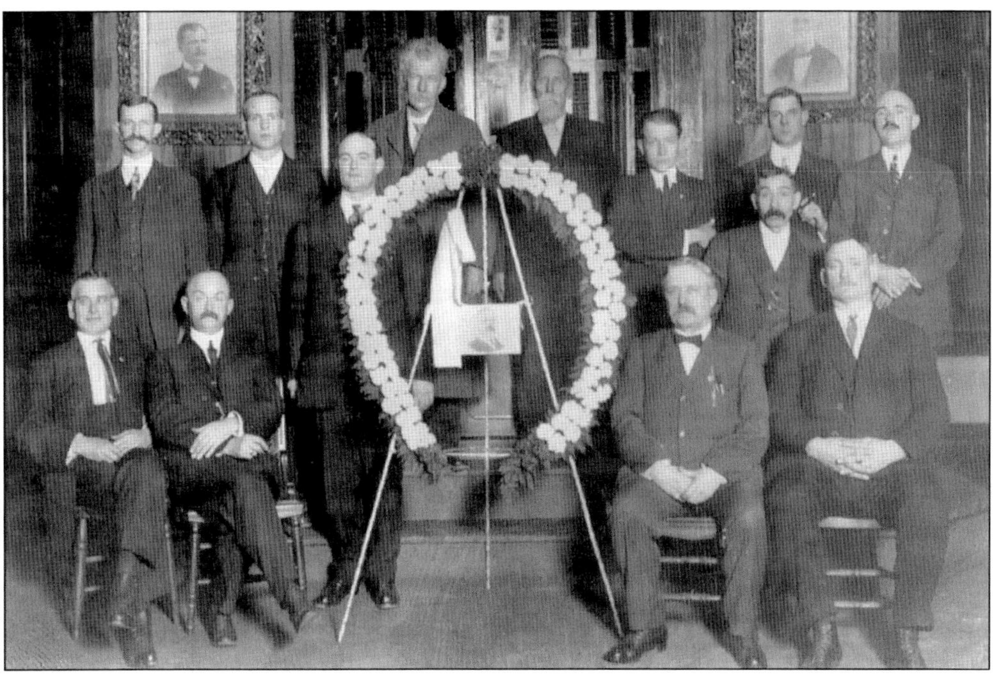

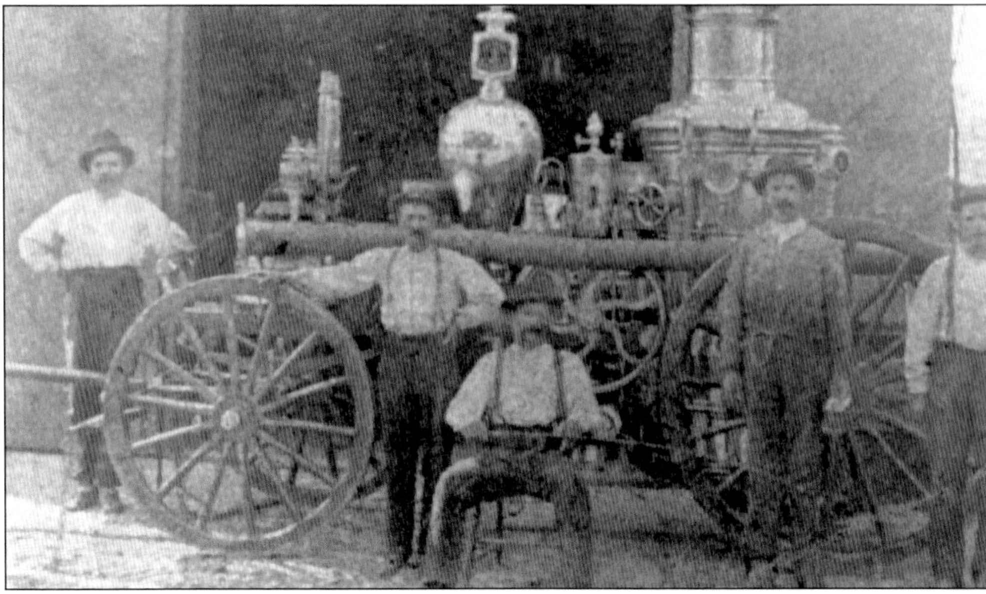

JEFFERSONVILLE FIRE DEPARTMENT. The city organized a fire department in 1835, but it operated more or less as a volunteer "bucket brigade" with limited equipment until July of 1871, when the city council passed an ordinance calling for the department's professionalization. The Great Chicago Fire in October of 1871 no doubt vindicated the city's decision. (Photo: Jeffersonville Fire Department)

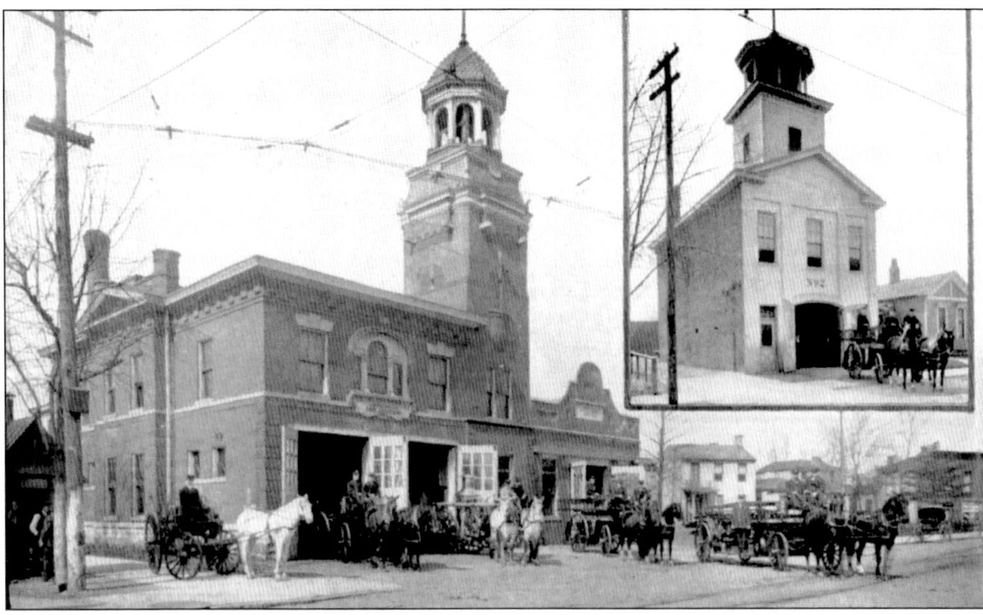

JEFFERSONVILLE'S FIRE STATIONS. Jeffersonville's main fire station occupied the corner of Spring Street and Court Avenue across from Warder Park until it was demolished in the late 1960s during the urban renewal era. The main station and the engine house for Company Number 2 (inset) had tall towers for the dual purpose of drying out hoses and watching for fires in the city. Firemen used to stand watch during the night, ever vigilant against the threat of fire. (Photo: *Souvenir Jeffersonville, Ind.*)

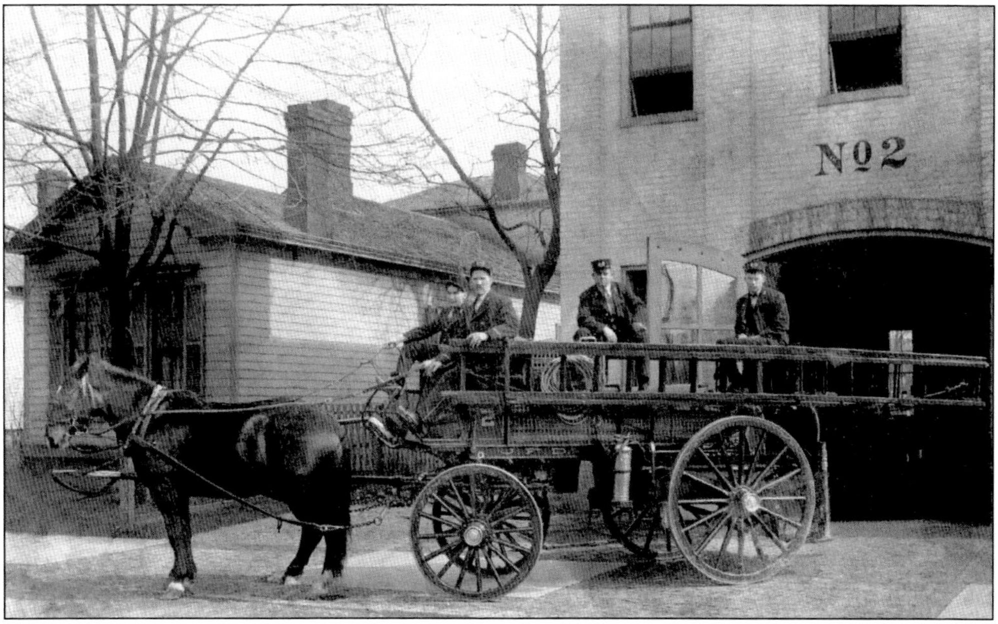

ENGINE COMPANY NUMBER 2. Jeffersonville's second fire station stood on the south side of the 500 block of Chestnut Sreet (a building still there, in altered form). It served as the Number 2 station until the city constructed Crestview Station in the early 1950s. Here the company members sit with their equipment in front of their station in this early 20th century photograph. Hoseman Arthur O'Neal sits at the rig's rear. (Photo: Martha O'Neal Beatty)

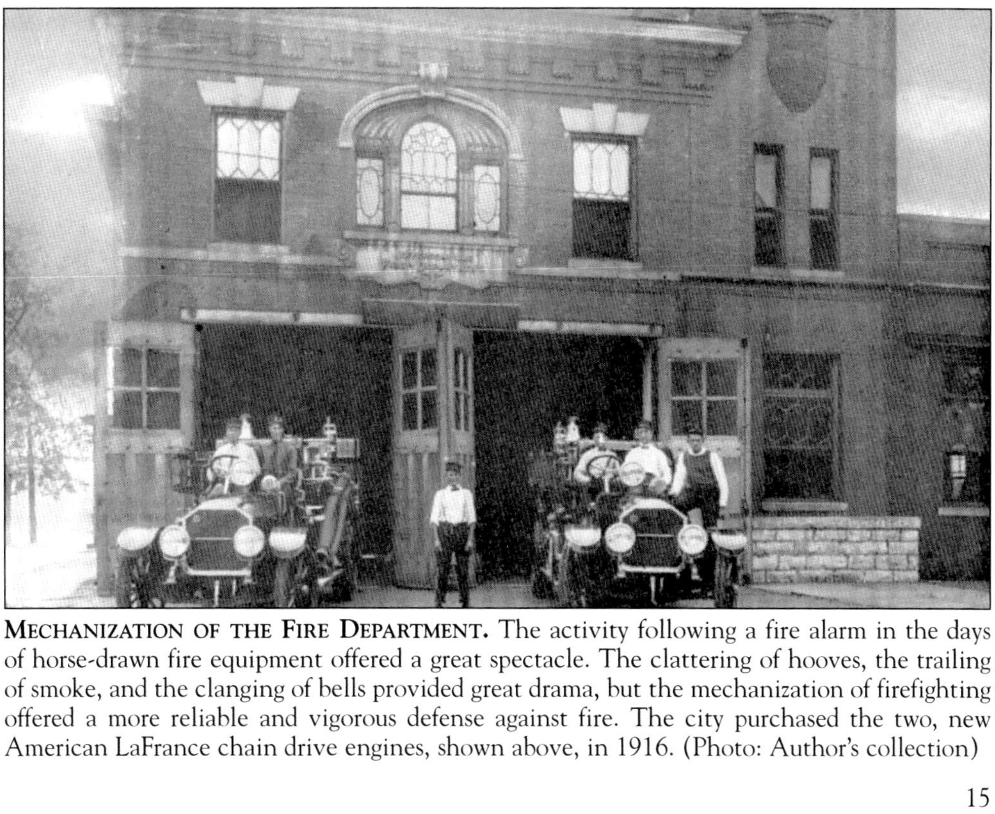

MECHANIZATION OF THE FIRE DEPARTMENT. The activity following a fire alarm in the days of horse-drawn fire equipment offered a great spectacle. The clattering of hooves, the trailing of smoke, and the clanging of bells provided great drama, but the mechanization of firefighting offered a more reliable and vigorous defense against fire. The city purchased the two, new American LaFrance chain drive engines, shown above, in 1916. (Photo: Author's collection)

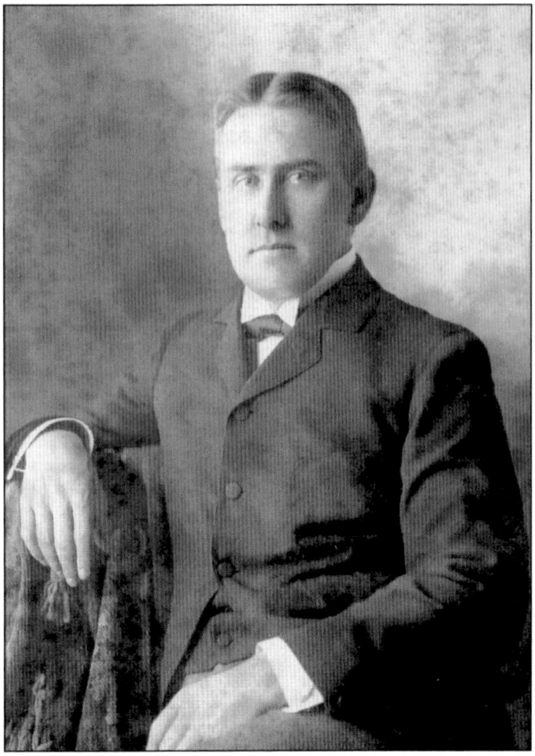

Dr. Charles Hancock. Many of Jeffersonville's older residents remember "Doc" Hancock, who lived from 1867 to 1938. He studied at the University of Louisville for a time, ranking first in his class, and graduated from the Medical College of Ohio at Cincinnati in 1887. After a short stint in Jasper, Indiana, he relocated to Jeffersonville where he continued to practice for 50 years. He also served as state senator in 1905 and 1906. (Photo: Jeffersonville Township Public Library)

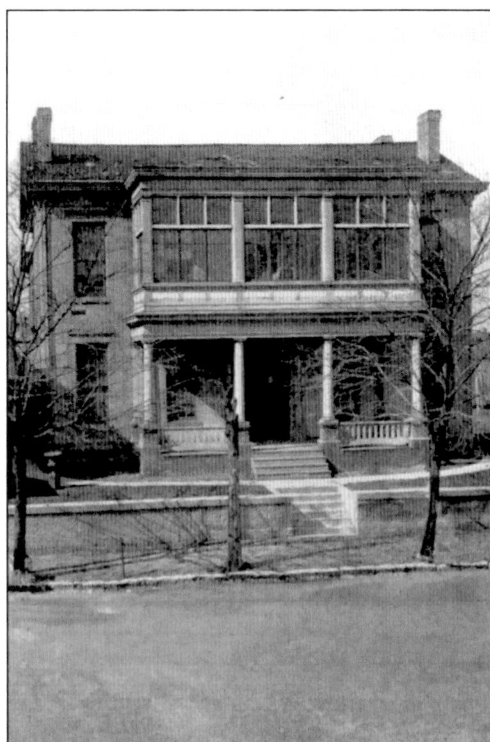

Jeffersonville Hospital. In July of 1892, a group of prominent women met at city hall to plan Jeffersonville's first public hospital. The committee raised funds and purchased the former home of lumber merchant P.F. Myers on Front Street, which they renovated for use as the Jeffersonville Hospital. The Methodist church later operated the facility, known then as Deaconess Hospital, but the institution closed by 1913. The building, in altered form, still stands at 415 East Riverside Drive. (Photo: Clark Memorial Hospital)

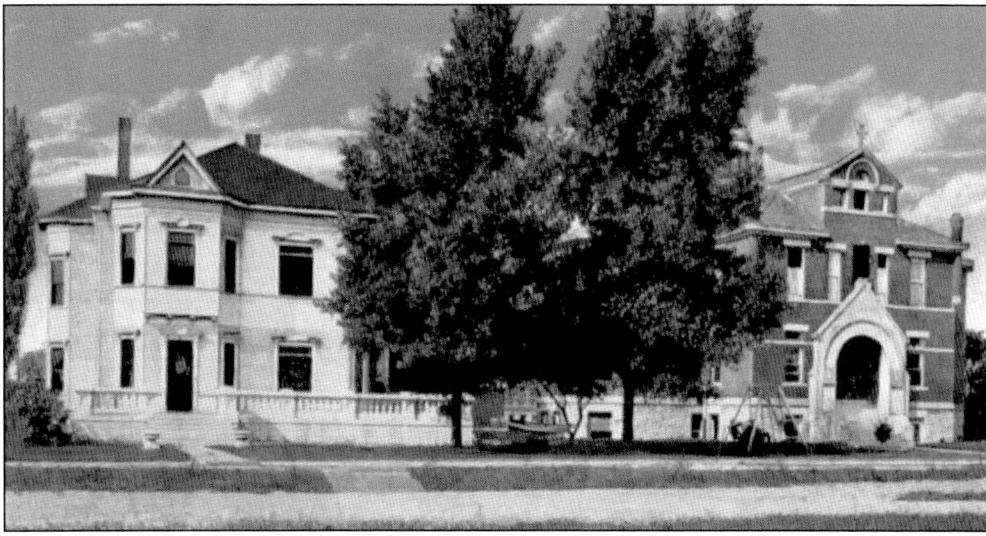

MERCY HOSPITAL AND SANITARIUM. The Sisters of Mercy opened a Roman Catholic hospital in the city in November of 1897 in a small home on East Chestnut Street. In December of 1898, the nuns relocated to a larger facility, the former residence of Mrs. Charles Rogers at Twelfth Street (now Sparks Avenue) and Missouri Avenue, depicted at left. The nuns sought also to care for the mentally ill, so they constructed a new brick facility, depicted at right, as a sanitarium in 1901. Their efforts proved short-lived, for within a few years the hospital and sanitarium closed. (Photo: Clark Memorial Hospital)

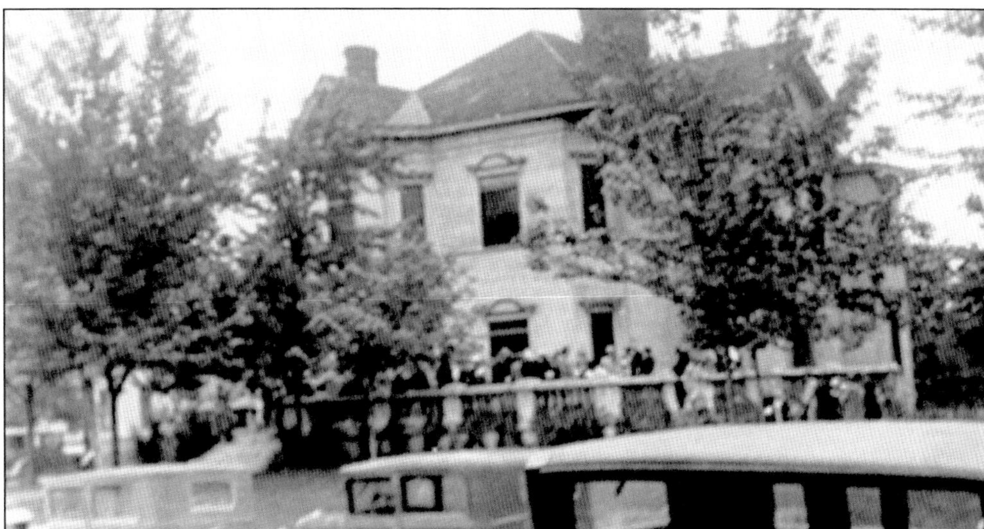

CLARK COUNTY MEMORIAL HOSPITAL. With Jeffersonville's medical facilities both closed, the city's newly formed Rotary Club organized the drive for a new hospital. In 1919, the club began an effort to purchase the former Mercy Hospital building for $45,000, utilizing funds from a special bond and the donations of churches, civic organizations, and local citizens. The hospital's dedication ceremonies on June 15, 1922, seen above, drew "the biggest crowd ever seen in the Spring Hill neighborhood," according to one eyewitness. Organizers dedicated the hospital to the memory of those servicemen who gave their lives in the recent world war. (Photo: Clark Memorial Hospital)

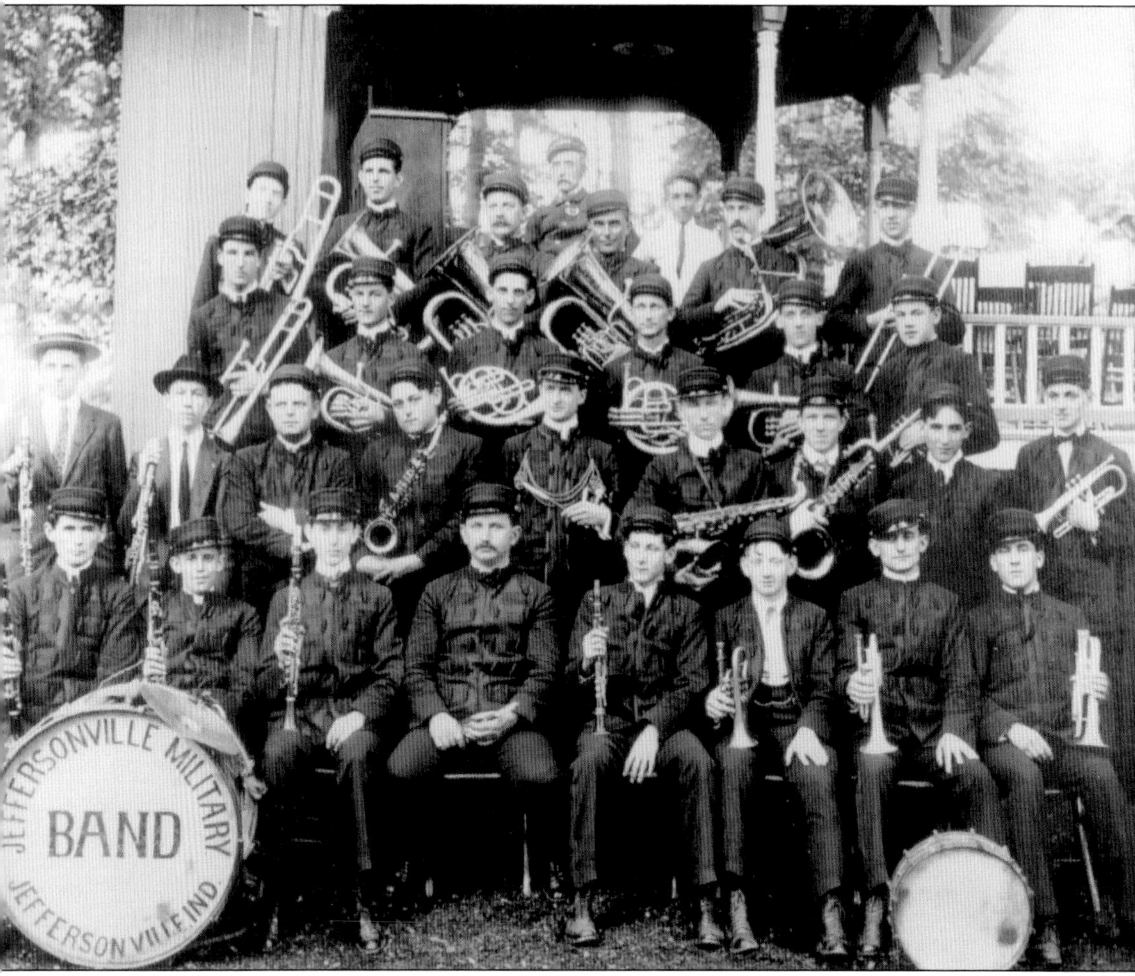

JEFFERSONVILLE MILITARY BAND. The band, pictured here in 1904, performed on many Sunday afternoons and special occasions. Pictured from left to right are the following: (front row) William Humphrey, Addie Knapp, Nick Worrell, Ed Rauth, Dan Smith, George Straw, ? Leibeck, and Norman Howard; (second row) Reuben Knight, Philip Higdon, Charles Williams, Conrad Storz, Prof. Henry H. Dreyer (the conductor), Rutledge Worrell, James B. Prewitt, Rolla Bowman, and William Gallrein; (third row) Charles Duble, Elmer Keeble, Joe Morrow, William Worthington, Lee Mathews, and Tony Cowling; (fourth row) Albert Keller, Froman Coots, Lawrence Keeble, Otto Voit, George Kincaid, and George Smith; (standing in the rear) M. Howell and David Stiglitz (not members of the band). (Photo: E.M. Coots' Sons Funeral Home)

Opposite: **CLARK COUNTY COURTHOUSE.** Territorial Governor William Henry Harrison created Clark County on February 3, 1801. The tiny town of Springville, which has since ceased to exist, served briefly as the first county seat. Jeffersonville became the second seat on June 9, 1802, and the county built a courthouse in the approximate location of the 1881 city hall. Charlestown, laid out in 1808, secured the seat in 1812 but the honor returned to Jeffersonville in 1878 after a bitter fight. The city donated land north of New Market Street (now Court Avenue), between Watt Street and Meigs Avenue for the courthouse above. The building lost its tall cupola and spire in the 1930s after a lightning strike. (Photo: *Souvenir Jeffersonville, Ind.*)

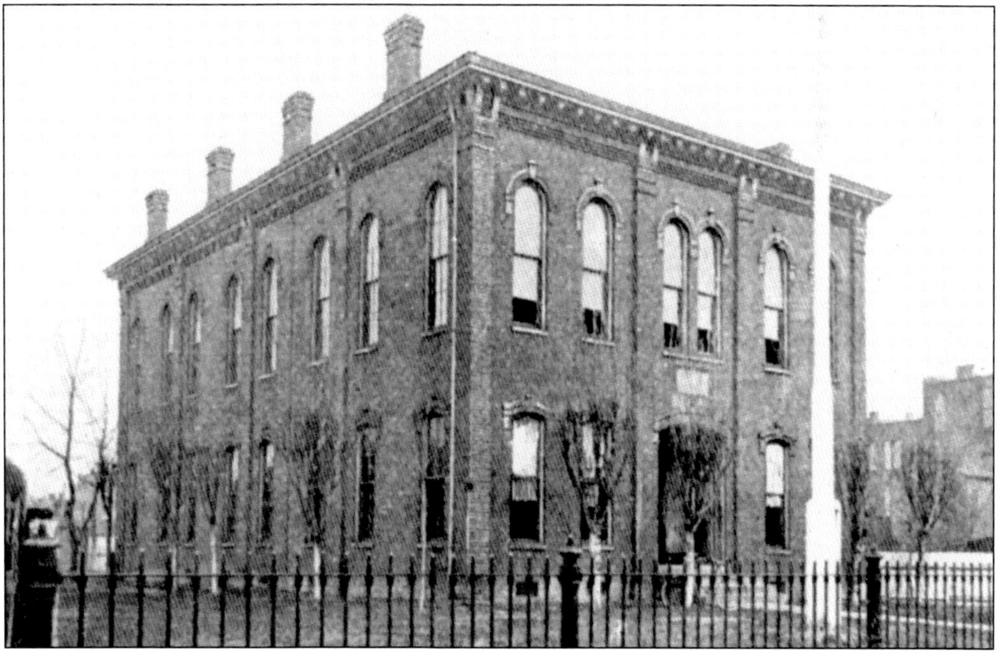

JEFFERSONVILLE CITY HALL. The city constructed this facility, its third city hall, in 1881 during the Luther F. Warder administration. The building sat on the north side of the block on Market Street bounded by Spring and Pearl Streets. City government used the building until 1935, when it moved to the annex of the courthouse, depicted below. (Photo: Jeffersonville Township Public Library)

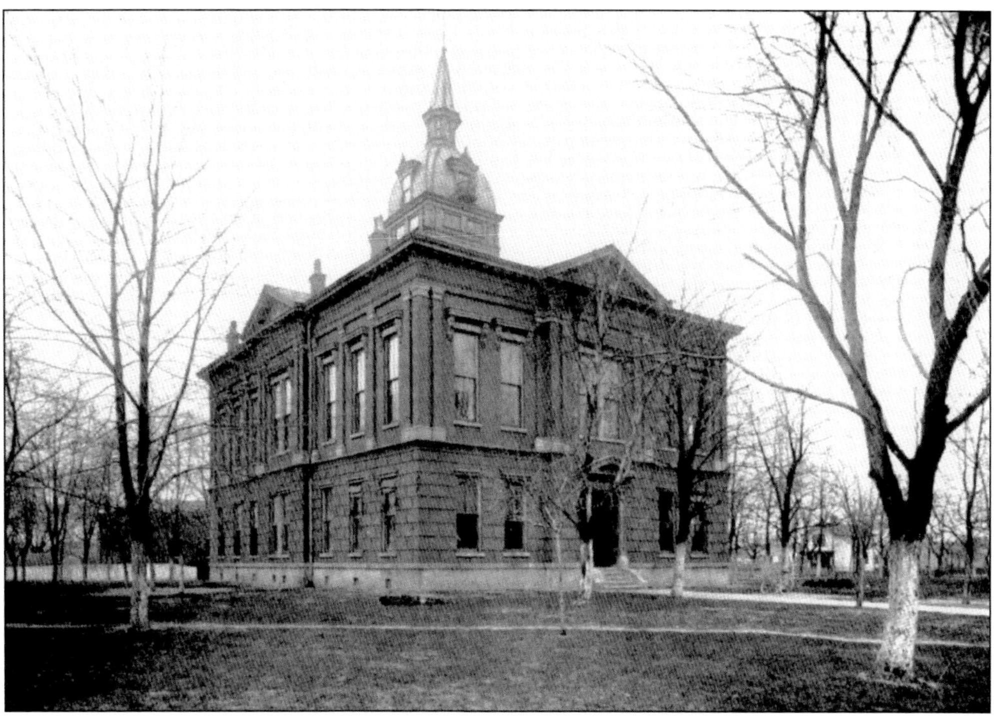

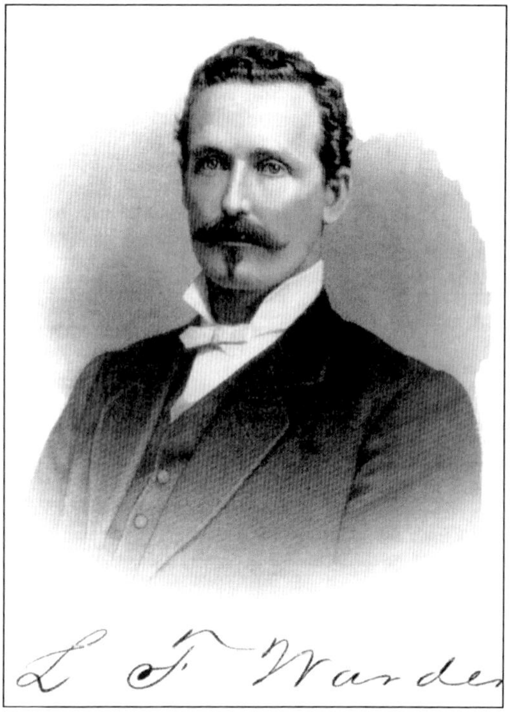

LUTHER F. WARDER. The city of Jeffersonville had in Luther Fairfax Warder one of its hardest-working and most colorful mayors. His administration of the city, from 1875 to 1883 and again from 1887 to 1891, exhibited great "boldness of enterprise and breadth of view," according to one source. Warder bolstered civic pride through his efforts at reestablishing Jeffersonville as the seat of Clark County in 1878, building a new city hall in 1881, and laying out a beautiful new park in the city's old market square the same year. He also strengthened the city's key commercial interests through financial assistance to such companies as the Ohio Falls Car Works and the Jeffersonville Plate Glass Company. Warder, however, generated some controversy for his agnosticism and temper. He once attacked the editor of a Jeffersonville newspaper over a slanderous article. (Photo: *History of the Ohio Falls Cities and Their Counties*)

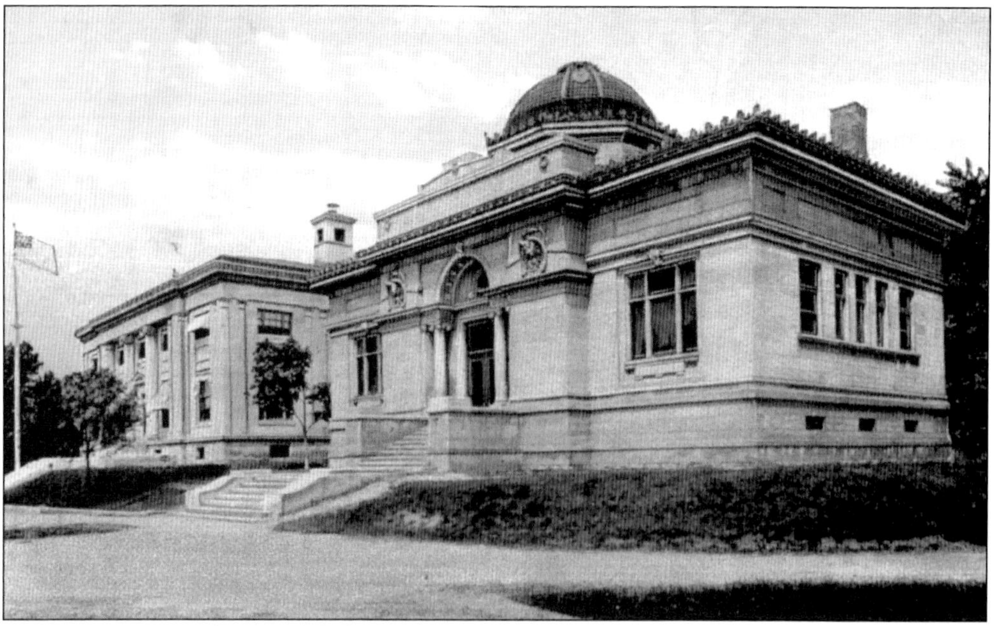

WARDER PARK. A hard tack bakery for the Union Army during the Civil War operated in Jeffersonville's old market square, which occupied the block north of today's Court Avenue between Spring and Wall Streets. The city rewarded Mayor Warder's beautification efforts and other accomplishments by christening the new park in his honor in 1881. The city chose the north end of the park for two key buildings in the early 20th century, the Carnegie Library, seen at right and begun in 1903, and the Post Office, seen at left and completed in 1912. (Photo: Terry Stackhouse)

ARTHUR LOOMIS. The locally renowned architect Arthur Loomis was born in Westfield, Connecticut, in 1859, but came west to Jeffersonville with his family at about the time of the Civil War. Loomis received his education in Jeffersonville's schools and joined the firm of Louisville architect Charles J. Clarke about 1880, eventually rising to become a partner of the firm in 1891. Loomis designed a number of notable buildings on both sides of the river, including St. Paul's Episcopal Church, the Citizens Bank and Trust building, the Masonic Temple, the Carnegie Library in Jeffersonville; and the Todd Building (an early skyscraper), the Speed Art Museum, and several buildings of the Southern Baptist Seminary in Louisville. Loomis moved to Louisville in about 1910 and died there in 1935. (Photo: Kentucky Board of Architects)

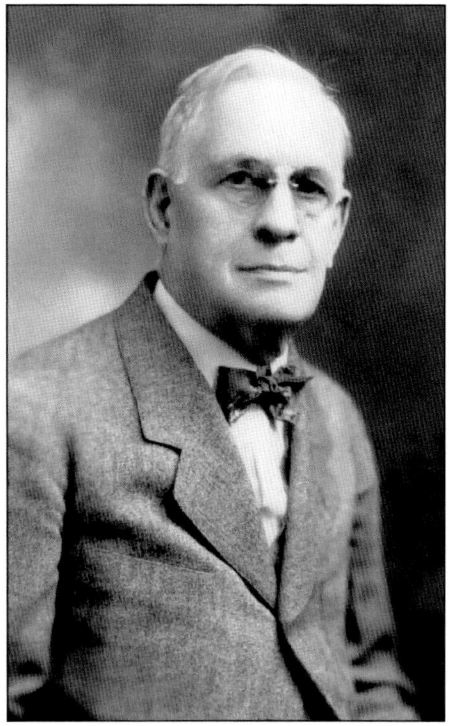

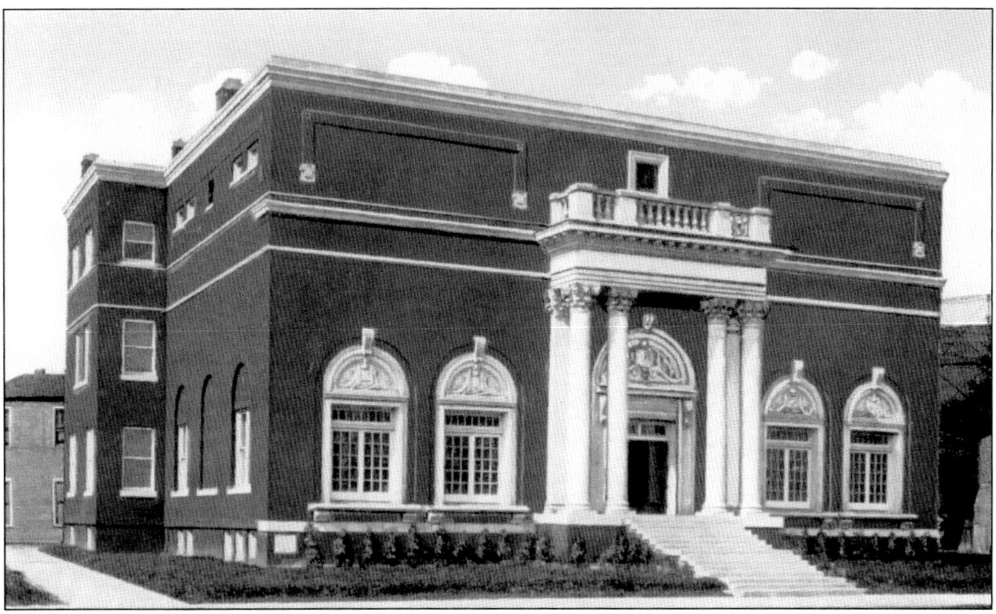

MASONIC TEMPLE. Masons organized a lodge in Jeffersonville as early as 1819, but it failed to thrive and closed within 10 years. Masons reorganized and formed the Clark Lodge, Number 40, in 1835. They met in several locations over the years before building a lodge building all their own, the impressive building on Spring Street across from Warder Park depicted above. The distinctive building, which was designed by architect Arthur Loomis in the neoclassical style and built in 1926, served the masons until 1996, when the lodge moved to a new facility on Park Place. (Photo: Bob Weber)

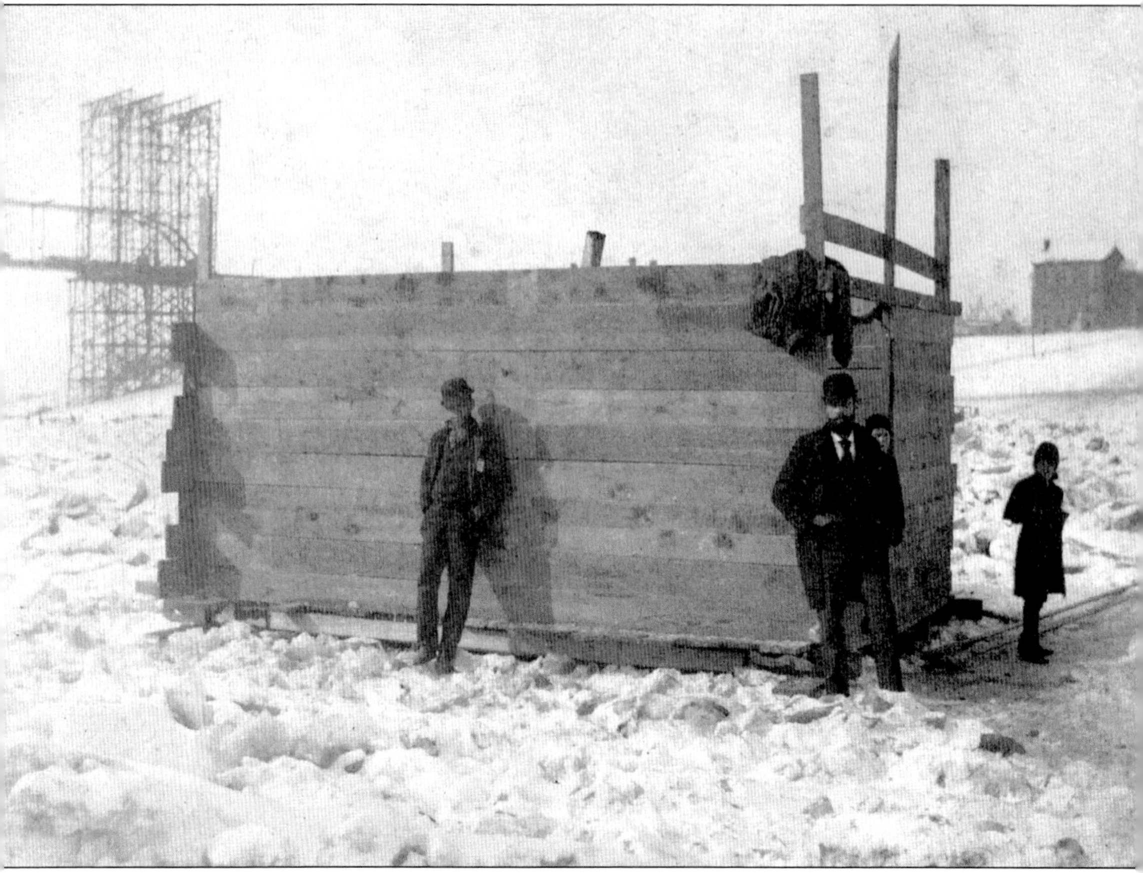

A DRINK "ON THE ROCKS." Jeffersonville once offered numerous places where residents and travelers alike could go for drinks and a night of entertainment. By 1909, there were 58 saloons in the county, 43 of which abided in Jeffersonville. One critic, writing in the 1940s, pronounced "[T]here is a sad, moldering degeneracy on the river front of Jeffersonville…where businesslike gambling establishments…and dingy marriage parlors jostle a superabundance of taverns." One brilliant proprietor looked forward to the ice that choked off river traffic in the winter and hauled a portable saloon onto the Ohio River for brave customers, seen here in this January 1893 image. (Photo: Charles R. Leap)

Opposite: **THE MARRIAGE INDUSTRY.** Lax enforcement of the law in Jeffersonville also allowed the "marriage industry" to thrive here. Magistrates such as Oscar L. Hay, "the Marrying Squire" above, operated the parlors along Court Avenue and catered to out-of-state business, particularly from Louisville and rural Kentucky. "At one time," according to longtime Indiana writer Cliff Robinson of the *Courier-Journal*, "the magistrating business was so good they had runners out meeting all the trolley cars, ferryboats and trains." The city required no waiting period and a deputy county clerk actually worked from 6 PM to 6 AM to process late-night licenses. An estimated 80 percent of marriages in the county at one time involved out-of-county couples. Business dropped considerably after the Indiana Supreme Court demanded enforcement of an 1852 law forbidding the issuance of marriage licenses to out-of-state women. (Photo: Terry Stackhouse)

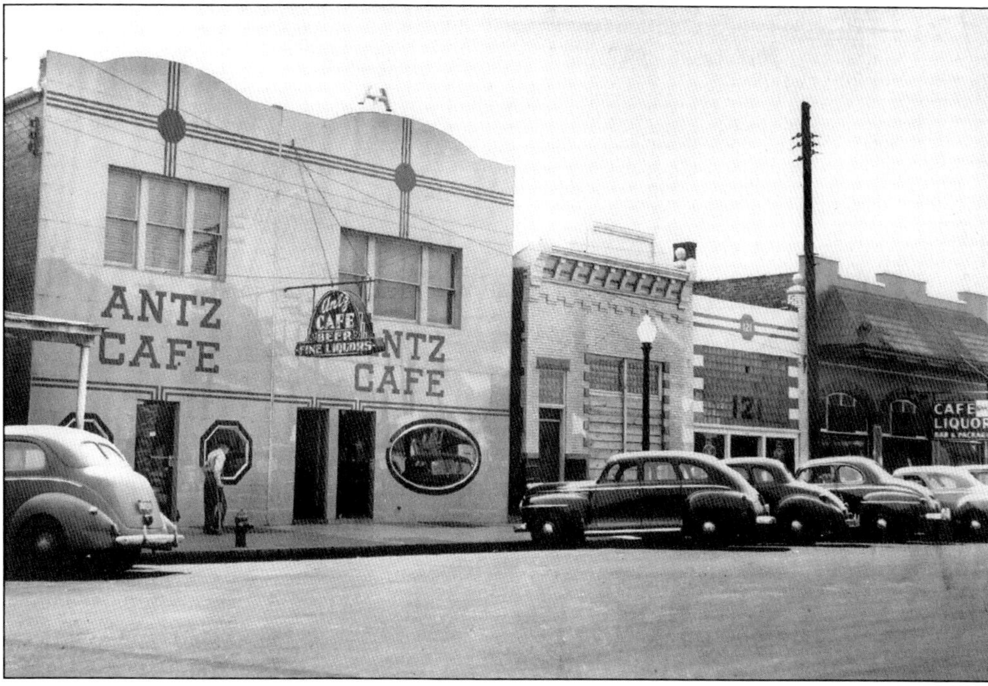

JEFFERSONVILLE'S GAMBLING HALLS. Jeffersonville will always be remembered as a gambling town on account of its "decades of decadence" in the 1930s and 40s. Some have dubbed the city "Little Las Vegas," but Jeffersonville's brand of "wide-open, we-dare-you-to-close-us-down" illegal gaming, as characterized by journalist Mike King, more resembled the corruption and decadence of a northerly neighbor, thus calling to mind the sobriquet "Little Chicago." Five casinos operated within a single block of West Court Avenue: the Antz Cafe, the 119 Club, the 121 Club, the 125 Club, and the Court Cafe. These halls and others such as the Municipal Bar offered roulette, craps, and other games, as well as betting on races across the country. Local and state officials crashed the long-running party by 1948 (see page 122). (Photo: *Courier-Journal*)

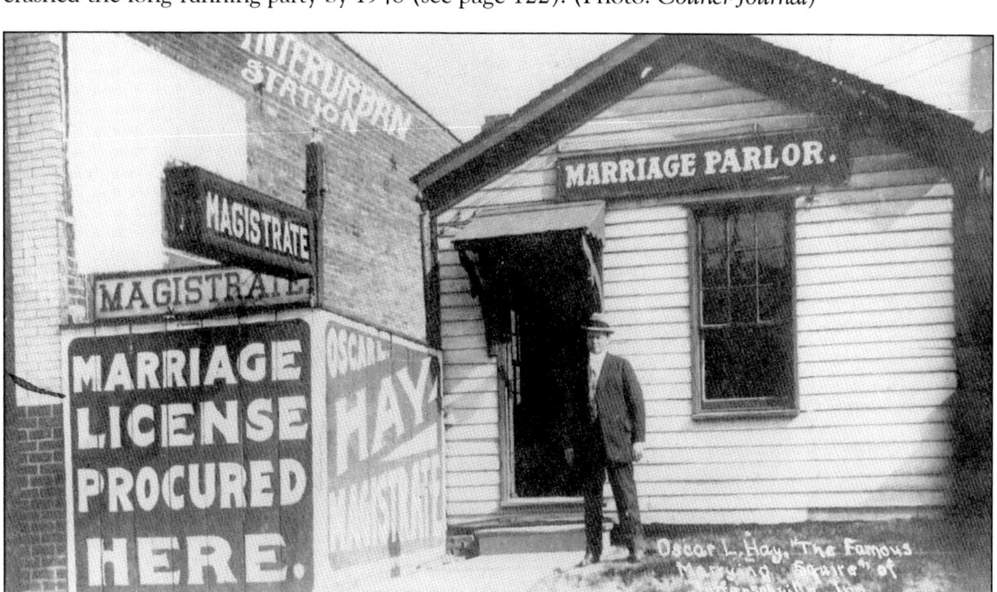

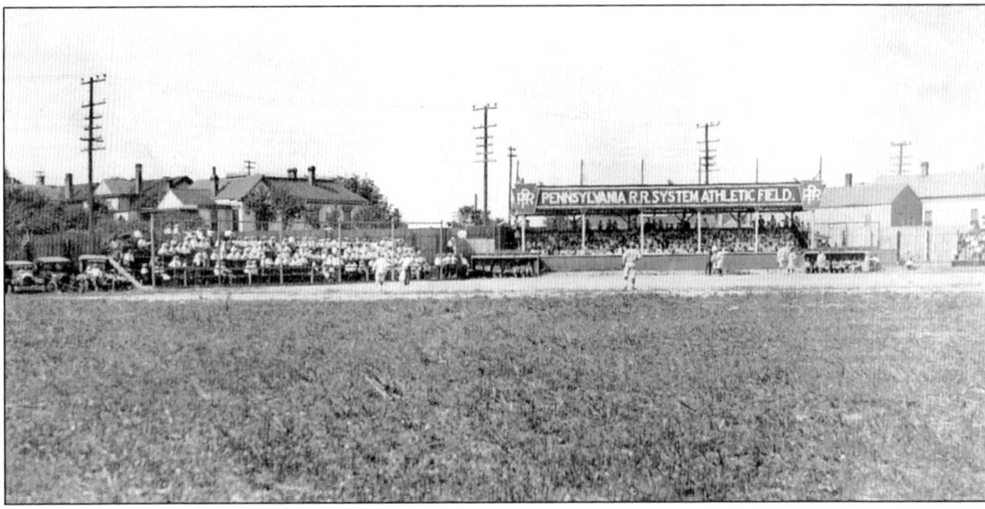

PENNSY FIELD. The local division of the Pennsylvania Railroad erected a ball field in 1923 at the block bounded by Ninth, Tenth, Watt, and Locust Streets to provide a home field for its team in the company's league. Although the league folded after four seasons, many other teams in the city used old Pennsy Field until the flood waters of 1937 destroyed it. (Photo: Clarksville Historical Society)

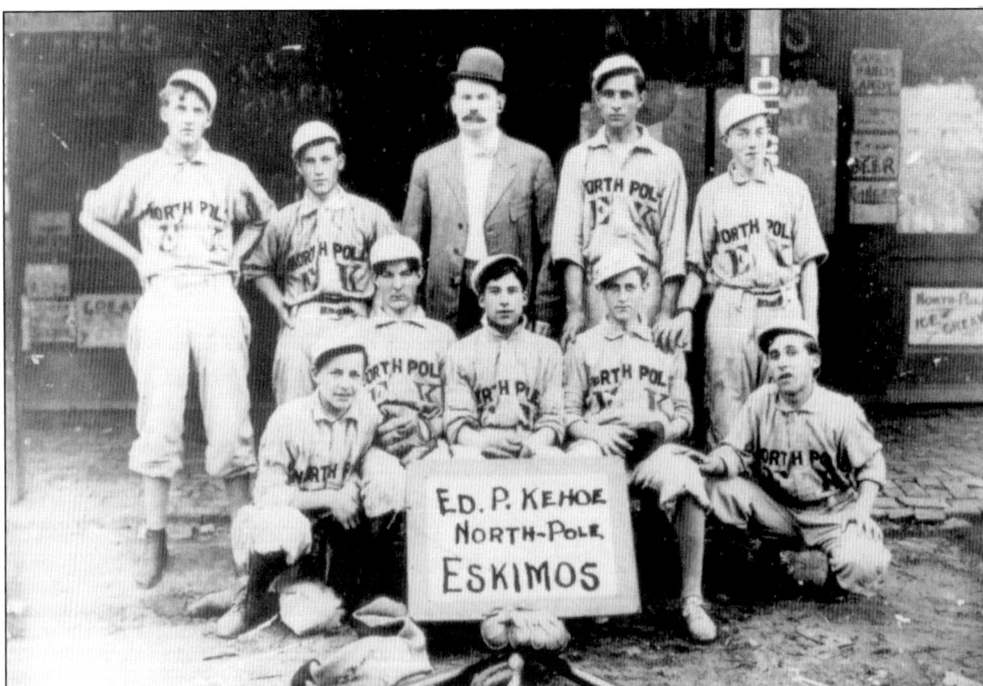

NORTH POLE ESKIMOS. One of many local teams in the golden days of baseball was the "North Pole Eskimos," sponsored by grocery store owner Ed P. "Doc" Kehoe. The team members, posing here in front of their sponsor's shop at 901 Watt Street, were from left to right: (front row) James Heuser, Dude Chapman, Frank Williams, Charles Hazard, and Victor Weber; (back row) Norman Howard, Virgil Weber, Kehoe, unidentified, and Raymond Fogarty. (Photo: Dennis and Debbie Duffy)

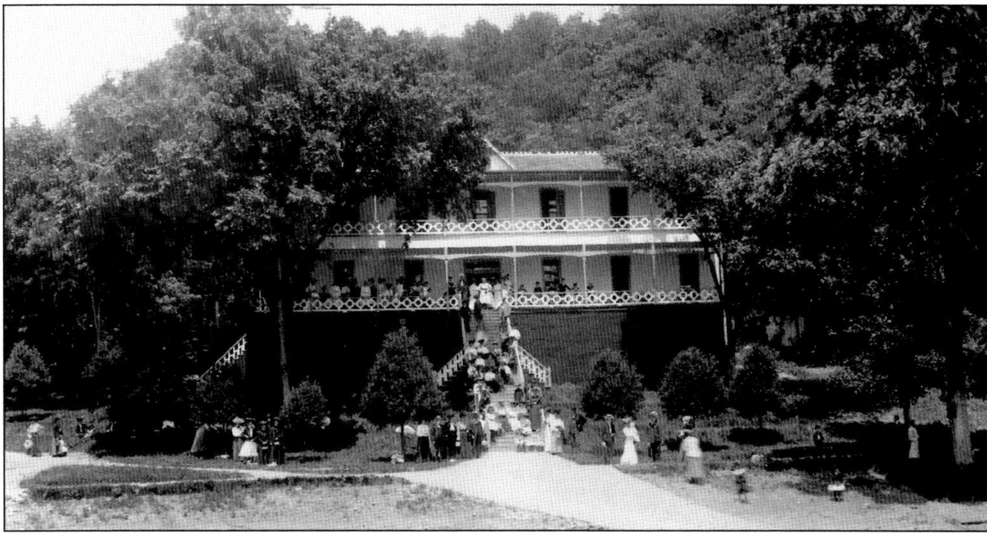

ROSE ISLAND. Citizens of Jeffersonville and its Falls Cities neighbors sought escape from the Ohio Valley's muggy summers in the late 19th century by taking the ferry to a shady retreat on a small peninsula at the confluence of Fourteen Mile Creek and the Ohio River. The Louisville and Jeffersonville Ferry Company, in an effort to stimulate its business, purchased and enlarged the grounds, known then as Fern Grove, in the late 1880s. The park thrived on church picnics and family outings, but Louisville business owner David B.G. Rose purchased the property in 1923 with bigger plans in mind. Rose renamed the resort Rose Island and spent $250,000 on improvements to the facility, which included the hotel seen above. Travelers could reach the remote park by car, as seen in the 1926 photograph below, but most preferred to enjoy the leisurely ride aboard the steamer *America*, which hauled up to 4,000 people to the resort at a time. (Photos: University of Louisville Photographic Archives)

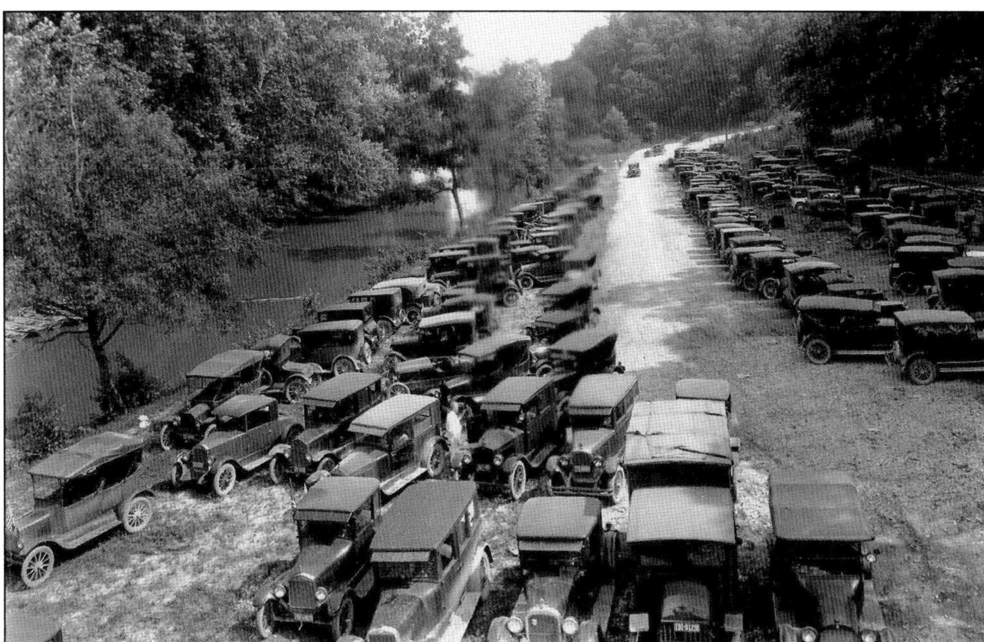

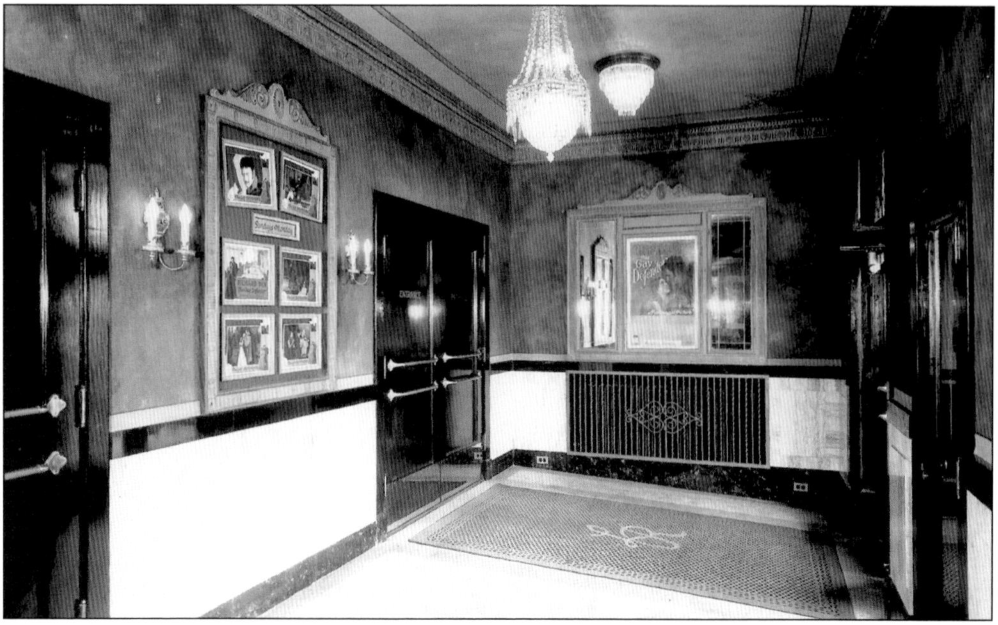

LeRose Theater. Jeffersonville's movie palace, built in the Renaissance Revival style in 1920, was originally operated by ice-cream merchant Michael Switow's Jeffersonville Amusement Company. Switow also owned Jeffersonville's older Dream Theater. The LeRose (335–339 Spring Street) and the Dream (403 Spring Street) were so close to each other that some patrons recall creating their own double features by watching movies at both theaters in one day. These photos illustrate the inside of the theater and its lobby in 1928. The exterior (see page 123) featured elaborate brick and stonework in its façade. (Photos: University of Louisville Photographic Archives)

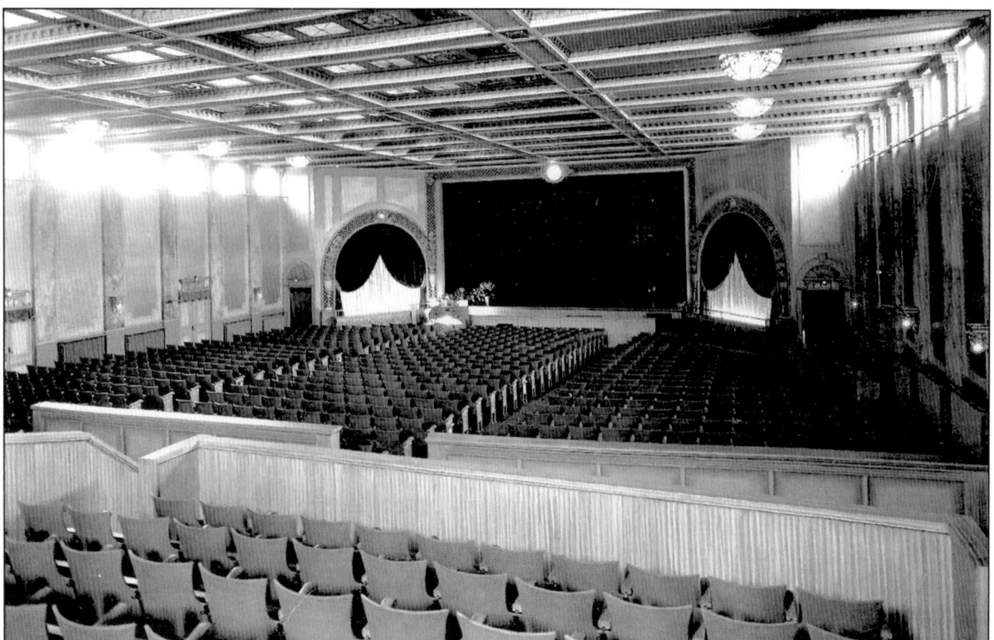

Two

TRAVELING

RIVER, RAIL, AND ROAD

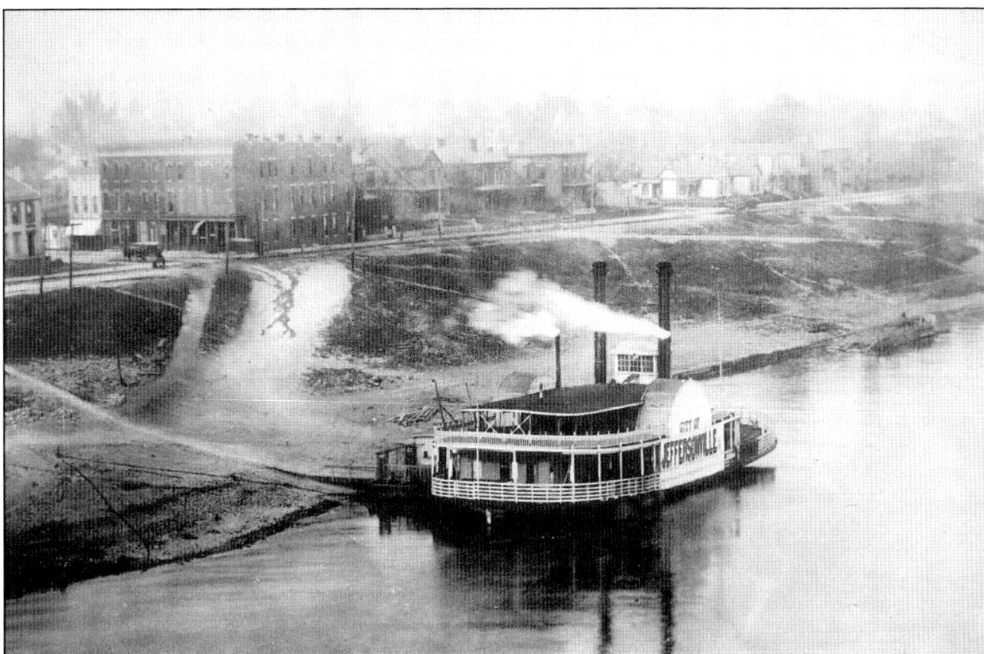

THE FERRY TO LOUISVILLE. The city's first licensed ferry began plying the river in 1802. The first ferries relied on horses, poles, oars, or sails to cross the river until the 1830s, when steamers made their local appearance. The Jeffersonville to Louisville route proved one of the more hazardous routes across the Ohio, for if a ferry lost power or steering, the falls just below the city might smash a wooden hull to splinters. In addition to human travelers with their horse-drawn carriages and later automobiles, the ferries also transported herds of livestock driven down to the Spring Street dock, shown above, and ferried to the stockyards in Louisville. (Photo: University of Louisville Photographic Archives)

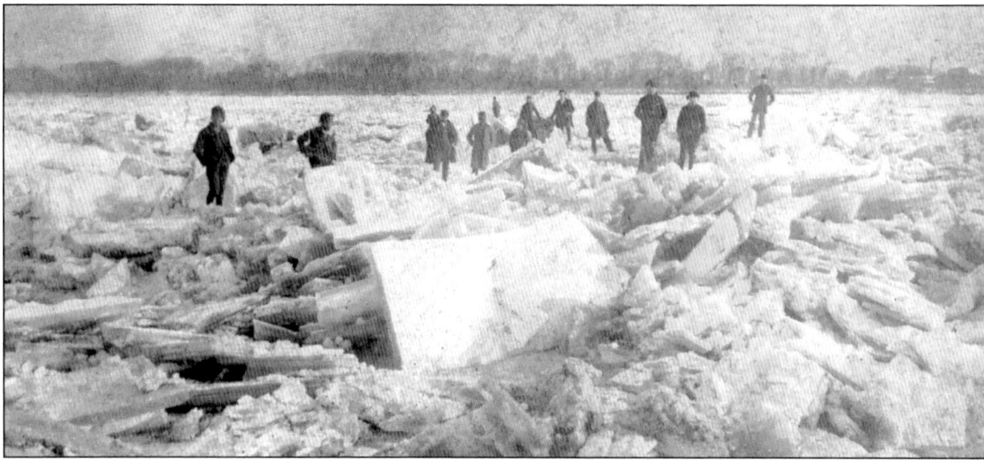

The Ice Gorge of January 1893. Ferries and other craft risked being whisked into the falls, blinded by fog, and carried away by flood (not to mention destroyed by a burst boiler). Ice represented another haunting specter to river traffic. Many a wooden river vessel suffered a crushing death in the ice gorges that groaned downstream after a thaw. The photo above shows a number of unidentified brave souls testing the safety of the January 1893 ice gorge on the river. (Photo: Charles R. Leap)

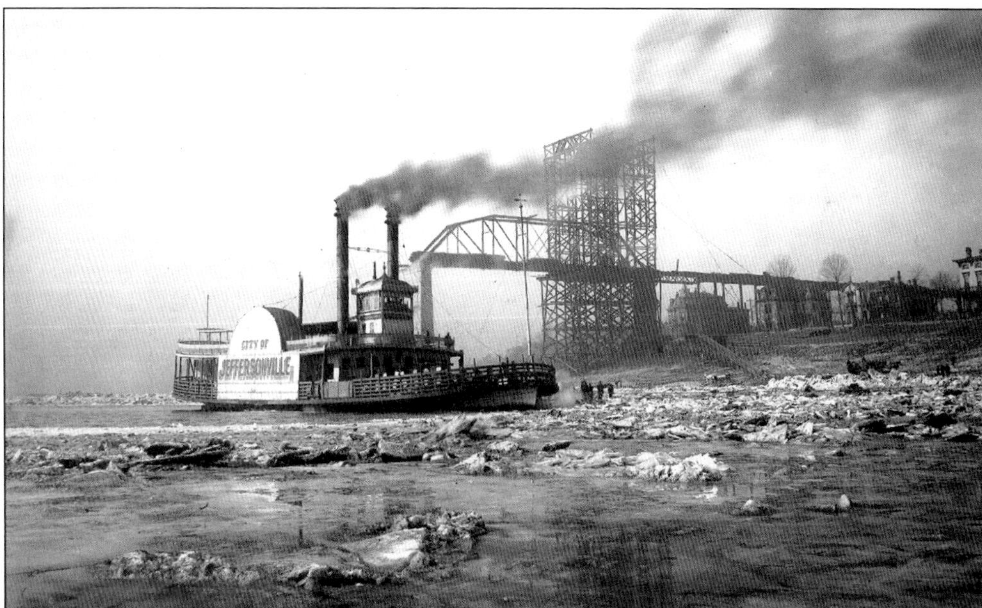

City of *Jeffersonville* Ferry in the Ice. The *City of Jeffersonville* sits below the still incomplete Big Four Bridge at Jeffersonville in the January 1893 ice gorge in this image. The gorge broke loose that month causing great destruction along the Ohio River. Spectators along the riverbank watched helplessly as many barges and steamers were crushed by the ice or driven into the new bridge's piers. Captain Mike Duffy and his crew aboard the steamer *Hotspur* attempted to get their craft to shore, but were instead carried downstream on a "most thrilling ride" in the grinding, cracking ice. The ice forced the craft ashore near the new bridge above, allowing the crew to clamber safely to land, but Captain Duffy fell into the ice-choked water, where he nearly suffered crushing and drowning. (Photo: University of Louisville Photographic Archives)

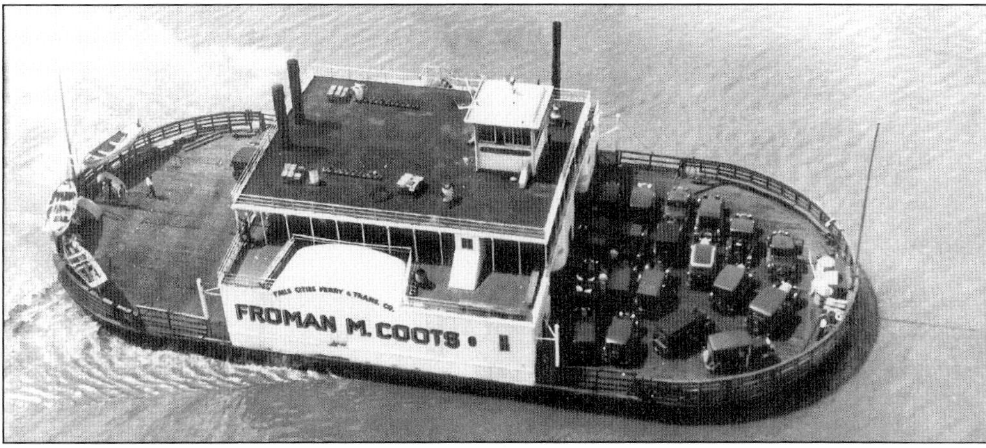

FROMAN M. COOTS FERRY. This unusual view from above catches the *Froman M. Coots* with a load of vehicles and passengers, on its journey across the Ohio River. The photographer stood atop the unfinished Municipal (now Clark Memorial) Bridge on May 25, 1929, for this shot. Froman M. Coots, the son of E.M. Coots' Sons Funeral Home founder Edwin M. Coots, served as an officer of the Falls Cities Ferry and Transportation Company, which operated from December 1920 to December 1929. Coots and other Jeffersonville businessmen advocated building the bridge, but formed the company to keep ferry service alive until the bridge's completion. (Photo: E.M. Coots' Sons Funeral Home)

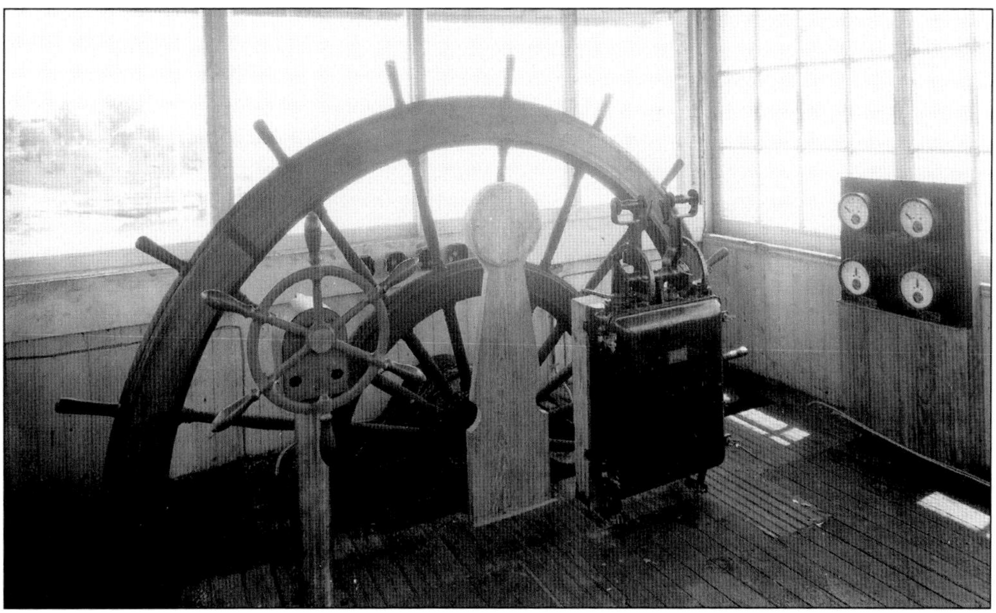

PILOT HOUSE OF THE FROMAN M. COOTS. The *Froman M. Coots* approaches the Indiana shore in this image shot from within the craft's pilot house. The ferry began life in the Howard Yards as the steamer *W.S. McChesney, Jr.* in 1912. It operated in St. Louis until 1920, when the Falls Cities Ferry and Transportation Company purchased it for local use. The company refitted it with a diesel-electric drive system and renamed the craft in 1925. It operated until the end of ferry service. According to author Alan Bates, the rheostats in the black box seen to the right of the large pilot wheel produced "an impressive display of arcs and sparks directly under the pilot's arm…with each change of speed or direction." (Photo: University of Louisville Photographic Archives)

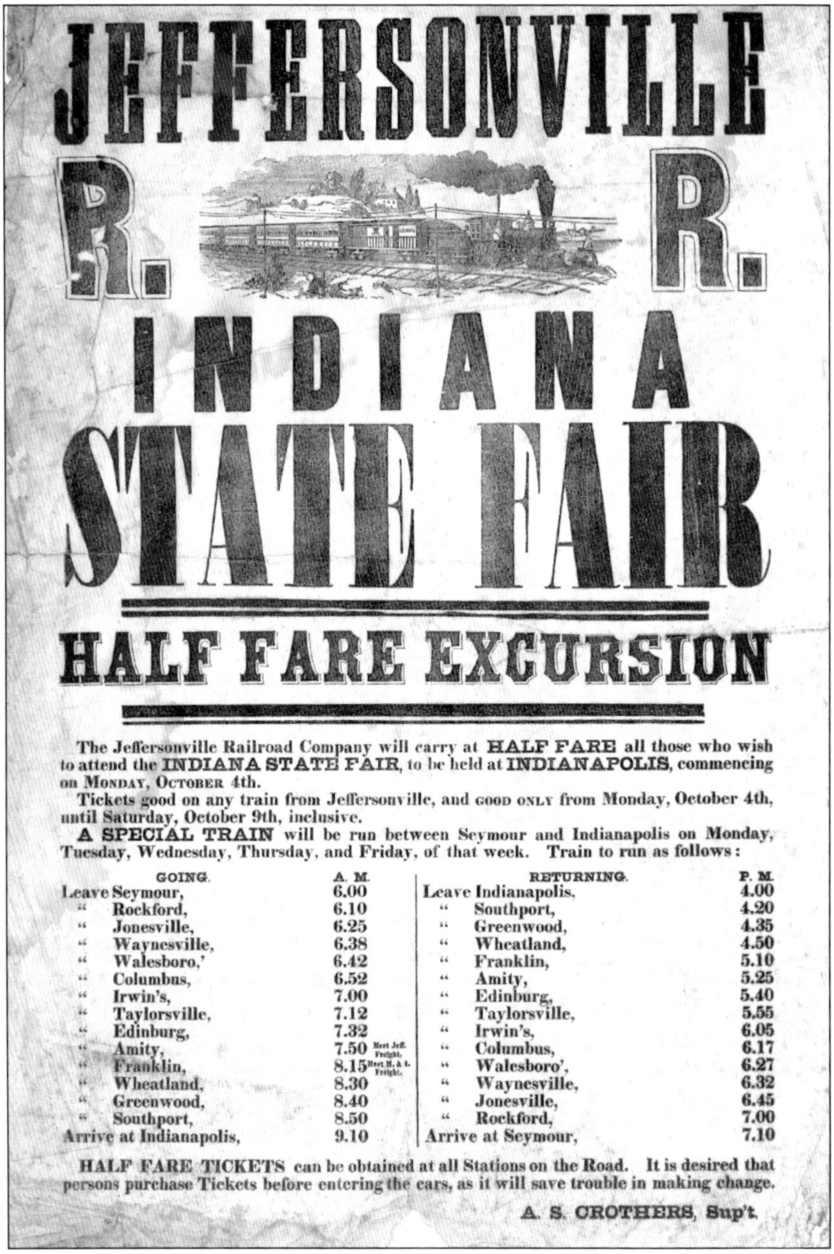

JEFFERSONVILLE

R. R.

INDIANA

STATE FAIR

HALF FARE EXCURSION

The Jeffersonville Railroad Company will carry at **HALF FARE** all those who wish to attend the **INDIANA STATE FAIR**, to be held at **INDIANAPOLIS**, commencing on MONDAY, OCTOBER 4th.

Tickets good on any train from Jeffersonville, and GOOD ONLY from Monday, October 4th, until Saturday, October 9th, inclusive.

A SPECIAL TRAIN will be run between Seymour and Indianapolis on Monday, Tuesday, Wednesday, Thursday, and Friday, of that week. Train to run as follows:

GOING.	A. M.	RETURNING.	P. M.
Leave Seymour,	6.00	Leave Indianapolis,	4.00
" Rockford,	6.10	" Southport,	4.20
" Jonesville,	6.25	" Greenwood,	4.35
" Waynesville,	6.38	" Wheatland,	4.50
" Walesboro,'	6.42	" Franklin,	5.10
" Columbus,	6.52	" Amity,	5.25
" Irwin's,	7.00	" Edinburg,	5.40
" Taylorsville,	7.12	" Taylorsville,	5.55
" Edinburg,	7.32	" Irwin's,	6.05
" Amity,	7.50 Meet Jeff. Freight.	" Columbus,	6.17
" Franklin,	8.15 Meet M. & I. Freight.	" Walesboro',	6.27
" Wheatland,	8.30	" Waynesville,	6.32
" Greenwood,	8.40	" Jonesville,	6.45
" Southport,	8.50	" Rockford,	7.00
Arrive at Indianapolis,	9.10	Arrive at Seymour,	7.10

HALF FARE TICKETS can be obtained at all Stations on the Road. It is desired that persons purchase Tickets before entering the cars, as it will save trouble in making change.

A. S. CROTHERS, Sup't.

JEFFERSONVILLE RAILROAD AND ITS SUCCESSORS. The rail era began for Clark County with the organization of the Jeffersonville Railroad in 1849. The railroad reached 67 miles north to Columbus in 1852 and entered Indianapolis by 1853. The broadside above advertises special fares for service to Indianapolis for the 1858 state fair. The line merged with a major competitor in May of 1866 to form the Jeffersonville, Madison and Indianapolis (J.M. and I.) Railroad. The completion in 1870 of the bridge at Clarksville over the Ohio River, with the J.M. and I. as a principal stockholder, provided the first direct rail link with the South at the falls. The Pennsylvania Railroad acquired the line entirely in 1890 and merged it with the rest of its lines west to form the Pittsburgh, Cincinnati, Chicago and St. Louis Railway. (Photo: Jefferson County Historical Society)

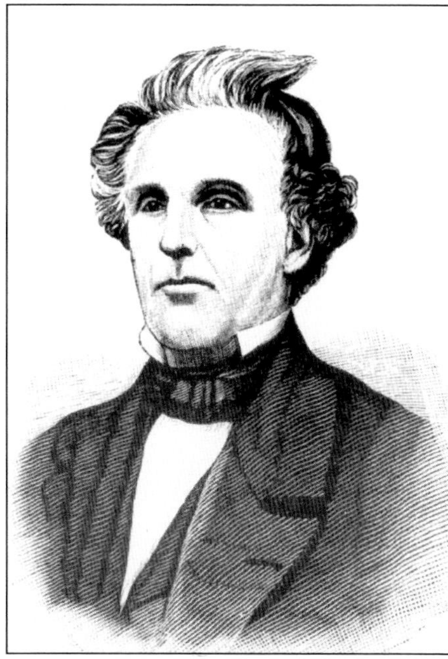

WILLIAM G. ARMSTRONG. The Jeffersonville Railroad's first president, William Goforth Armstrong, was a son of Col. John Armstrong, who had served at Fort Finney (see page 86). Born in 1797 in Columbia, Ohio, the younger Armstrong moved to Bethlehem in northeastern Clark County, Indiana, by 1820, where he managed a farm and store. He also served in the House of Representatives and Senate during that time. In 1841, he took a job at the federal land office in Jeffersonville and moved to this city, where he soon joined with other businessmen who sought to bring the railroad to the county. Armstrong, as railroad president, played a key role in raising the capital for the company, despite the local scarcity of wealth at the time. He retired in 1853, served on the Jeffersonville city council from 1855–1857, and died in 1858. (Photo: *History of the Ohio Falls Cities and Their Counties*)

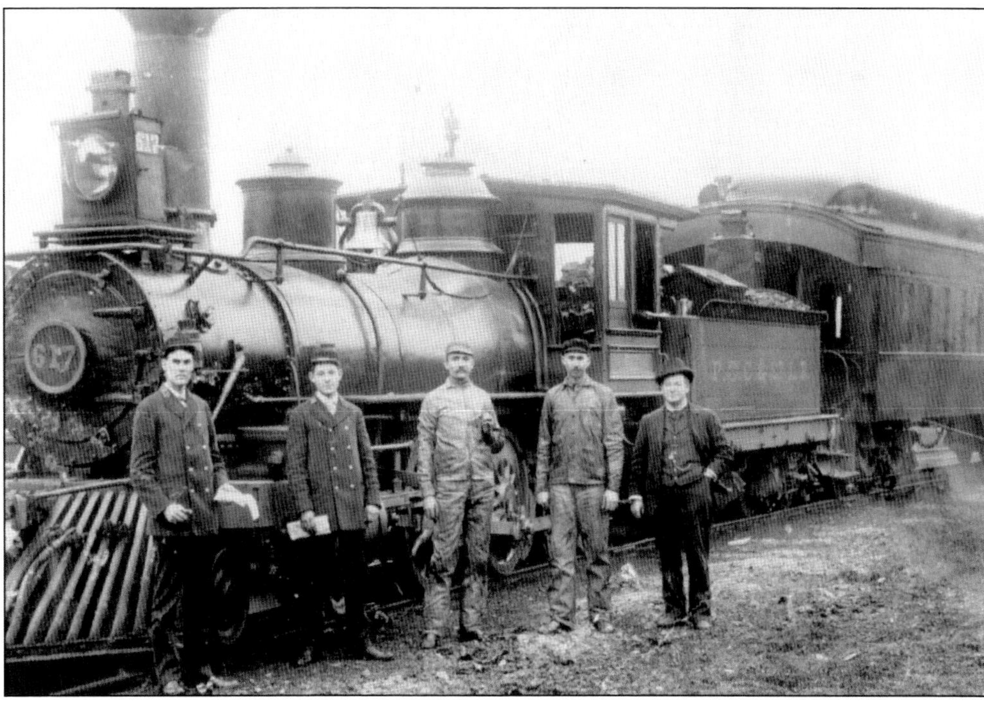

THE DINKY. The J.M. and I., and after 1890, the P.C.C. and St. L., operated a commuter route through the Falls Cities from 1867 to 1921. This steam railway line, known popularly as "the Dinky" for its small trains, ran through Jeffersonville, Clarksville, New Albany, and Louisville on tracks without facilities for turning the engine around. As a result, the train traveled backward on some sections of the route. In 1909, the Dinky offered 19 round trips at hourly intervals between Jeffersonville and Louisville over the Pennsylvania Railroad Bridge at Clarksville. (Photo: Clarksville Historical Society)

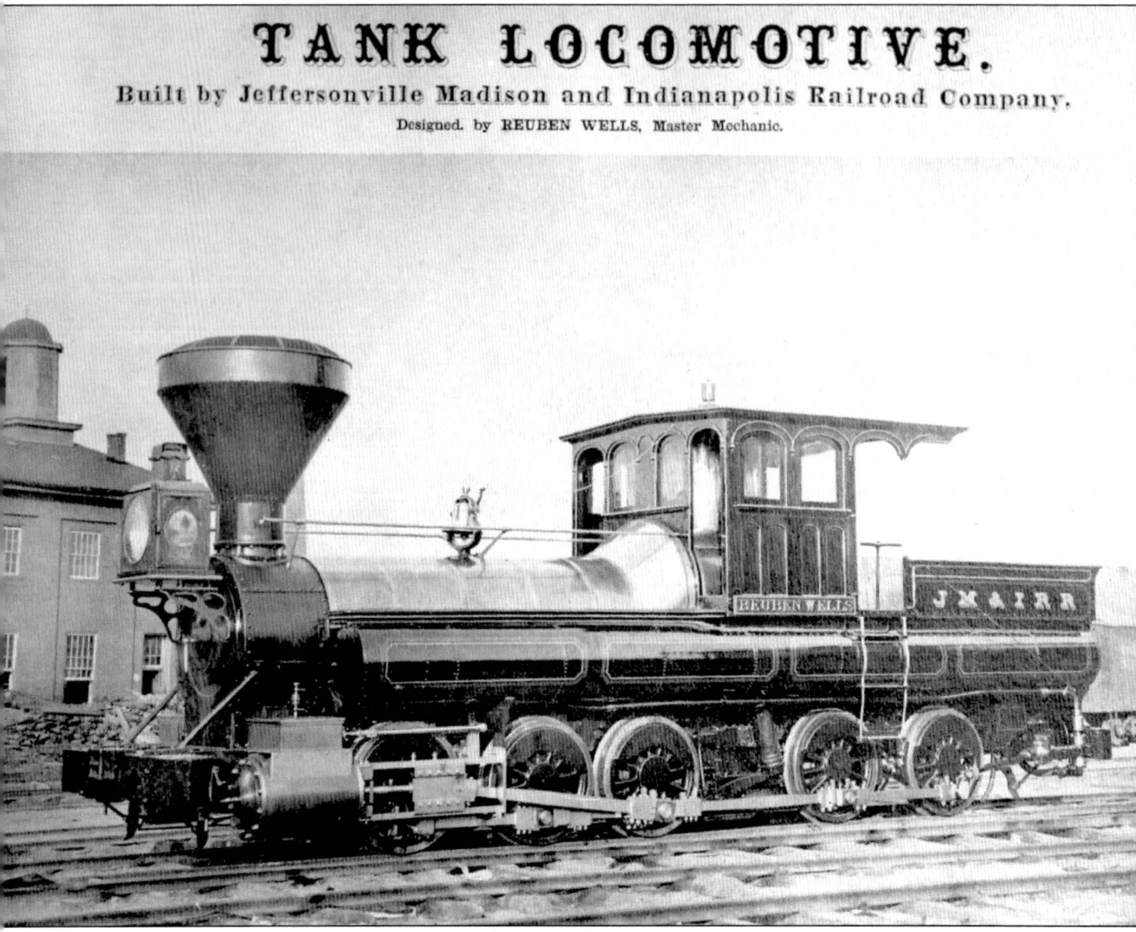

THE *REUBEN WELLS.* The Jeffersonville Railroad, and its successor the J.M. and I., built 28 locomotives between 1860 and 1881 at its Jeffersonville shops, located north of New Market Street (now Court Avenue) between Wall and Walnut Streets. The railroad's master mechanic, Reuben Wells, designed many of them, including the locomotive named for him and pictured above. The *Reuben Wells*, constructed in 1868 as the heaviest locomotive at the time, was the first engine to operate on the steep Madison incline by adhesion alone. Up to that time, the railroad used first horse-drawn and then a cog system on the 5.9 percent grade. The tank engine rolled on 10 driving wheels, later modified to 8, and weighed 56 tons. The Jeffersonville resident received worldwide accolade for his engineering achievement. The wood-burning locomotive operated regularly until 1898 and was replaced by a coal-burning engine in 1905. Visitors to the Indianapolis Children's Museum can see this Jeffersonville creation, which has been carefully preserved and put on display. This builder's photo of the locomotive likely depicts the engine at the Jeffersonville shops. (Photo: Jefferson County Historical Society)

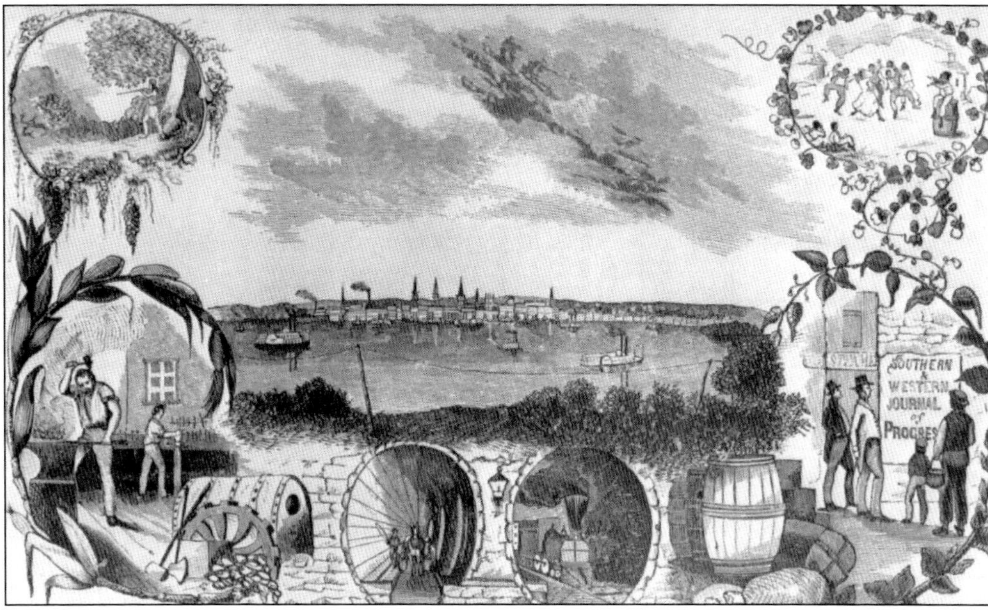

PLANS FOR A GREAT TUNNEL UNDER THE OHIO. The Ohio River offered a valuable water route for travel east and west, but it presented a tremendous obstacle from north to south. Planners as early as the 1850s imagined ways of getting trains across the river, including the scheme above, which called for a "Great Tunnel" of two tubes to pass beneath the river, but it never materialized. The Civil War halted efforts at building a permanent route across the river, but the military did operate a pontoon bridge for the transport of troops and supplies for a short time during the war (see pages 90–91). The first iron bridge across the river opened in 1870 at Clarksville. (Photo: *Progress of the Republic*)

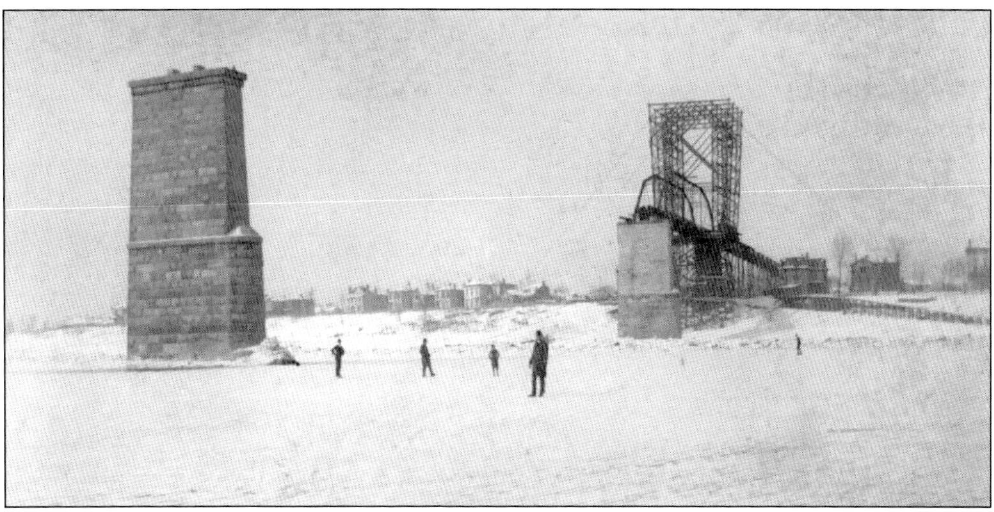

SPANNING THE OHIO AT JEFFERSONVILLE. The 1870 bridge at Clarksville and another at New Albany in 1886 already offered an uninterrupted route across the Ohio, but business interests in Jeffersonville planned for their own route from the city. Bad luck plagued construction from the start. Sixteen men died in two accidents in the caissons built below water level to construct the bridge piers seen completed above in 1893. A worse accident would strike later during construction of the bridgework between the piers. (Photo: Charles R. Leap)

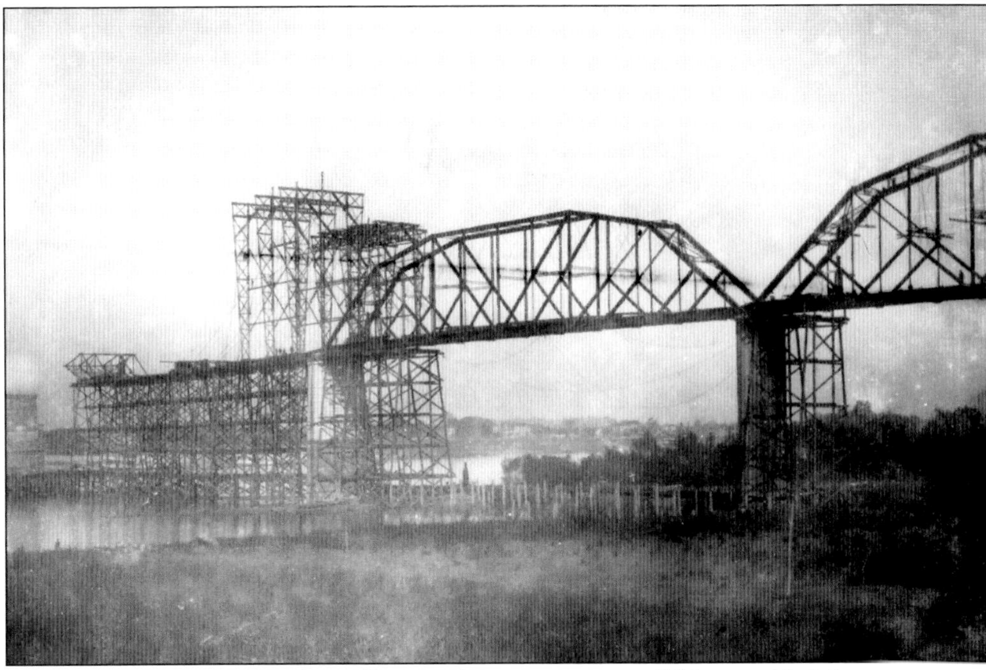

BRIDGING THE PIERS. This photo illustrates how enormous scaffolding enabled the construction of the ironwork between bridge piers. The Phoenix Bridge Company, ironically, began construction in 1888 and proceeded for seven difficult years. The Cleveland, Cincinnati, Chicago and St. Louis Railway, known popularly as the Big Four, eventually took over construction, which was interrupted by accidents and the financial panic of 1893. (Photo: University of Louisville Photographic Archives)

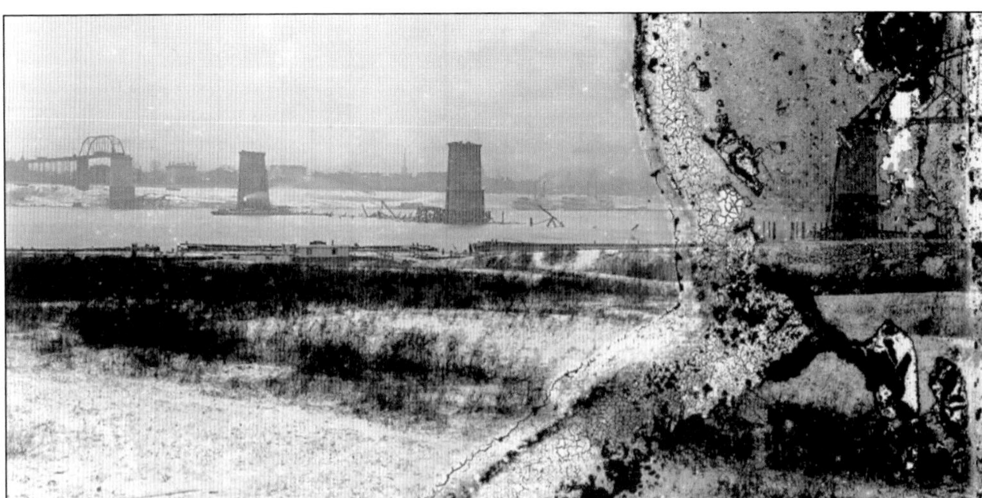

THE BRIDGE COLLAPSE. The worst accident to strike the bridge took place on December 15, 1893, after a gale swept through the Falls Cities. The great winds loosened a crane and it fell into the structure supporting an incomplete bridge span. The unlucky chain of events caused that span and its neighbor a short time later to collapse into the river. The accident plunged 41 men into the water, far below, killing 21 of them. The photograph above, from a damaged negative, shows the bridge in ruins. (Photo: University of Louisville Photographic Archives)

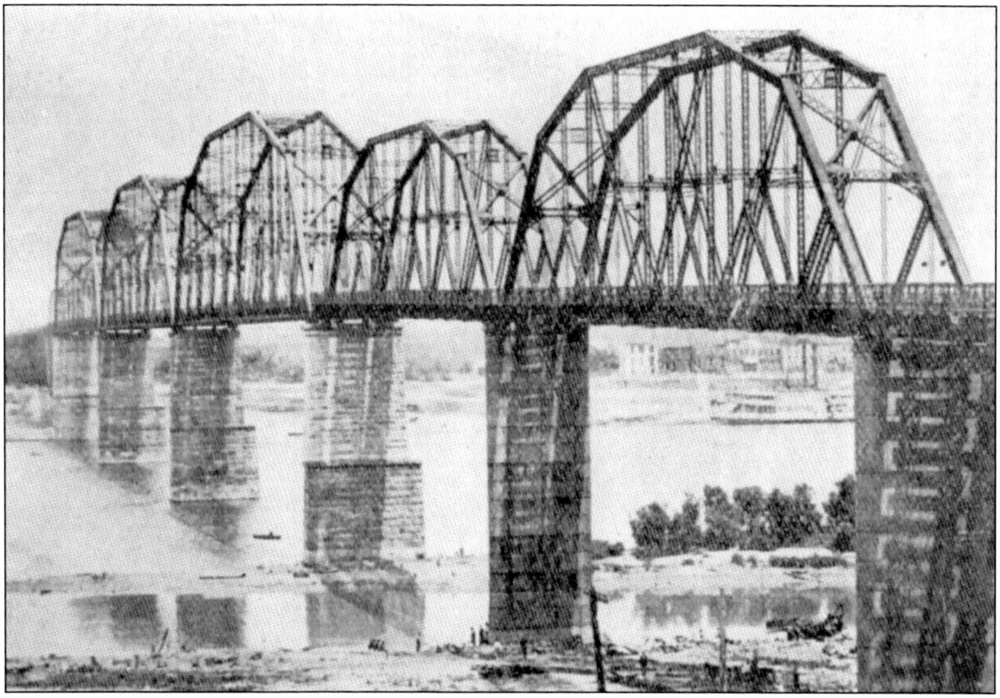

COMPLETION OF THE BRIDGE. The bridge reached completion in September of 1895. It extended 2,525 feet across the river and 77.5 feet above pool stage. The bridge proved inadequate for the increasing weight of traffic over it by the 1920s, so engineers reconstructed it on its original piers using a brilliant plan that utilized the old spans as supporting structures for the new ones. The rebuilding process lasted only one year from 1928 to 1929, compared to the original's seven years. (Photo: Jeffersonville Township Public Library)

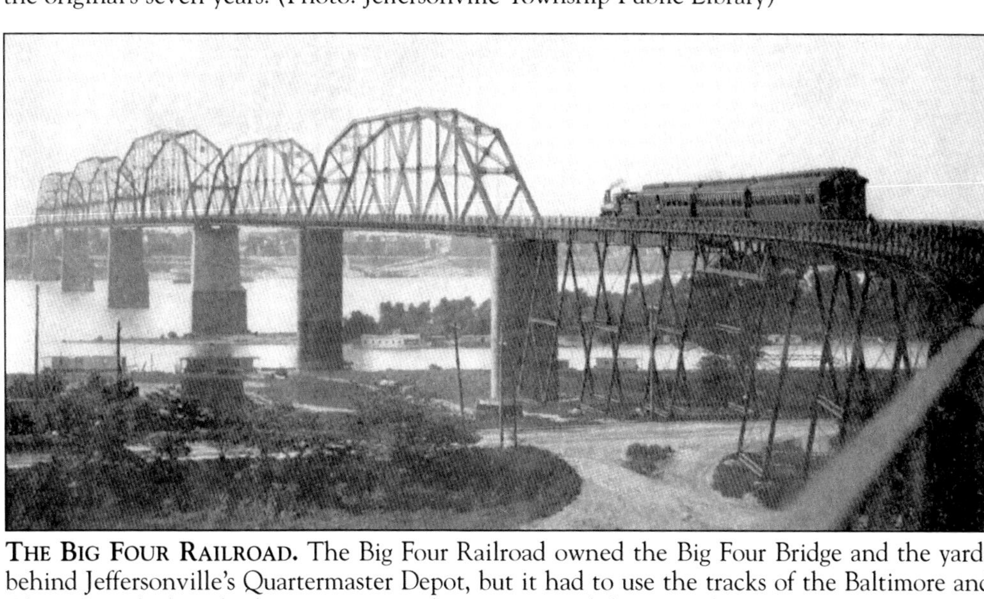

THE BIG FOUR RAILROAD. The Big Four Railroad owned the Big Four Bridge and the yards behind Jeffersonville's Quartermaster Depot, but it had to use the tracks of the Baltimore and Ohio to reach them both. Here, a steam locomotive and three coaches approach the bridge on the Louisville side, with Jeffersonville in the background. The Big Four Railroad evolved later into the New York Central. (Photo: Charles R. Leap)

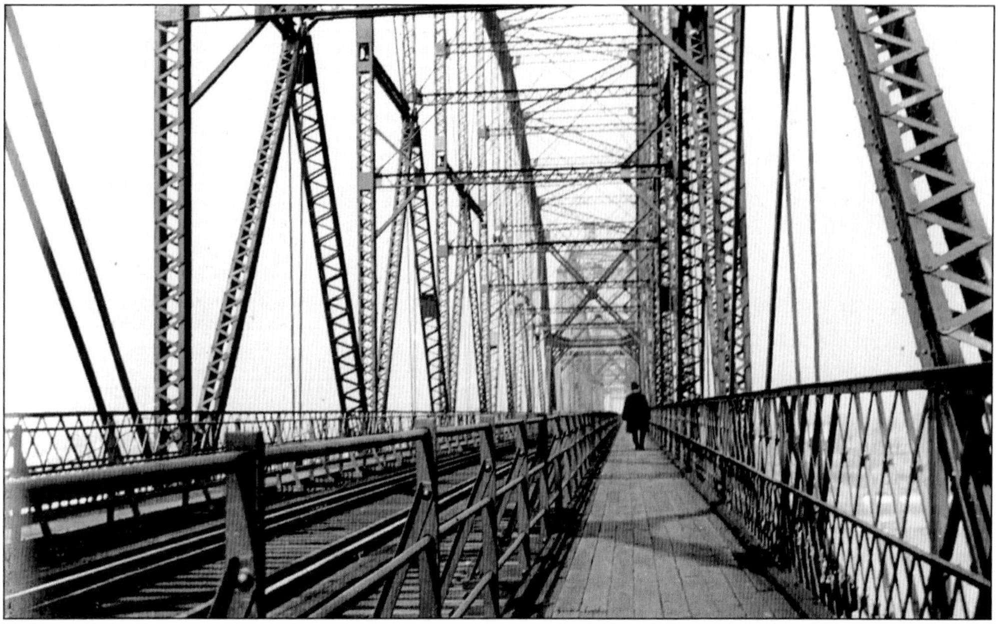

PEDESTRIAN GATEWAY TO LOUISVILLE. The Big Four Bridge served the railroad as a single-track crossing, but it also accommodated pedestrians, as seen in this early-20th-century image. (Photo: University of Louisville Photographic Archives)

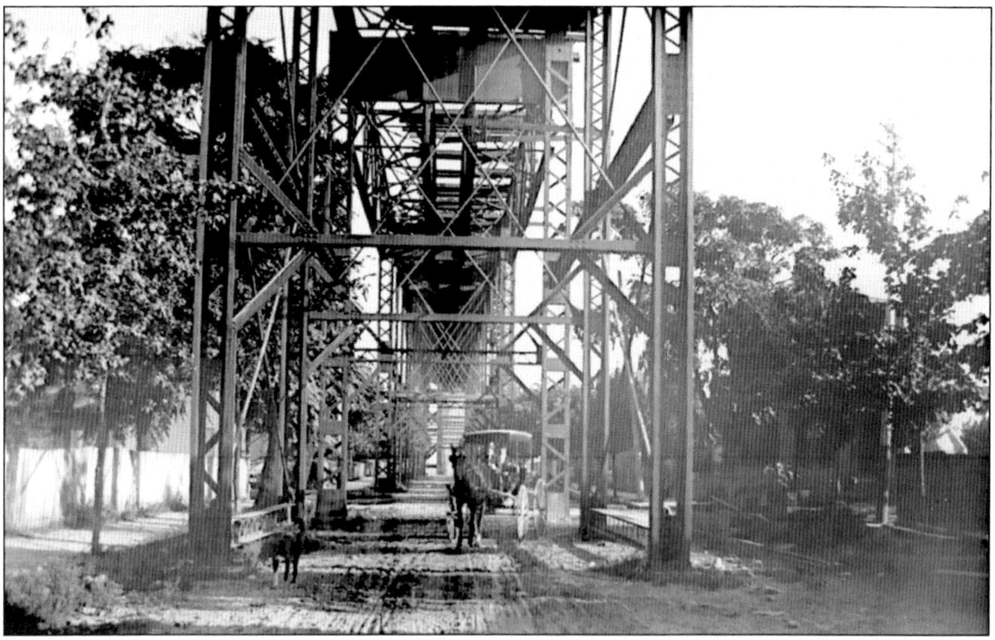

HORSE AND CARRIAGE UNDER THE BIG FOUR BRIDGE. Pedestrians and rail traffic enjoyed the direct link to Louisville from Jeffersonville offered by the Big Four Bridge, but carriages, and later automobiles, still had to take the ferry or drive all the way to the Kentucky and Indiana Bridge in New Albany. A horse-drawn carriage treads the dirt roadway at Mulberry and Chestnut Streets beneath the Big Four Bridge in this photograph from the late 19th century. (Photo: University of Louisville Photographic Archives)

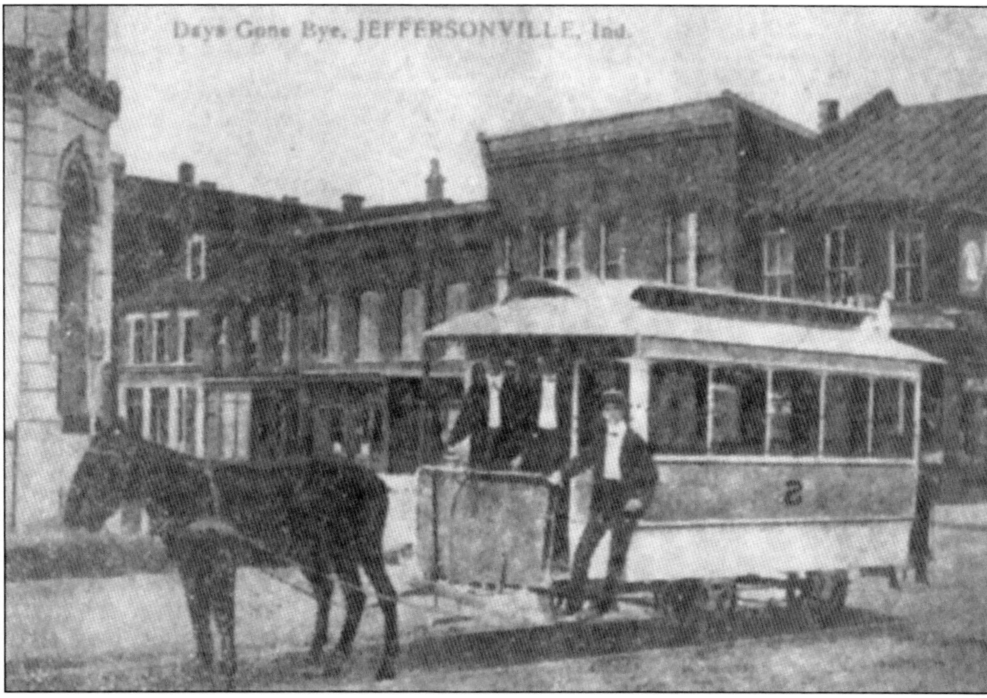

DOWNTOWN BY MULE. Jeffersonville's first system of streetcars relied on mules for motive power. Historian Lewis Baird observed that the mule trolley was the "butt of all jokers," but it "paved the way" for the more modern electric service that replaced it. The old mule trolley made its last trip on May 1, 1904. A photographer shot this image at the corner of Market and Spring Streets in about 1890 for a postcard. (Photo: Jeffersonville Township Public Library)

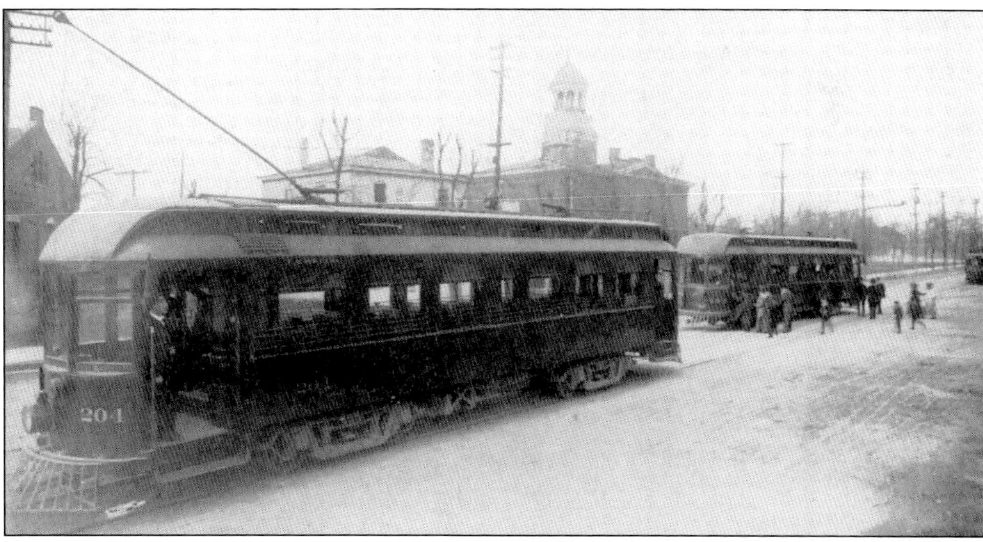

ELECTRIC TROLLEY SERVICE. The Louisville and Southern Indiana Traction Company expanded public transportation within the city and provided another commuter option among the Falls Cities alongside the Dinky. The company operated lines on Spring Street, Court Avenue, Chestnut Street to Port Fulton, Missouri Avenue, and Sixth Street. The local American Car and Foundry Company plant built many of the railway's cars. (Photo: *Souvenir Jeffersonville, Ind.*)

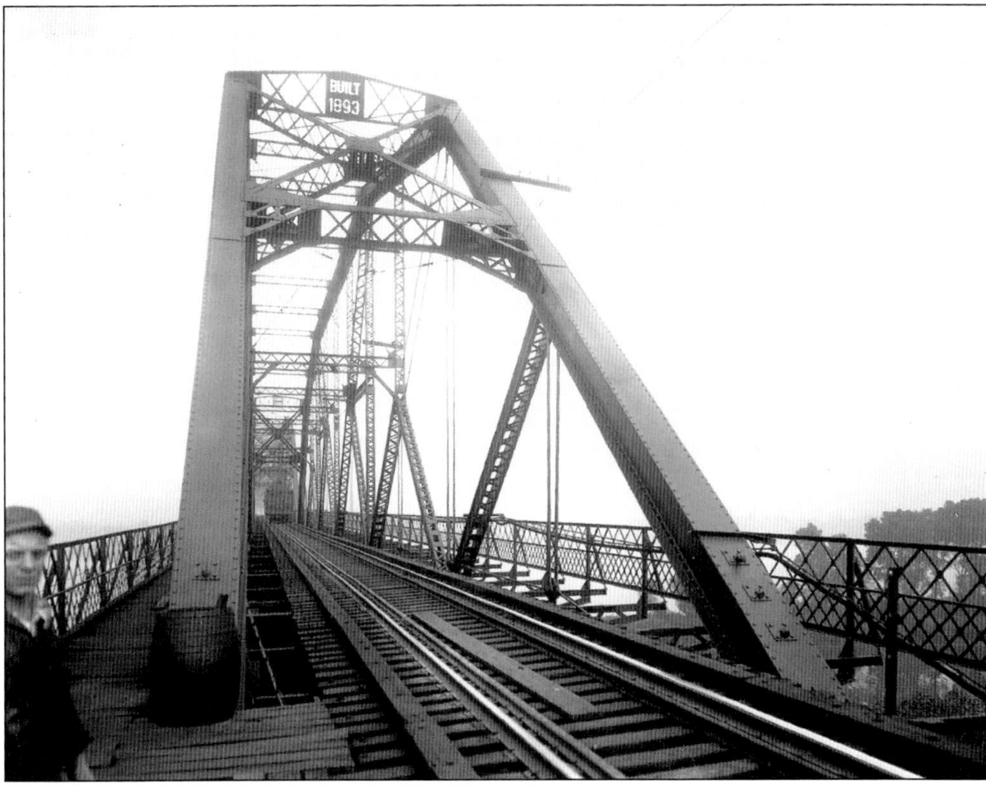

INTERURBAN CONNECTION WITH LOUISVILLE. The Louisville and Southern Indiana Traction Company built a new approach to the Big Four Bridge from Court Avenue in September of 1905, allowing its trolleys to cross into Louisville. This photo from October 4, 1919, catches a trolley as it crosses the bridge. The trolley system gave way to bus service in the 1930s. (Photo: University of Louisville Photographic Archives)

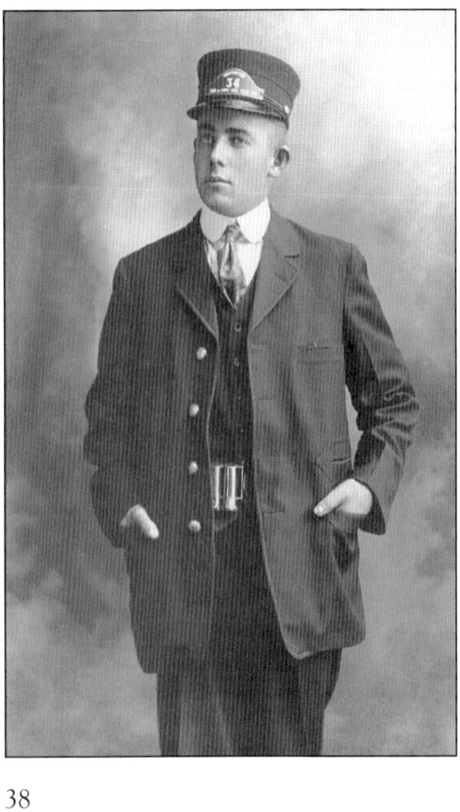

CONDUCTOR ON THE INTERURBAN. A young conductor of the Louisville and Southern Indiana Traction Company in his uniform, complete with a change holder on his belt, strikes a relaxed pose for the photographer. (Photo: Sellersburg Public Library)

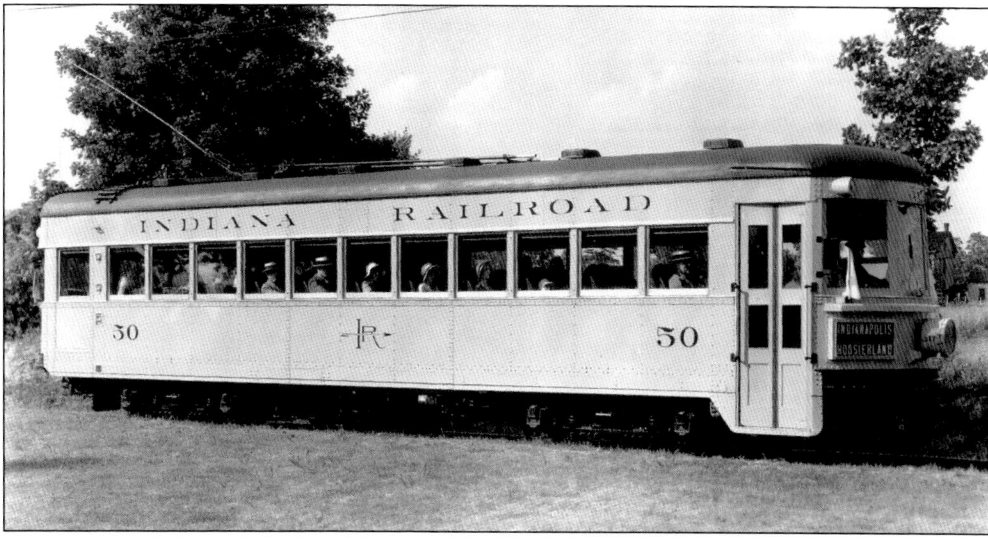

RIDING THROUGH HOOSIERLAND ON THE INTERURBAN. In 1921, the Louisville and Southern Indiana Traction Company merged into Interstate Public Service Company (later Public Service Company of Indiana). This provided Jeffersonville its first direct interurban service over one line to Indianapolis, and any number of other destinations served by the capital's massive traction terminal. A giant corporate consolidation took place between 1928 and 1930, which led to the formation of the state-wide Indiana Railroad system, controlled by utilities magnate Samuel Insull. The photograph above shows Indiana Railroad car 50, among many manufactured at American Car and Foundry's local plant. Most interurban cars maintained a traditional coach-style bench seat arrangement to maximize capacity, but the photograph below shows the interior of a series of cars that featured a special lounge seating arrangement put into service in 1931. (Photos: University of Louisville Photographic Archives)

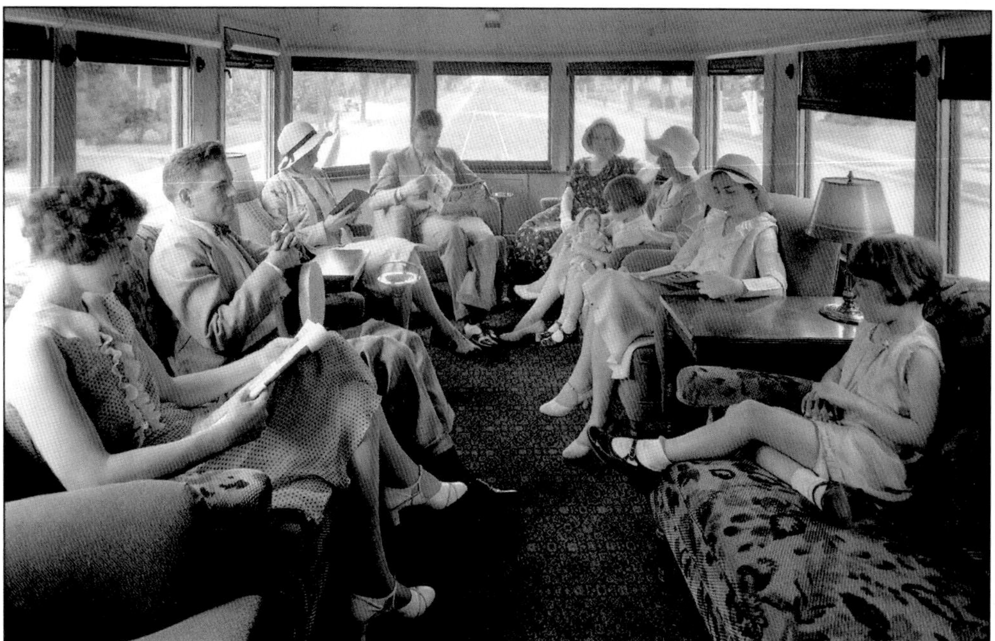

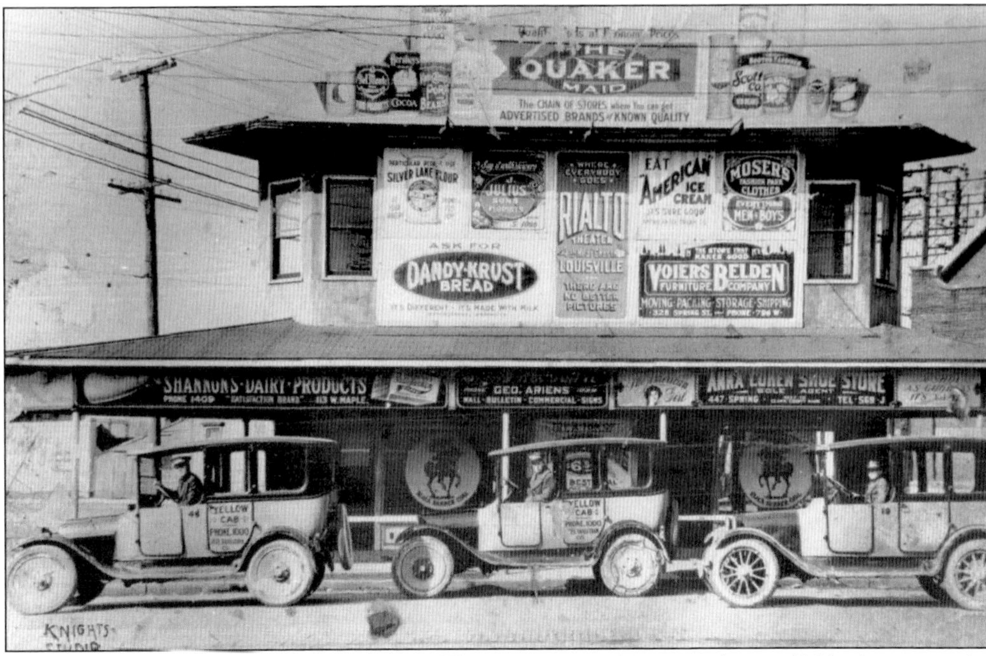

TAXICABS AT THE FLATIRON BUILDING. The Flatiron Building, in the small block surrounded by Court Avenue and Sixth and Kentucky Streets, has housed many businesses in its years. This photo, taken in 1924, shows three Yellow Taxis operated by the Jeffersonville Taxi and Transportation Company. The unusual triangular building, said to be perhaps the smallest city block in the country, may have been an interurban station at one time. (Photo: Jeffersonville Township Public Library)

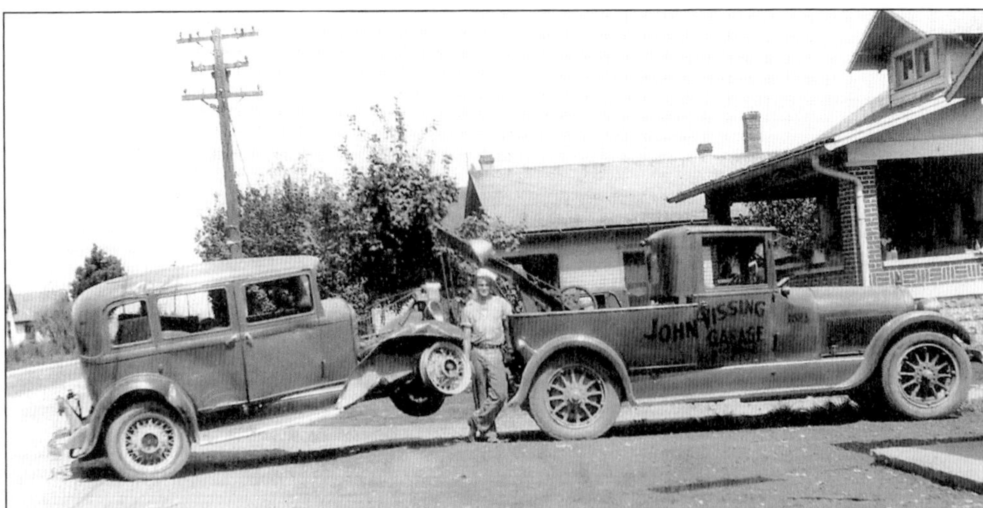

RISE OF THE AUTOMOBILE. The Howard family owned Jeffersonville's first automobile in the 1890s, but automobile usage accelerated only with the economic boom of the 1920s. A whole range of garages, sales agencies, and gas stations supplanted the old blacksmith shops and livery stables of the horse age. Pictured here is a wrecker belonging to Vissing's Automobile Sales and Service, started in 1927 by John Vissing. (His son, Richard, served as mayor of Jeffersonville from 1964 to 1983.) The agency sold Studebakers for most of its first 30 years. (Photo: Jack Vissing)

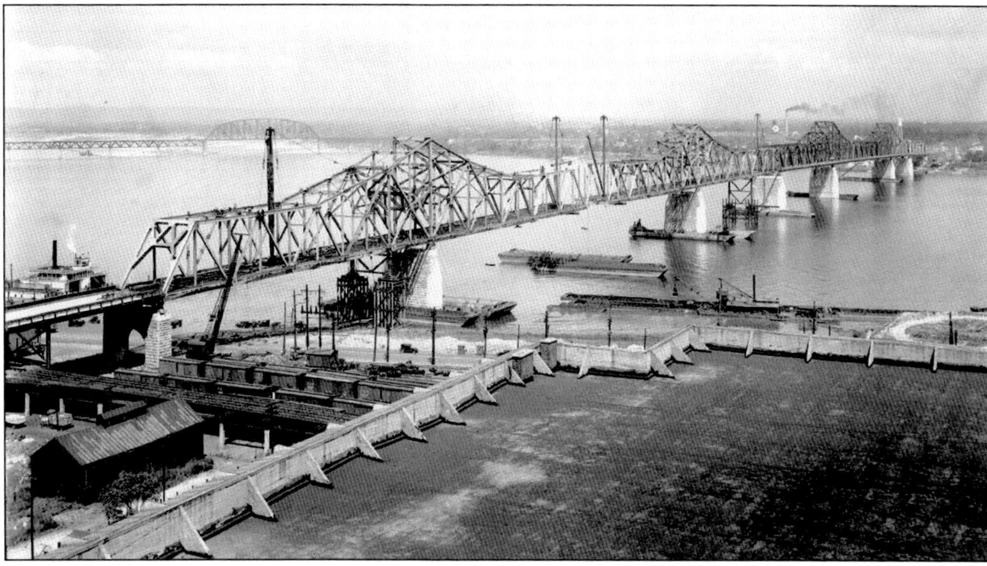

CONSTRUCTION OF THE MUNICIPAL BRIDGE. Despite increasing automobile usage in the 1920s, drivers still had to depend on the ferry if they wanted to cross the river. Discussion of a dedicated automobile bridge began in the mid-1920s, but soon bogged down over the question of whether it should be a free or toll bridge. The Louisville Bridge Commission, formed by the Kentucky General Assembly in 1926, sought but failed to receive voter approval on a bond issue for construction. When the measure failed, the commission obtained private funding, thus requiring the establishment of tolls on the bridge. The American Bridge Company of Pittsburgh began construction in June of 1928 using plans designed by the Philadelphia engineering firm Modjeski and Masters. (Photo: University of Louisville Photographic Archives)

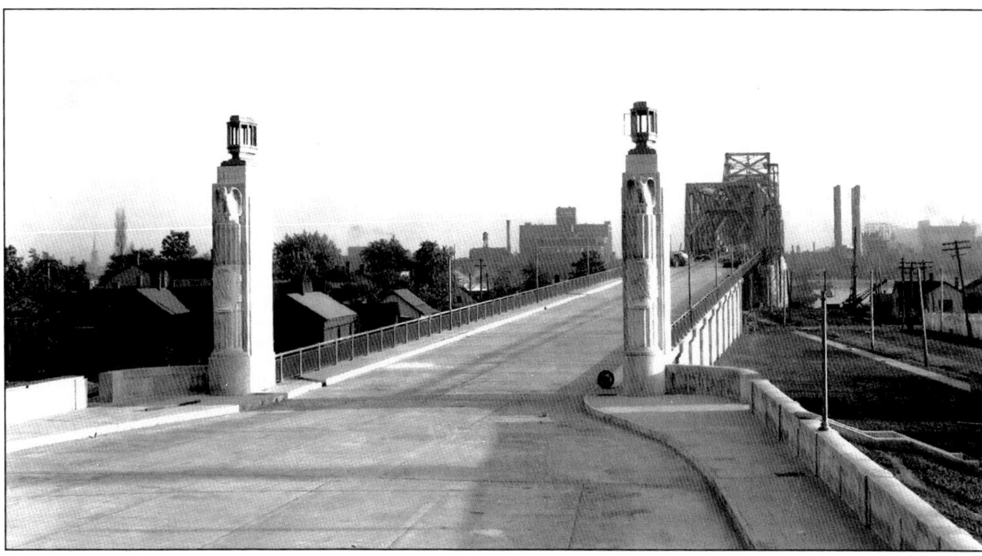

APPROACH TO THE INDIANA SIDE OF THE BRIDGE. The new bridge offered automobiles and pedestrians a direct route between Louisville at Second and Main Streets and Jeffersonville at Illinois Street (now Southern Indiana Avenue). It cost $4.7 million to construct. This photograph depicts the Indiana bridge approach and its art deco pylons capped by decorative lights. (Photo: University of Louisville Photographic Archives)

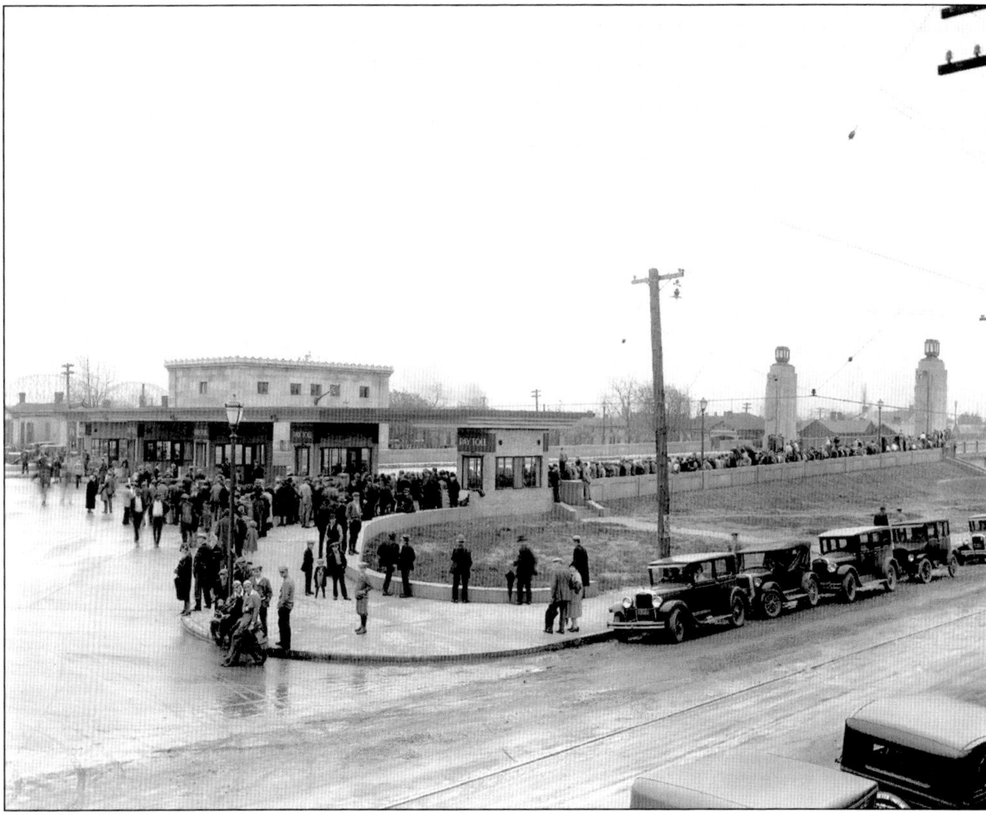

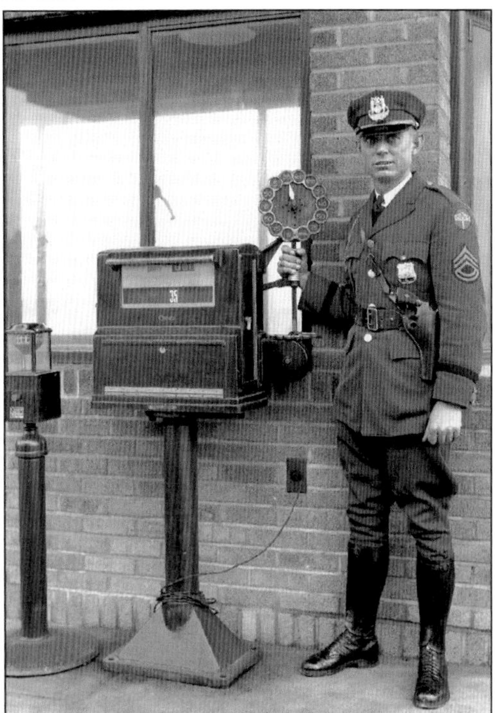

OPENING DAY ON THE MUNICIPAL BRIDGE. Opening ceremonies for the new bridge took place on October 31, 1929, just two days after the great stock market crash. Despite the financial gloom and rainy weather, many residents lined up to cross the bridge on its first day, as seen in this photo. A few of Jeffersonville's residents remain who remember walking across the bridge and receiving a commemorative token to mark the occasion. (Photo: University of Louisville Photographic Archives)

PAYING THE TOLL. The original toll schedule adopted by the Louisville Bridge Commission charged pedestrians 5¢ and passenger automobiles 35¢ for one-way passage. Trucks paid a graduated rate, increasing from 35¢ to a maximum charge of $1.50 depending on tonnage. The toll schedule also provided for horse-drawn vehicles, which paid according to the number of horses used, but did not allow any animals to be driven across, such as cattle. (Photo: University of Louisville Photographic Archives)

Three

LEARNING

SCHOOLS AND THE LIBRARY

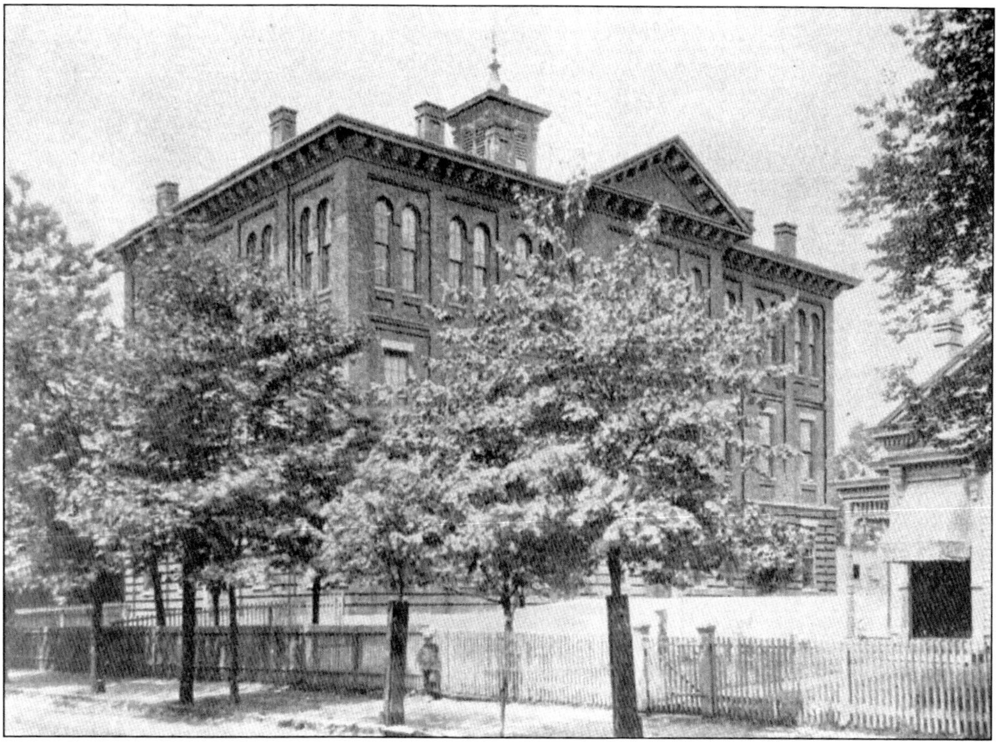

CHESTNUT STREET SCHOOL. Indiana's new constitution of 1851 required that the General Assembly provide for "a general and uniform system of Common Schools, wherein tuition shall be without charge, and equally open to all." As a result, Jeffersonville created its public school system in 1852 with two buildings, a two-story school on Mulberry Street opposite Chestnut Street and an identical building on the northwest corner of Maple and Watt Streets. Jeffersonville's first high school classes met at Mulberry Street School in 1868, but moved to the new Chestnut Street School, depicted above, just two years later. Elementary classes also met at Chestnut Street School. Jeffersonville High School's first class of five students graduated in 1872. (Photo: Jeffersonville Township Public Library)

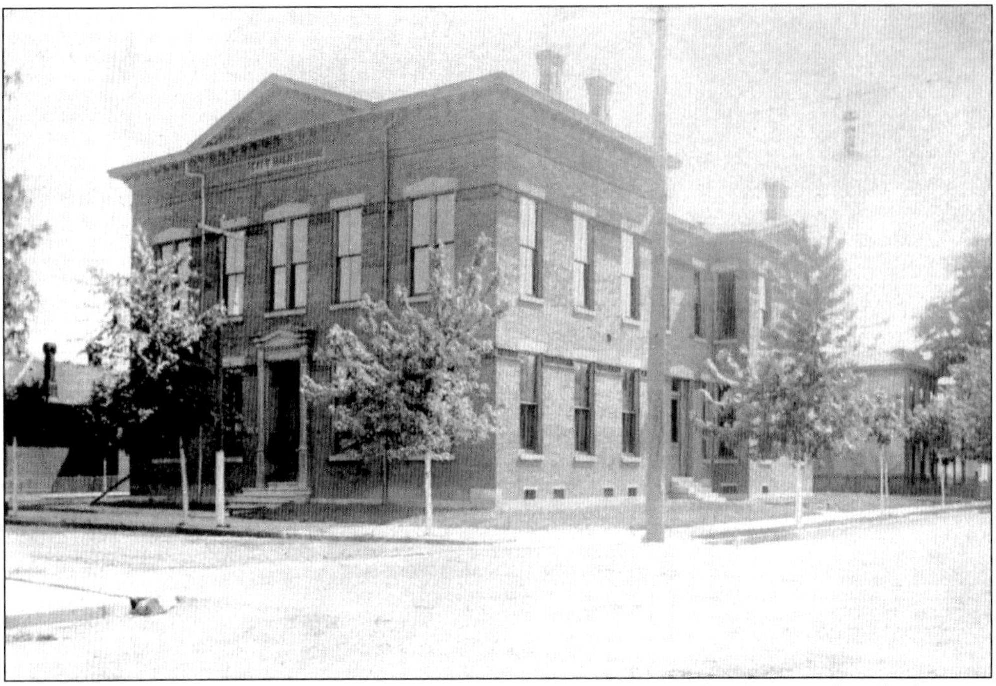

JEFFERSONVILLE'S THIRD HIGH SCHOOL. The city built a new school at Pearl and Chestnut Streets, shown above, for its secondary students in 1882. This school served Jeffersonville's high schoolers until 1911, when the new Court Avenue high school building opened. The Pearl and Chestnut Streets facility continued service as a junior high school until 1932 and was razed three years later. (Photo: Jeffersonville Township Public Library)

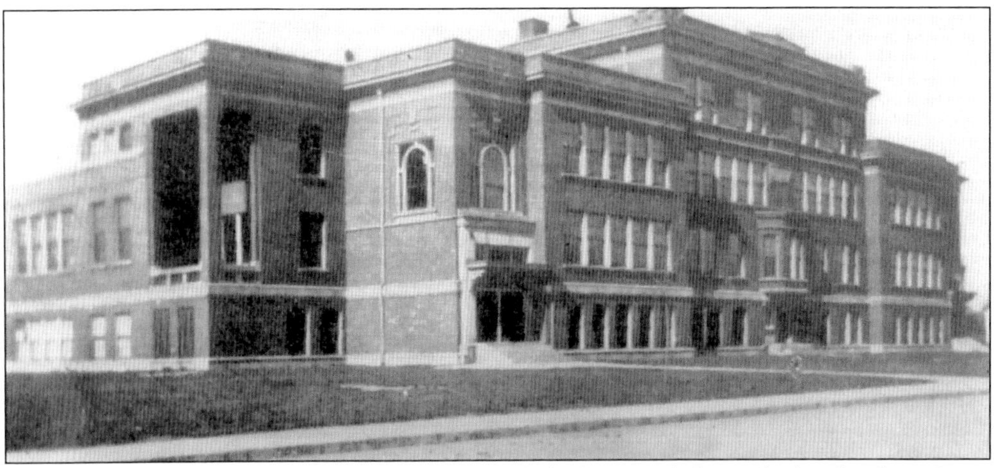

HIGH SCHOOL ON COURT AVENUE. Jeffersonville built a much larger high school on Court Avenue to accommodate rising enrollment and increasing curriculum improvements. Officials laid the building's cornerstone on March 30, 1910, and the new building opened for classes in January of 1911, just nine months later. The facility saw major additions through the years, including a girls' gymnasium, a junior high school, a field house (now known as the Nachand Field House), and a commercial building. The city opened its current high school on Allison Lane in 1971 and five years later, demolished the old main school building on Court Avenue, refurbishing the other buildings there for continued use. (Photo: Author's collection)

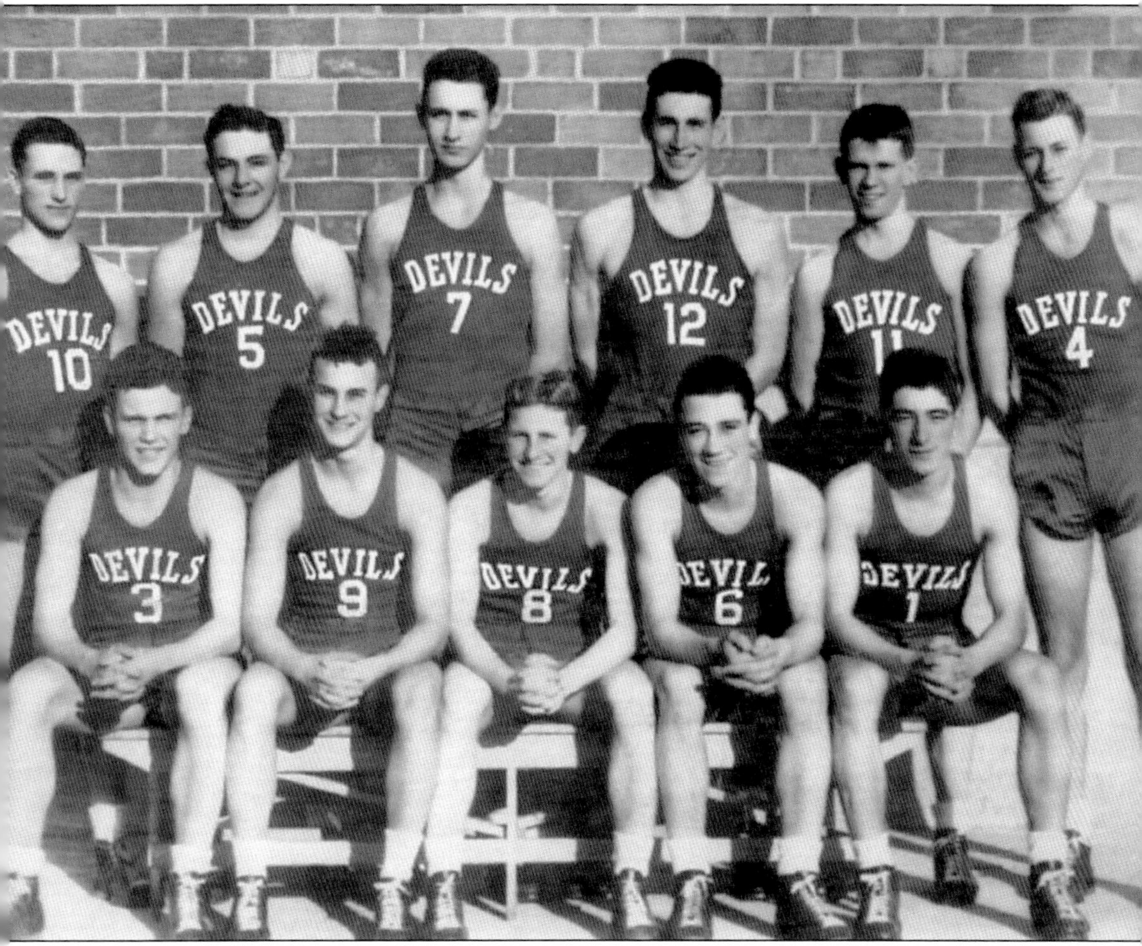

RED DEVILS AT STATE. Jeffersonville High School's boys' basketball program began in about 1906. The 1934–35 squad, pictured here, was the first Jeffersonville team to advance to the Indiana state basketball championship game. The undefeated Red Devils suffered a heart-breaking loss by the score of 23–17 to Anderson in that game. Schimpff's Confectionery in downtown Jeffersonville was "Red Devil Central" for away games, and the store registered approximately 3,000 phone calls for game updates during one tournament. The photo above hung for many years at the store on Spring Street, which generations of students enjoyed as a hangout. Team members pictured from left to right are as follows: (front row) Wilbur Davis, Kenny Groth, Ike Reynolds, Howard "Buddy" Phillips, and Fritz Hubbuch; (rear) Glennie Phillips, Junie Andres, Lindley Brubeck, Homer "Tubby" Thompson, C. Rauth, and Bill Johnson. Not pictured is coach Janis P. "Hunk" Francis. (Photo: Schimpff's Confectionery)

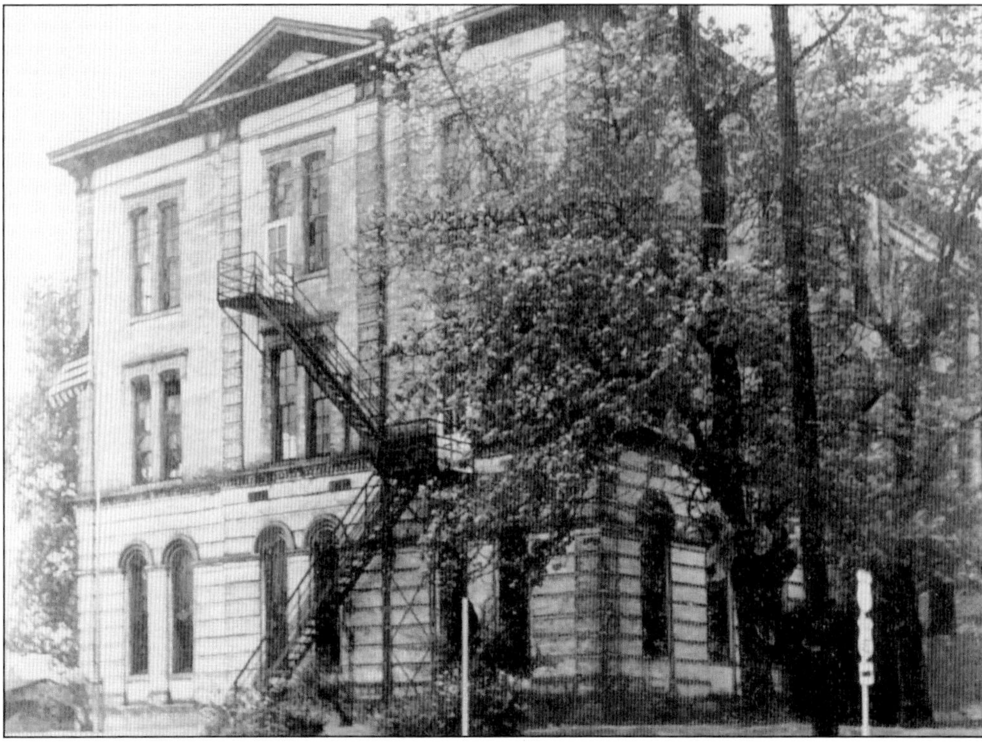

Rose Hill School. The city constructed Rose Hill School in 1874 on a small hill at Indiana Avenue and Fourth Street. The three-story elementary school, built in the style of Chestnut Street School on page 43, was known by many people in its early days as Prison Hill School, on account of its proximity to the old Indiana State Prison. This photo depicts the school after 1908, when the State Department of Inspection ordered numerous fire safety improvements to the school, including the fire escape seen here. (Photo: Dennis and Debbie Duffy)

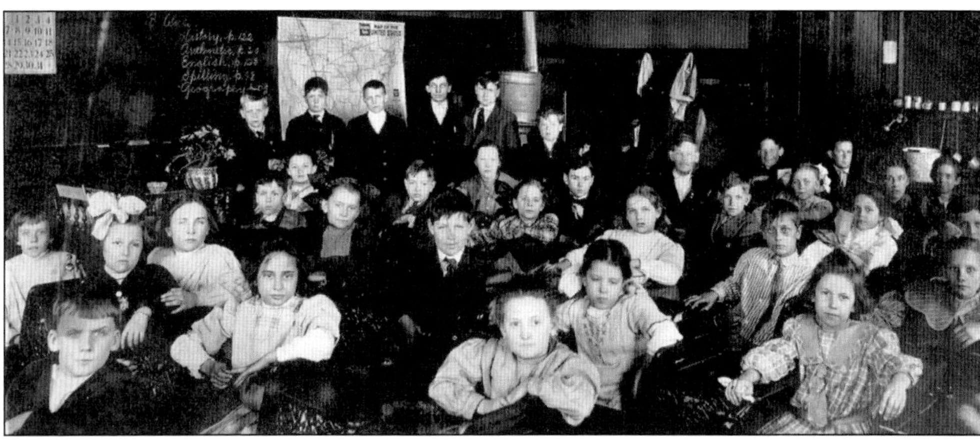

A Classroom at Rose Hill School. Students inside a classroom at Rose Hill School turn in their seats to pose for the camera in this 1911 image. A single stove in each classroom, seen here in the center rear, served as the building's only heat. The school had no running water or restrooms, so students used ladles to drink from water stored in large buckets, seen here at right. The school completed renovations in 1920 that added internal plumbing and restrooms. (Photo: Schimpff's Confectionery)

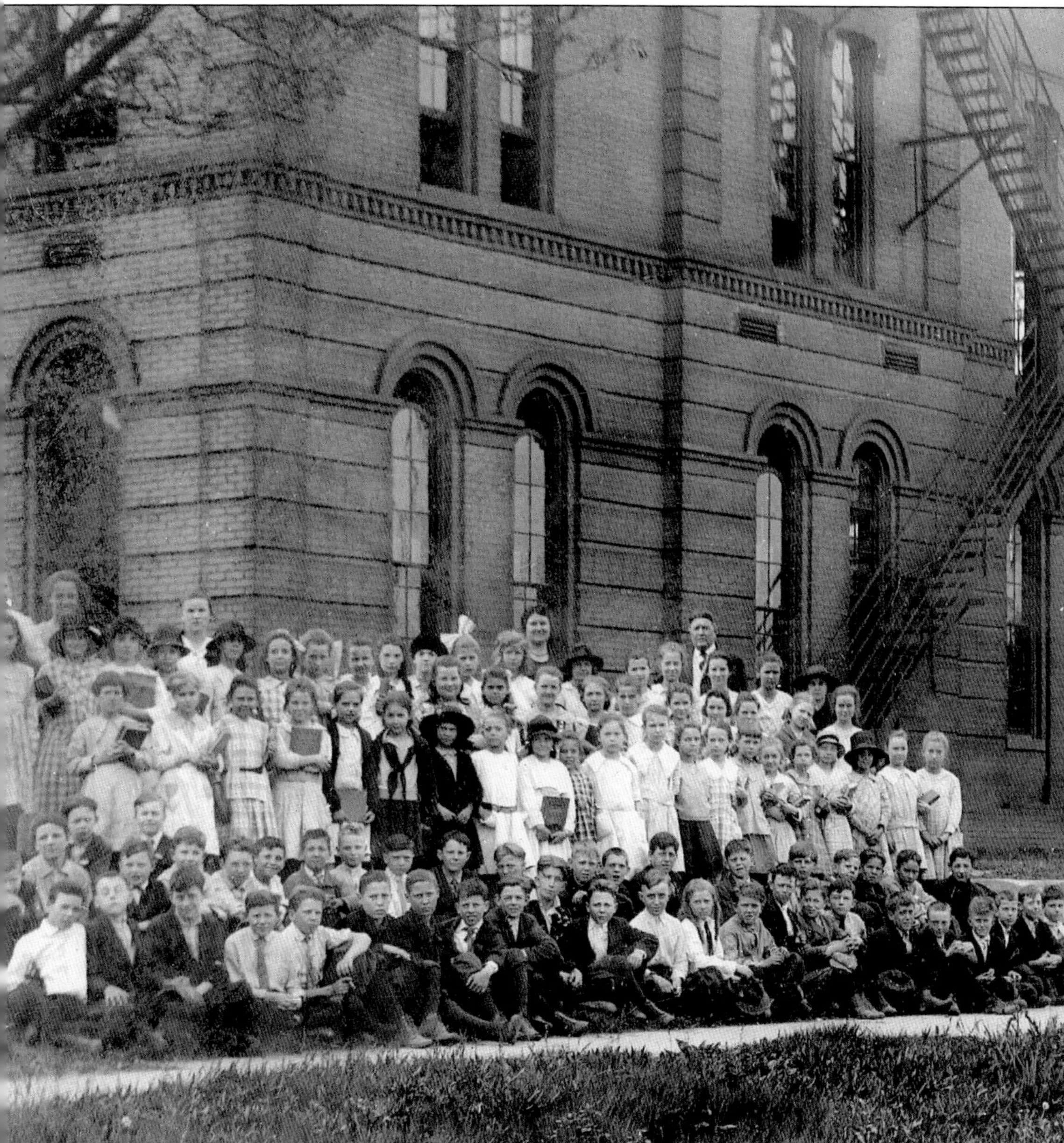

STUDENTS OUTSIDE ROSE HILL SCHOOL. The city removed Rose Hill School's second and third floors in 1950 as part of its effort to modernize the 75-year-old school building. Classes resumed in the reconstructed facility, but construction of what would become the Kennedy Bridge and its Court Avenue ramp just 10 years later led to the school's demise by the wrecking ball. Principal Robin M. Baggerly (top row, far right), who led the school from 1914 to 1939, poses outside the school with teachers and students in this photo from the mid-1910s. (Photo: Schimpff's Confectionery)

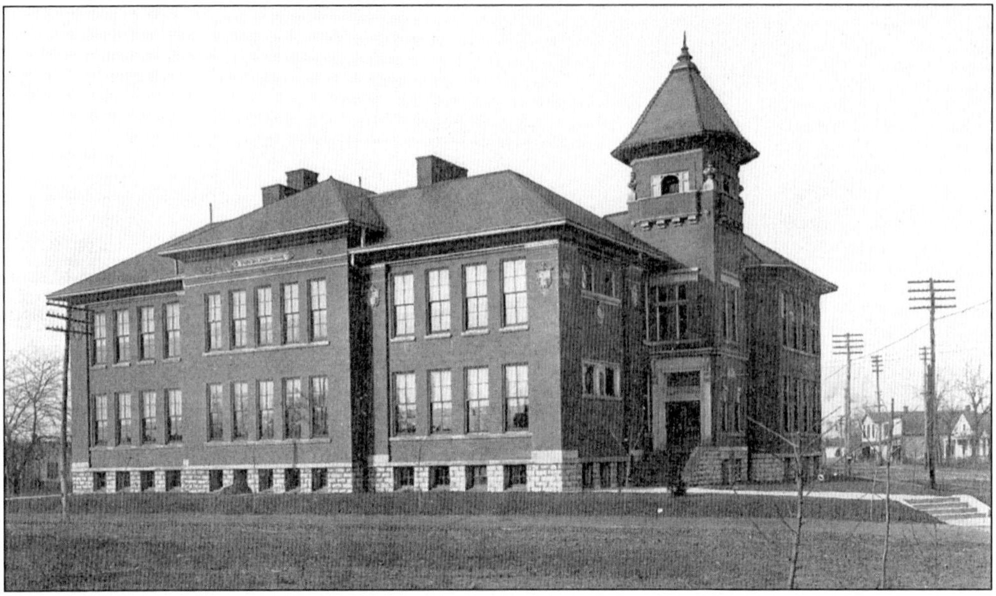

SPRING HILL SCHOOL. Jeffersonville built Spring Hill School in 1904 with great consideration for "sanitary and structural details." It was located west of Spring Street on Thirteenth Street. The photo below depicts a May Day celebration in about 1910 in which Lois Beeler, mother of funeral home owner William B. Scott, participated (see arrow). (Top photo: *Souvenir Jeffersonville, Ind.*; bottom photo: Scott Funeral Home)

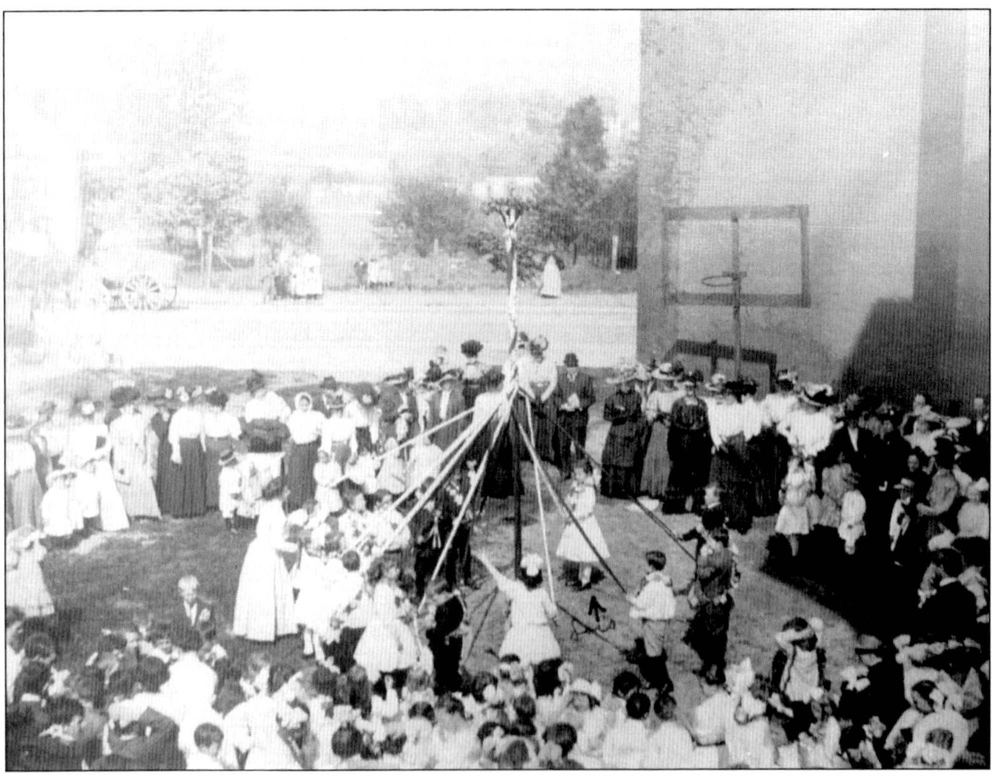

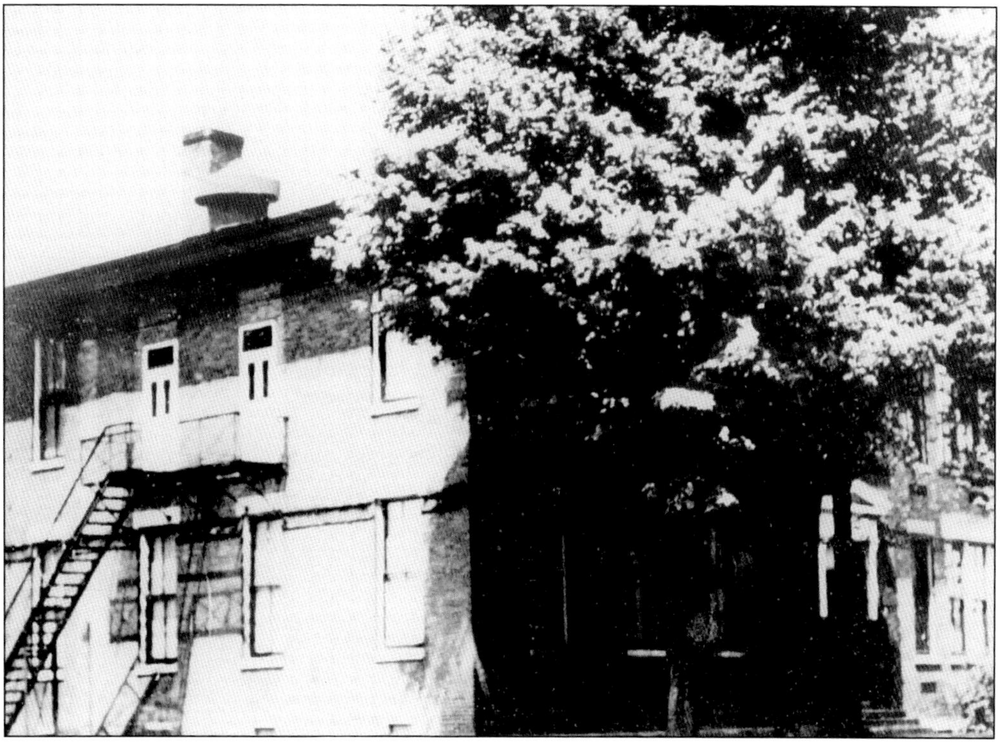

PORT FULTON SCHOOL. Port Fulton, located just to the northeast of Jeffersonville, existed as its own city until 1925, when its larger neighbor succeeded in annexing it. Port Fulton, consequently, operated its own school, the two-story structure seen above, which was built in 1880. The photograph below depicts two teachers and a group of students outside the school in about 1917. Identified persons in the photograph are Arthur Lee Smith (front row, third from left), Ellsworth Mitchell (front row, fifth from the left), and Charles Rau (front row, tenth from left). (Top photo: Dennis and Debbie Duffy; bottom photo: Naomi Mitchell)

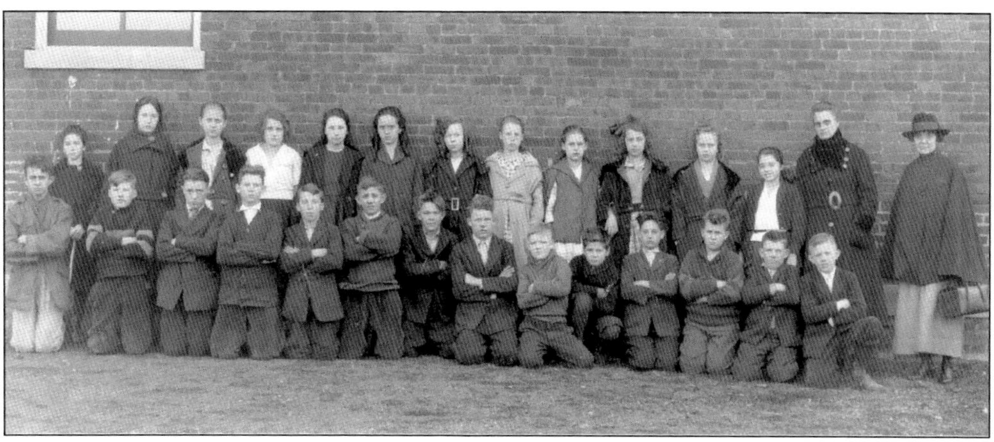

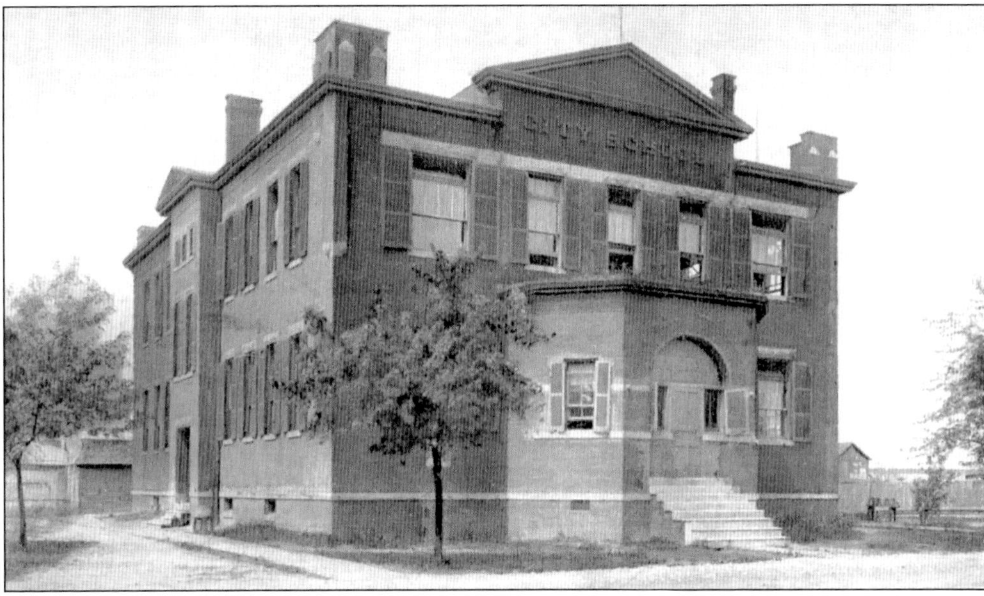

TAYLOR HIGH SCHOOL. Jeffersonville initiated a policy of segregating African-American students from the rest of its public school students in 1872. The city utilized the old Mulberry Street School for its African-American students until 1891, when Jeffersonville erected a new school for them, seen above. The facility, known officially as the City School and informally as Wall Street School, housed all of Jeffersonville's African-American elementary and high school students. The city renamed the school in 1924 for its beloved and longtime principal, Professor Robert Frank Taylor. (Photo: Bob Weber)

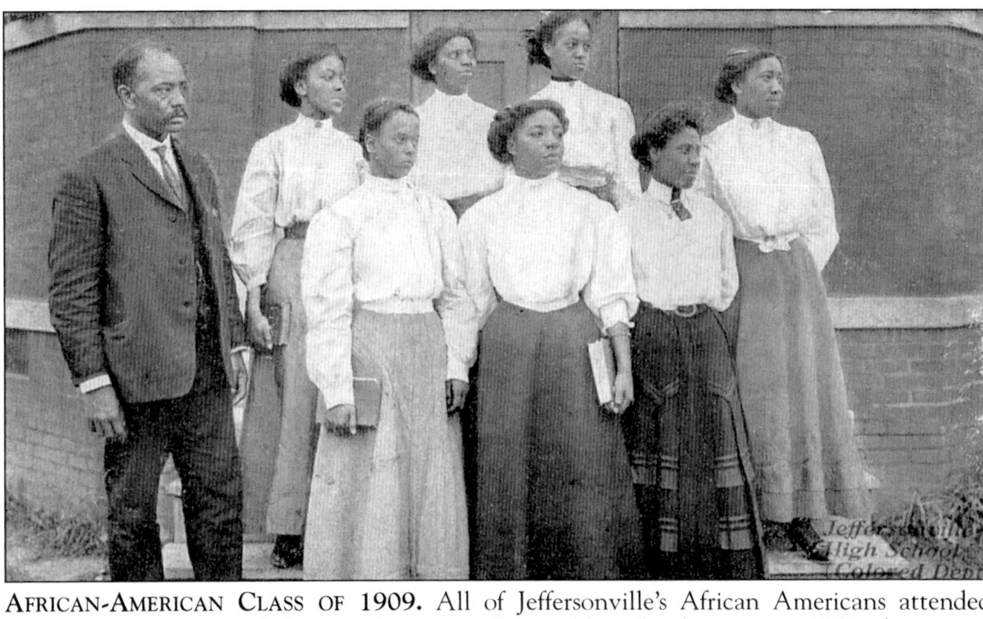

AFRICAN-AMERICAN CLASS OF 1909. All of Jeffersonville's African Americans attended Wall Street School until the city desegregated its public school system in 1952, three years after Indiana law banned segregated schools, but two years before the U.S. Supreme Court struck down segregation across the country. Pictured here is the school's Class of 1909 with an unidentified teacher. (Photo: Bob Weber)

PRINCIPAL ROBERT FRANK TAYLOR. Robert F. Taylor and two other students were Jeffersonville's first African Americans to graduate from high school. Administrators recognized Taylor's intelligence and appointed him a teacher in the "Colored Department" immediately after graduation in 1882. When the city constructed Wall Street School in 1891, Professor Taylor served as the school's first principal, a post he held until his death in 1926. Taylor could teach any of the school's subjects "with ease and efficiency," according to one source, and he was "loved and respected by pupils and citizens alike." (Photo: Doddie Ellis)

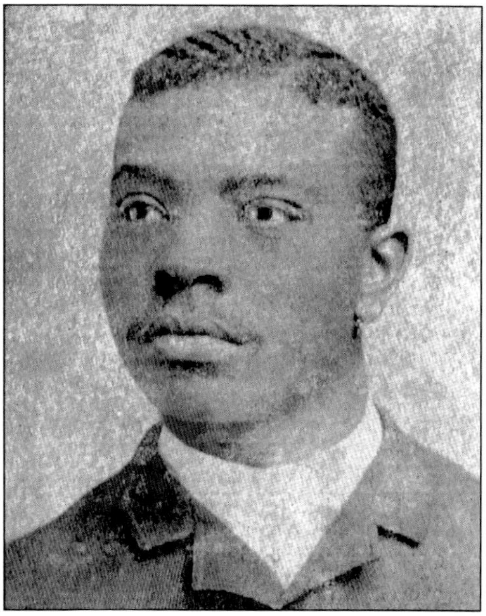

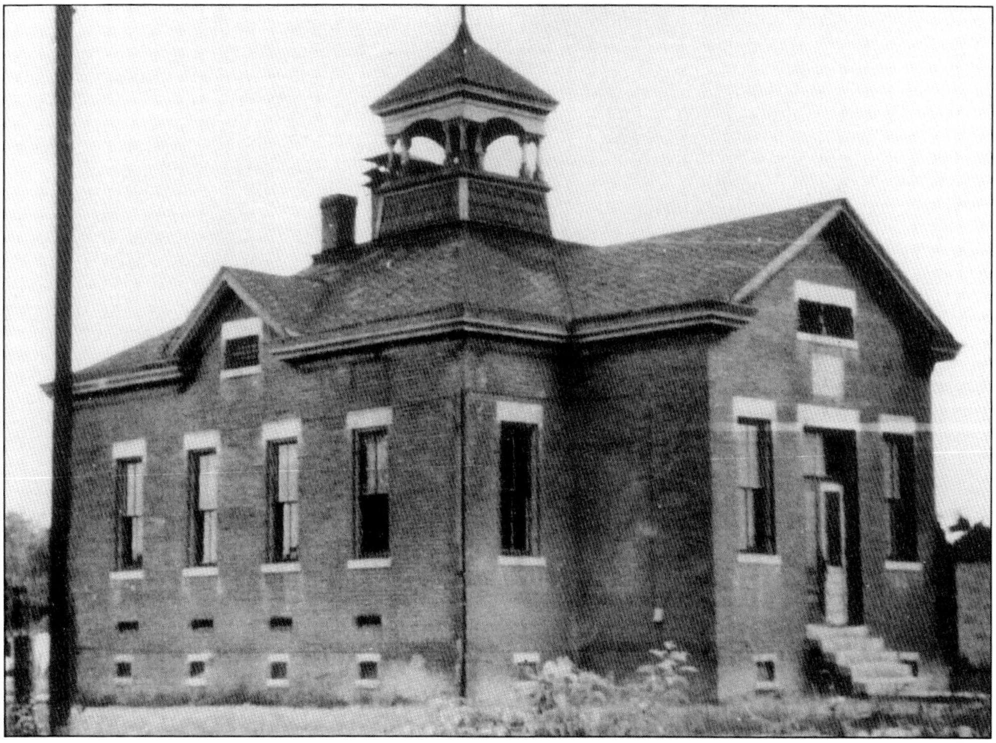

CLAYSBURG SCHOOL. Named for abolitionist Cassius Clay, Claysburg existed as an independent town from its founding in the middle of the 19th century to its annexation by Jeffersonville in 1948. It is one of Jeffersonville's traditionally African-American communities. Claysburg, like Port Fulton, operated its own school, seen in the photograph above. It stood until sometime after the 1948 annexation, when it became part of the Jeffersonville school system, but it was in poor condition by that time, with inadequate heating and outdoor toilets. (Photo: Dennis and Debbie Duffy)

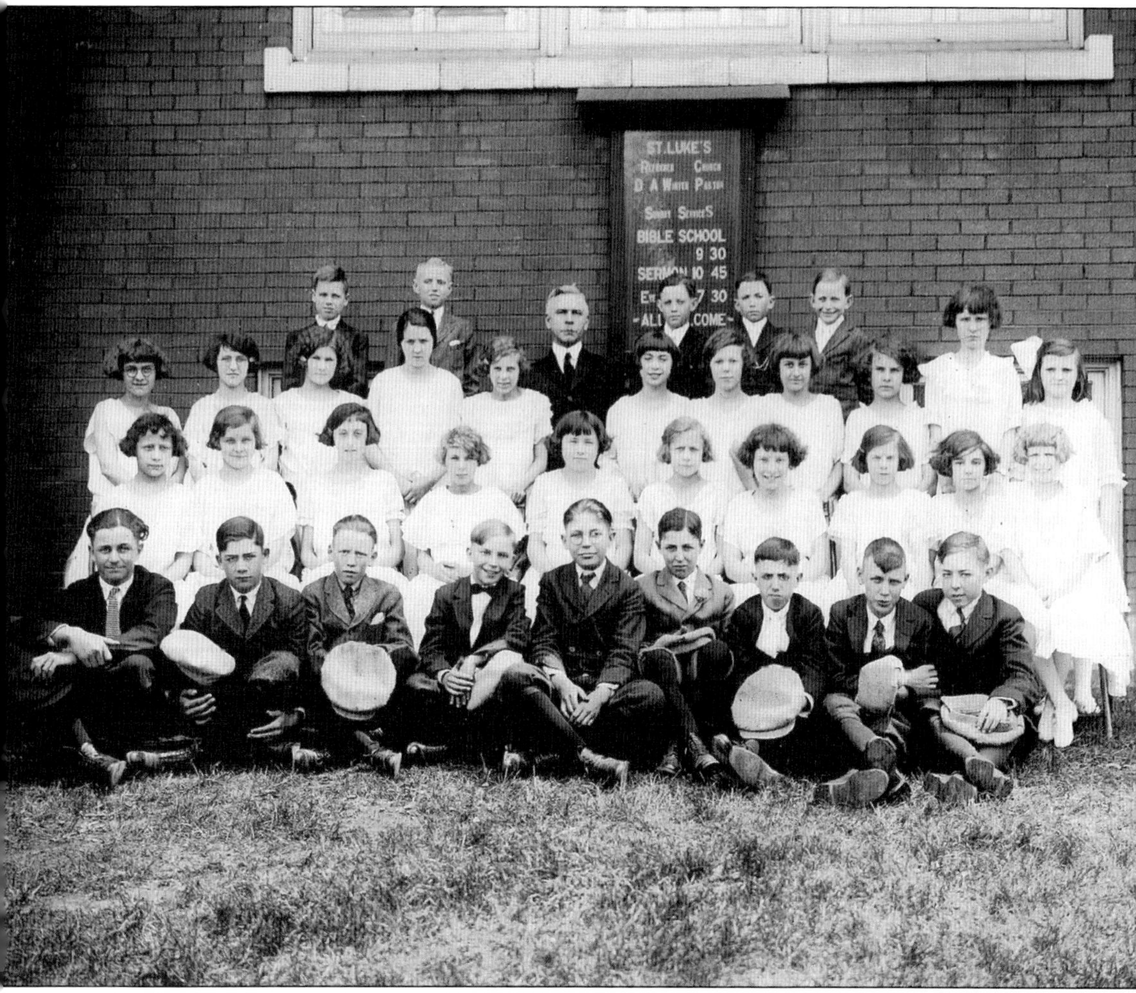

St. Luke's Church School. St. Luke's has operated a church school since 1870. Charles Schimpff served as the school's first general superintendent, a position he held for 46 years. Pictured in this photograph from April 13, 1924, are the following: (front row) Charles Hauser, John Andres, Frank Kaelin, Willie Kern, John Zurfluh, Earl Nagel, Oscar Kuntz, George James, and Harry Dyer; (second row) Doris Hassler, Alma Hauser, Madolyn Bixtenstien, Libby Rauth, Dorothy Schiller, Catherine Hassler, Edith Spangler, LaVerne Day, Doris Pangburn, and Myra Locke; (third row) Helen Williams, Margaret Kopp, Janet Locke, Mary Leach, Evelyn Rauth, Aileen Bales, Virginia Stemler, Charlotte Alben, Dorothy Brumbach, Freda Marie Higdon, and Alice Cain; (back row) William Phillips, Sherill Volmer, Rev. D.A. Winters, Ike Williams, Arthur Maloney, and Leonard Spooner. (Photo: St. Luke's United Church of Christ)

Opposite: **St. Augustine Catholic School.** St. Augustine operated a parish school from 1869 to 1969. Pictured here in this photograph from 1908 is a group of girls who called themselves "The Daisy Class." They stayed together throughout their school years. Pictured from left to right are the following: (front row) Margaret Kestler, Ellis Murphy, Mary Dean, Kate Linch, Anna "Midge" Duffy, and Margaret Kennedy; (back row) Rose Kennedy, Mary Dible, Alma Howes, Ivy Kimmick, and Gertrude Robards. (Photo: Dennis and Debbie Duffy)

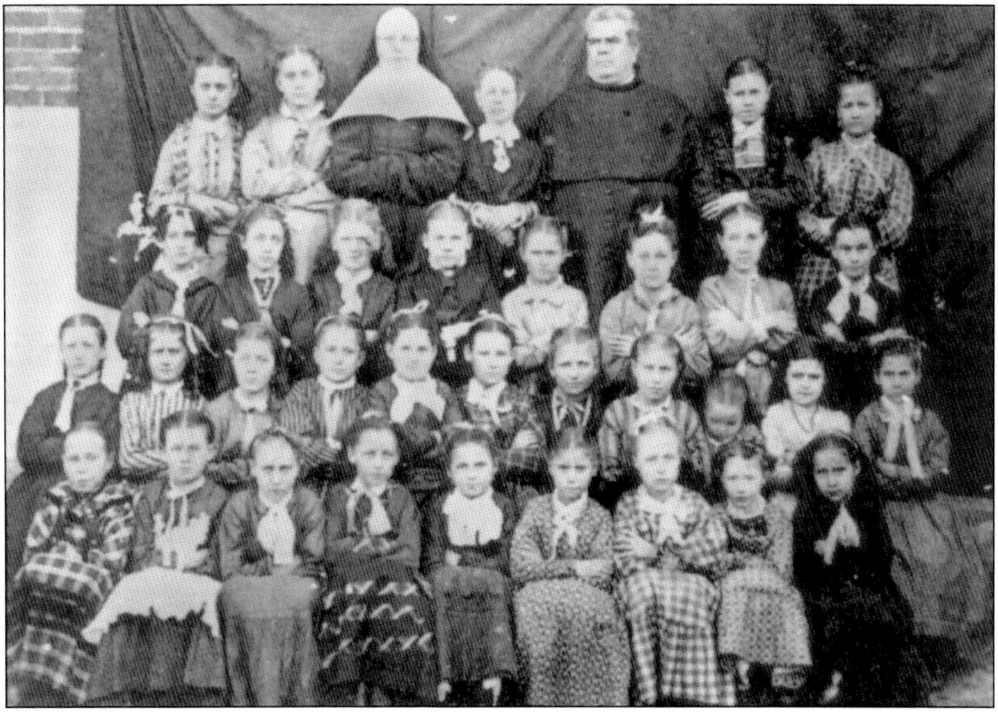

ST. ANTHONY CATHOLIC SCHOOL. Rev. Phillip Doyle, St. Anthony's third resident pastor, opened a parish school in 1860. Rev. Leopold Moczygemba and an unidentified nun join the first class at St. Anthony's new facility at Maple and Wall Streets for this 1876 photograph. The school closed for a time after the 1937 flood, but reopened and eventually relocated with the church to Clarksville where it operates to this day. (Photo: St. Anthony of Padua Church)

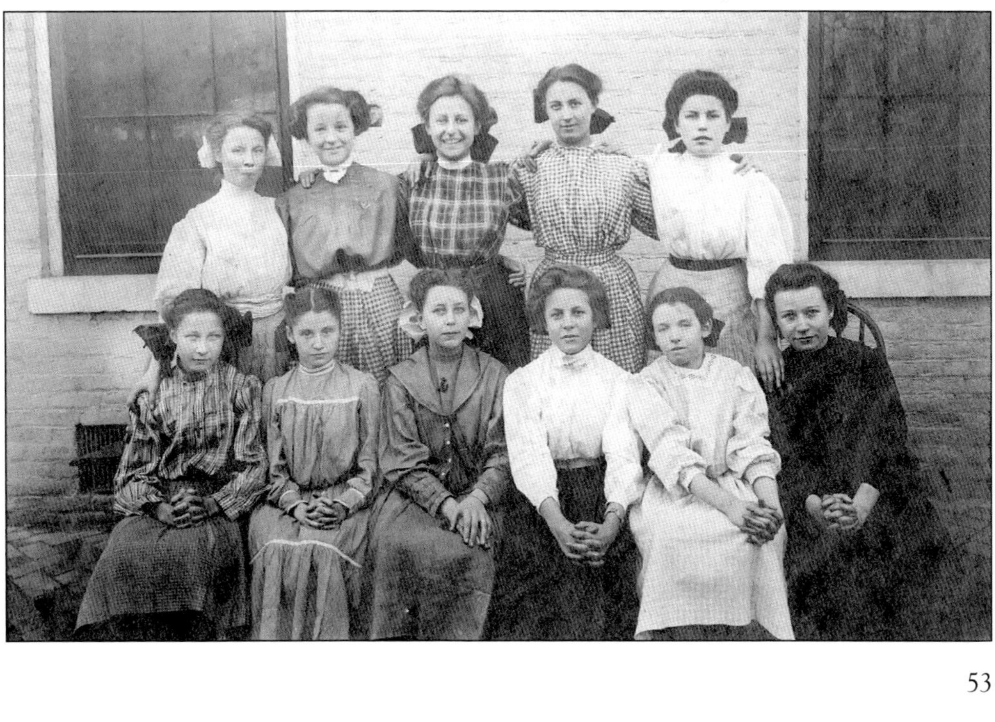

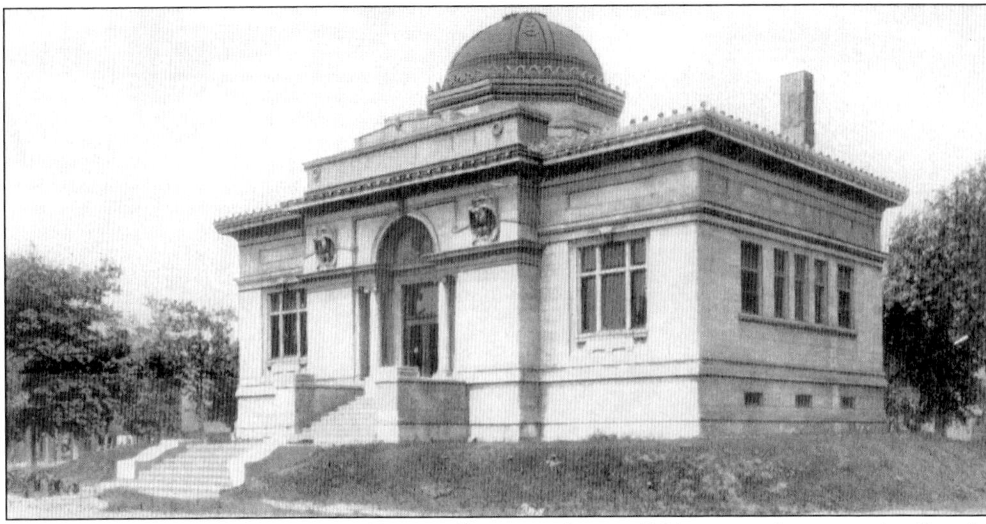

The Jewel of Warder Park. Jeffersonville enjoyed a small library in the trustee's office for some time in the 19th century, but it was, according to historian Lewis Baird, "a place where men loafed and smoked and discussed the ideas of the day," and "was no place where children or women could suitably visit." A new Jeffersonville Township Public Library officially opened on December 17, 1900, with 1,400 books in a room over the Citizens National Bank. The Carnegie Foundation soon donated $16,000 for the construction of a new library building, the copper-domed Beaux Arts landmark designed by Jeffersonville architect Arthur Loomis. Masonic officials laid the building's cornerstone on September 19, 1903, in Warder Park. (Photo: Jeffersonville Township Public Library)

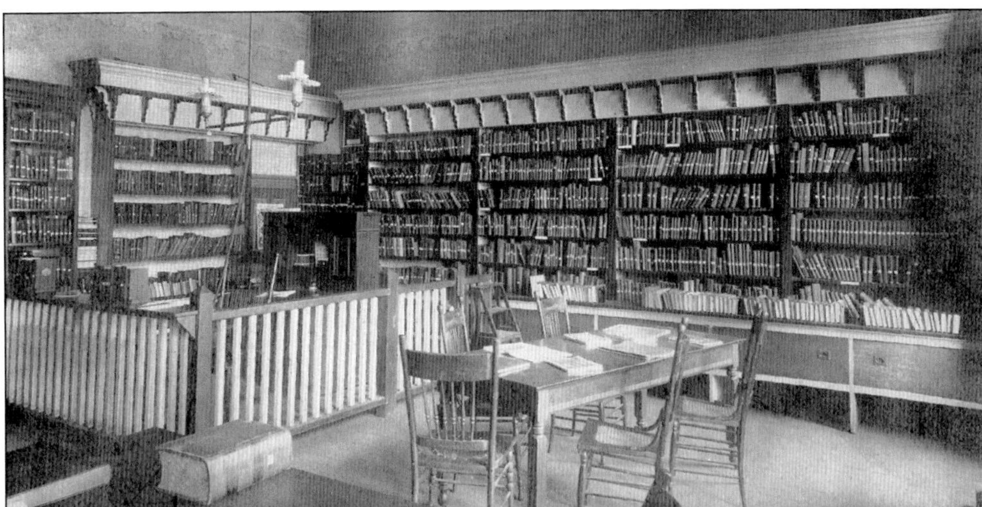

Interior of the Carnegie Library. The library boasted a collection of 3,869 volumes when it reopened to the public in January of 1905 after relocating to the Carnegie facility. Shown here in this early photograph is a room inside the library. Flood waters inundated the building in 1937 causing a near total loss of the library's collection. The library reopened in November of 1937 thanks to months of hard work and generous donations of money and books. The building served as the city's library until the completion of a new building just east on Court Avenue in 1969. (Photo: Jeffersonville Township Public Library)

Four

WORSHIPPING

CHURCHES AND CONGREGATIONS

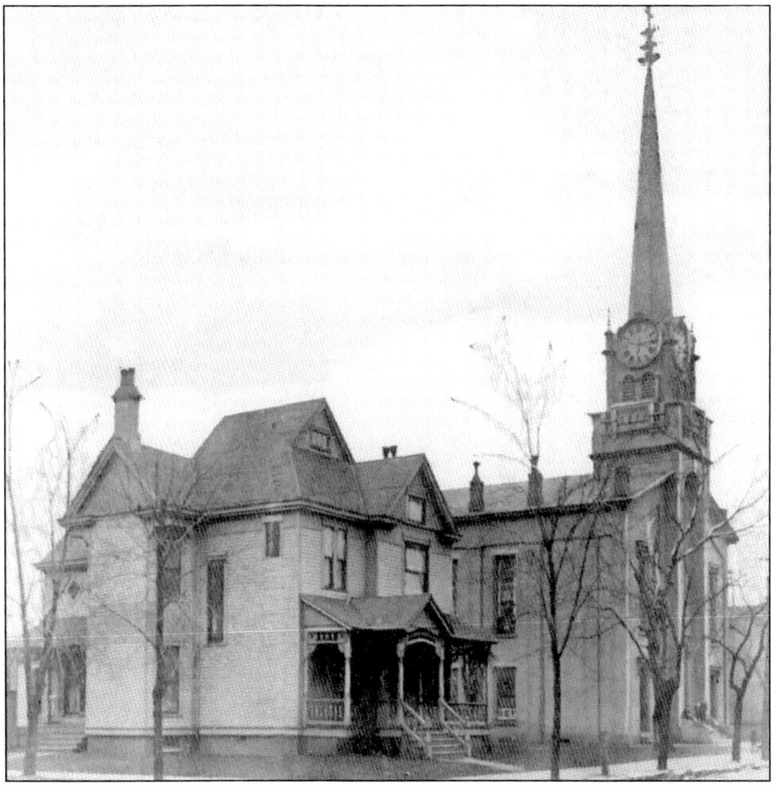

WALL STREET METHODIST EPISCOPAL CHURCH. The first recorded Methodist minister to preach in Jeffersonville came to the city in 1803. Four years later, Methodists organized a society in a house on the location of today's Wall Street United Methodist Church. The congregation attained station status in 1833, and the church completed its first house of worship two years later. The church grew over the next two decades forcing its leaders to plan a larger facility. The congregation completed its second church in stages between 1859 and 1865. The photograph above depicts this second church and its parsonage before 1900. The decision of church leaders to cap the church steeple with a cross (an uncustomary practice) caused great dissension, for many objected that it made the building look too much like a Catholic church. A prominent member of the congregation asserted that "the Catholics had no lien on the cross" and the matter subsided. (Photo: Author's collection)

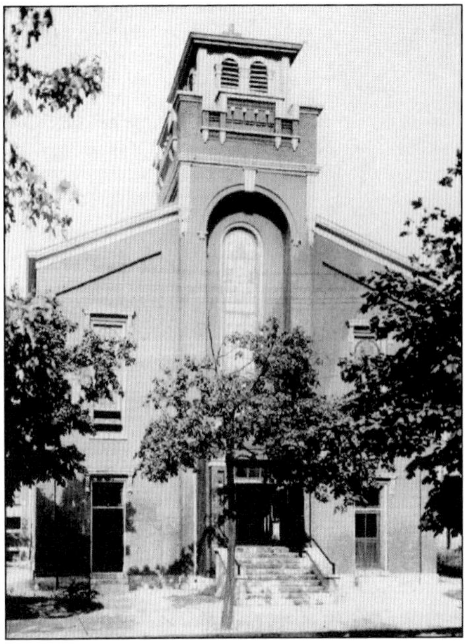

IMPROVEMENTS AT WALL STREET METHODIST. Some time after 1900, church leaders judged "the extremely lofty spire. . .to be unsafe." They removed it along with its clock, which no longer kept the correct time, and replaced it with the smaller bell tower seen above. In 1904, the church completed other extensive remodeling, which included the installation of stained glass windows and forced-air heat. The congregation has been known as Wall Street United Methodist Church since the religion's 1968 merger with the Evangelical United Brethren Churches. (Photo: Wall Street United Methodist Church)

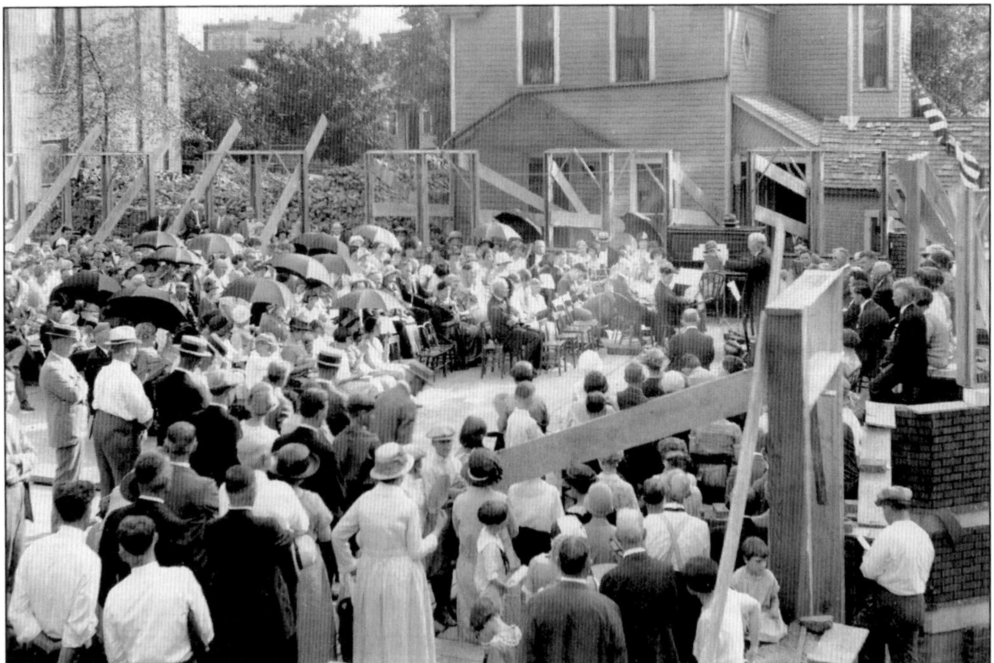

ANNEX DEDICATION CEREMONY. Homer M. Frank, chairman of Wall Street Methodist's building committee and longtime leader of the church's Troop 1 (Jeffersonville's first Boy Scout troop), remembered how the Scouts requested $500 to build a recreational annex near the church for their use, as their play was considered "more boisterous than was thought to be decorous in the house of worship." That small plan evolved into the construction of a much larger scale educational and recreational annex. The cornerstone laying ceremony in 1925, depicted above, drew hundreds of attendees, many of whom represented Jeffersonville's other churches. (Photo: Charles R. Leap)

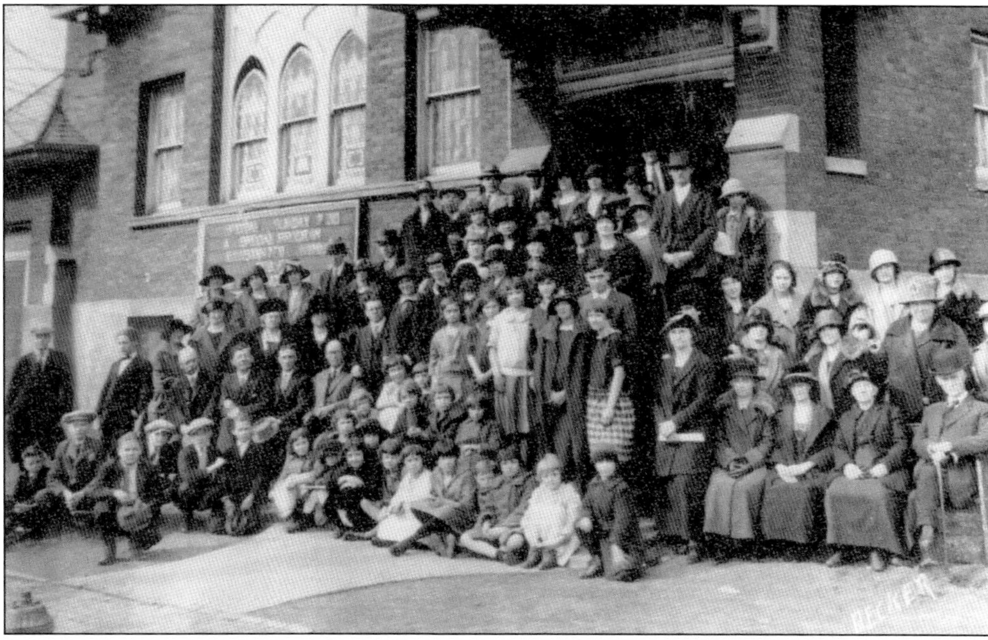

THE METHODIST CHURCH IN PORT FULTON. Port Fulton Methodist Episcopal Church began in May of 1849 as an offshoot of Wall Street Methodist. The congregation constructed its first church in July of 1851 at 200 Market Street (now Park Place). Membership grew rapidly in the late 19th century. As a result, the congregation built a new church, pictured above, between 1912 and 1914, on land donated by Edmonds J. Howard. It changed its name to Park Place Methodist Episcopal Church when the east end of Market Street was renamed Park Place and finally relocated to a new church further east on the street in 1962. Bethel A.M.E., one of the city's oldest African-American congregations, now worships at the facility. It was founded in Claysburg in 1842. (Photo: Violet Rogers)

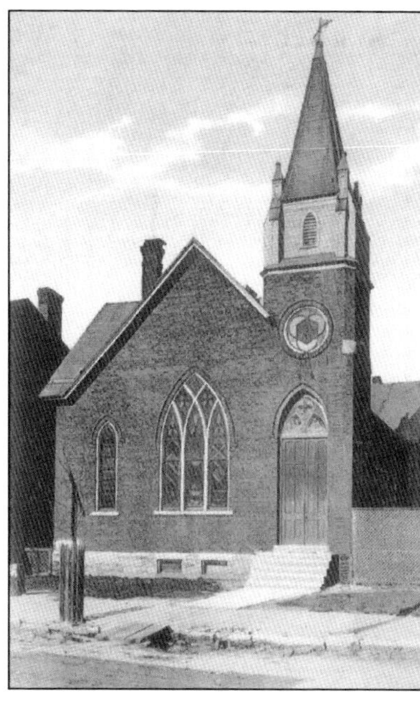

MORTON MEMORIAL METHODIST EPISCOPAL CHURCH. Morton Memorial also traces its origin to Wall Street Methodist. In 1868, 22 members of the mother church joined to form a Southern Methodist congregation later named Morton Chapel in honor of Dr. David Morton, who raised significant funds for the church. The congregation built its first church at Maple and Mulberry Streets and moved to a new church, pictured above, in 1893 on Locust Street between Maple and Court. The congregation relocated to Clarksville in 1950. (Photo: Bob Weber)

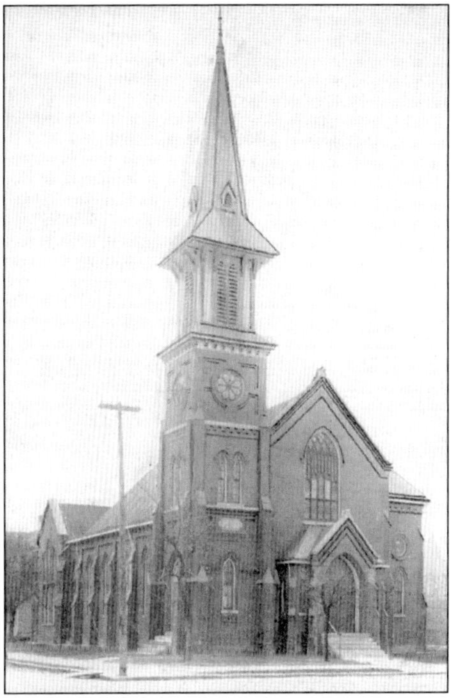

GERMAN METHODIST EPISCOPAL CHURCH. Jeffersonville's German-speaking Methodists organized in 1845 and built their own church on Locust Street in 1851. The congregation built a larger church in 1877 at Maple and Watt Streets, seen in the photograph at left. By 1909, the congregation had begun to lose its unique identity, for members had become more English than German in their language and customs. The 1937 flood devastated the church and members of its congregation were absorbed soon after by the city's other Methodist churches. Today, Jeffersonville's Seventh-Day Adventist Church worships at the facility, which has a much reduced steeple rising above it. (Photo: Bill Whittaker)

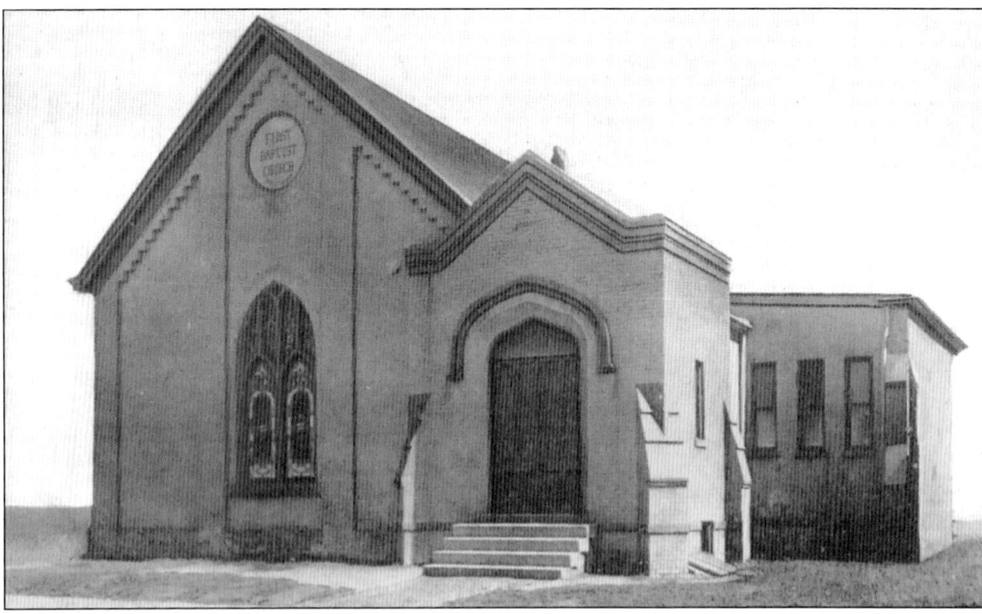

FIRST BAPTIST CHURCH. Jeffersonville's Baptists organized on June 22, 1839, at Jeffersonville's First Presbyterian Church and continued to worship there until relocating to their own facility. The congregation worshiped at various locations until 1880, when it relocated to West Maple Street. The church purchased from Mrs. J.G. Howard and remodeled a building there, which became the nucleus of the church depicted above. The First Baptist Church relocated in 1964 to a new facility on State Route 62, but it maintained a small ministry at the old church, now known as West Maple Baptist Church. The old church continued to stand on West Maple until some time after 1988, when it was razed to make way for a new facility. (Photo: Author's collection)

FIRST PRESBYTERIAN CHURCH OF JEFFERSONVILLE. In 1816, Rev. James McGready, a missionary from Pennsylvania, organized Jeffersonville's first Presbyterian church, known then as the Union Church of New Albany and Jeffersonville. The congregation broke up and moved to New Albany a year later. Jeffersonville's Presbyterians reorganized in 1830 and built a new church in 1832 (pictured on page 64 and occupied later by St. Luke's). By the late 1850s, the congregation needed a larger house of worship. The new structure rose up in the early 1860s to such a size that some criticized its scale. "I'm not building a church for today," asserted longtime elder James H. McCampbell. "I expect the church to last for years." The beautiful Gothic revival church, depicted at right in 1908, stands to this day at the corner of Chestnut and Walnut Streets. (Photo: First Presbyterian Church of Jeffersonville)

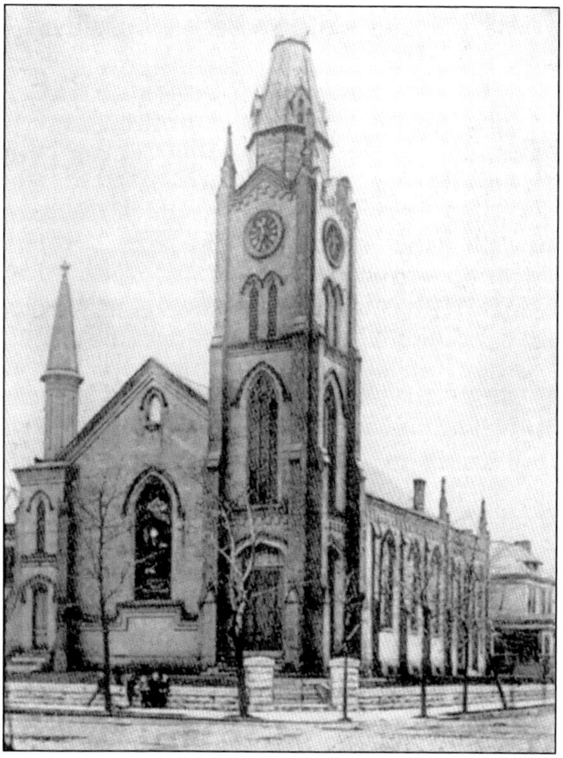

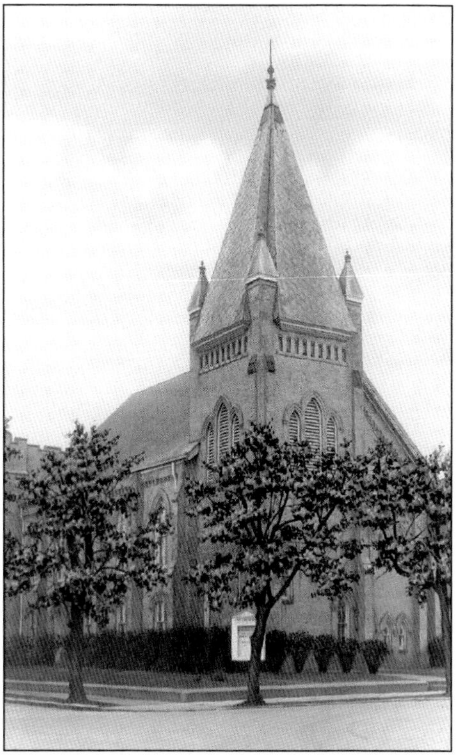

FIRST CHRISTIAN CHURCH OF JEFFERSONVILLE. Dr. Nathaniel Field, a prominent physician and civic leader in Jeffersonville, met with seven other Christians of the city on March 7, 1830, to organize the first "Church of Christ" in Jeffersonville. The congregation drew its inspiration from Alexander Campbell's New Testament-centered Restoration movement, begun in 1811. The congregation met in the old county courthouse at Market between Spring and Pearl until 1840 when it constructed a church on Telegraph (now Walnut) Street. The congregation worshiped there until 1884, when flood waters caused such great damage that the church built a new facility, dedicated later that year and pictured at left. First Christian worshiped in that church until 1973, when it relocated to a new facility on Middle Road. The Temple of Christ Apostolic Faith Church now owns the old church. (Photo: First Christian Church of Jeffersonville)

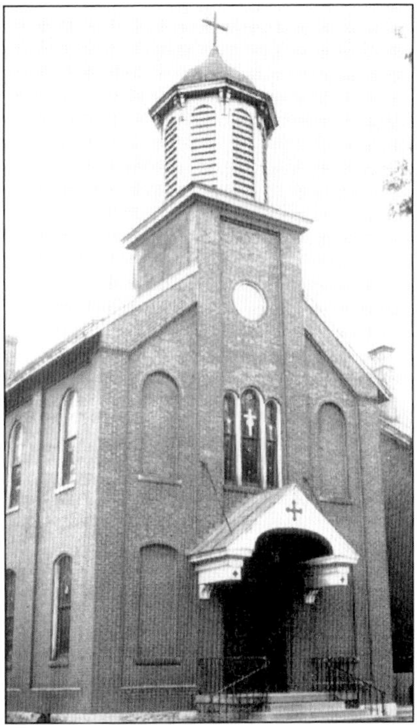

ST. ANTHONY OF PADUA ROMAN CATHOLIC CHURCH. Catholics had lived in Jeffersonville since its founding. They had to cross the river to Louisville to celebrate the sacraments, however, until October 18, 1851, when they opened their own church at the corner of Canal Street (now Meigs Avenue) and Maple Street. Rev. Augustine Bessonies served as the parish's first resident pastor from 1854 to 1857. The congregation built a new church, shown here, at Maple and Wall Streets in 1876. (Photo: St. Anthony of Padua Roman Catholic Church)

Opposite: **INTERIOR OF ST. ANTHONY.** This photograph depicts the interior of St. Anthony of Padua's 1876 church as it appeared in July of 1925 for Rev. Oderic Auer's silver jubilee as a priest. For many years it was considered Jeffersonville's German Catholic congregation. This church served the parish until 1949, when it moved to new facilities in Clarksville. The old church at Maple and Wall was demolished in 1965. (Photo: St. Anthony of Padua Roman Catholic Church)

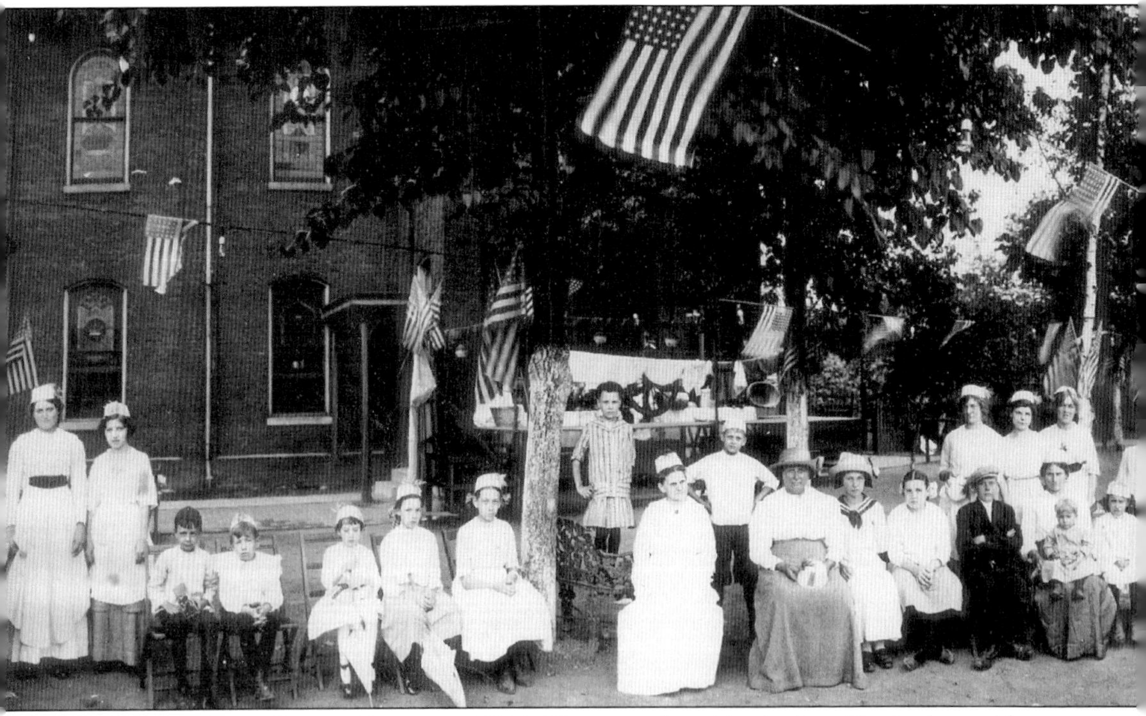

ST. ANTHONY PARISH PICNIC IN 1914. The annual parish picnic at St. Anthony, like many other churches, has highlighted the church's social calendar for many years. It has also provided a great material benefit on account of its financial contribution to the parish's budget. Among those depicted in this panorama from the July 27, 1914 picnic are Rev. Louis Hammer (the

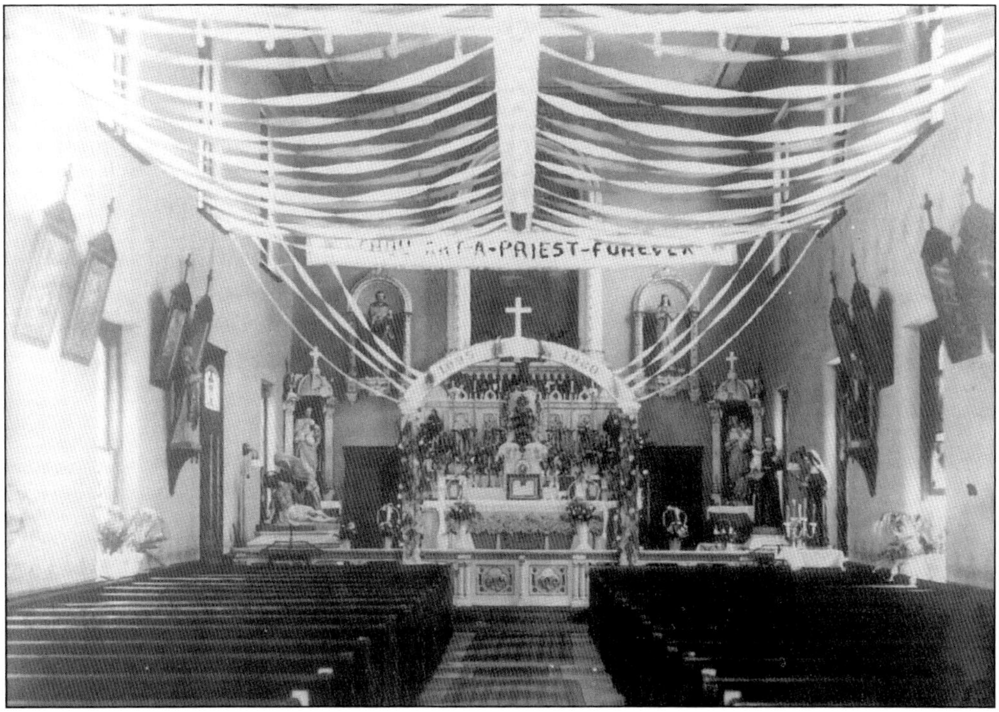

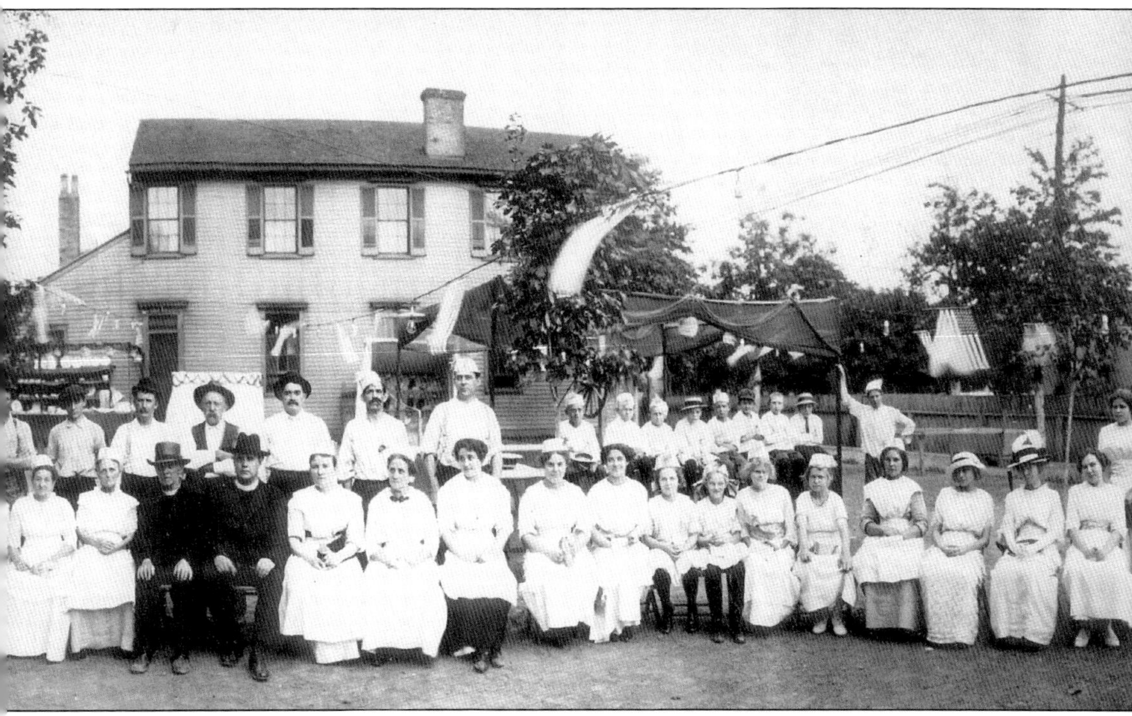

priest on the right), who was the parish's pastor at the time, and Joseph Bittner (the last boy on the right, standing with his arm raised), who would be St. Anthony parish's first casualty in World War I. (Photo: St. Anthony of Padua Roman Catholic Church)

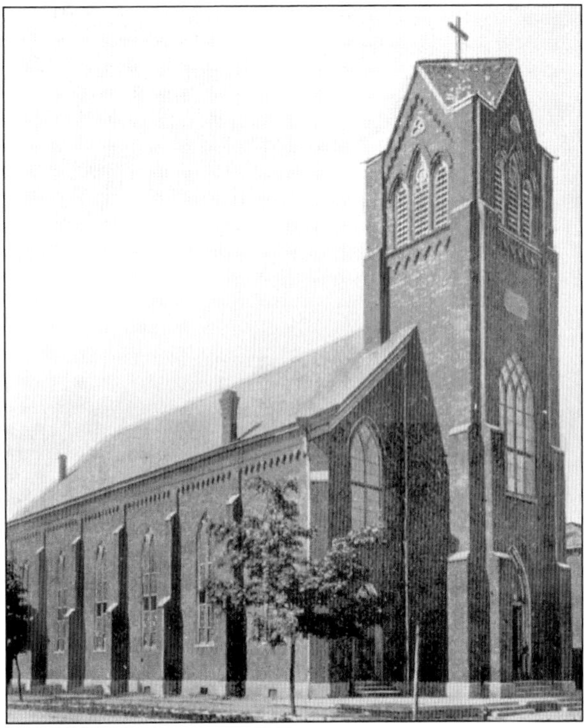

THE FIRST ST. AUGUSTINE ROMAN CATHOLIC CHURCH. Ethnic tension at St. Anthony of Padua Church between its Irish and German factions, coupled with the need for more space, led to the parish's division in the early 1860s. Those of mostly Irish descent relocated to a new building at Chestnut and Locust Streets. Bishop John Spalding of Louisville officiated at the laying of the cornerstone on October 8, 1863. The congregation chose St. Augustine as its patron saint, in honor of Rev. Augustine Bessonies. The new church received its formal blessing on St. Patrick's Day, 1868. Fire destroyed the church on December 9, 1903. (Photo: St. Augustine Roman Catholic Church)

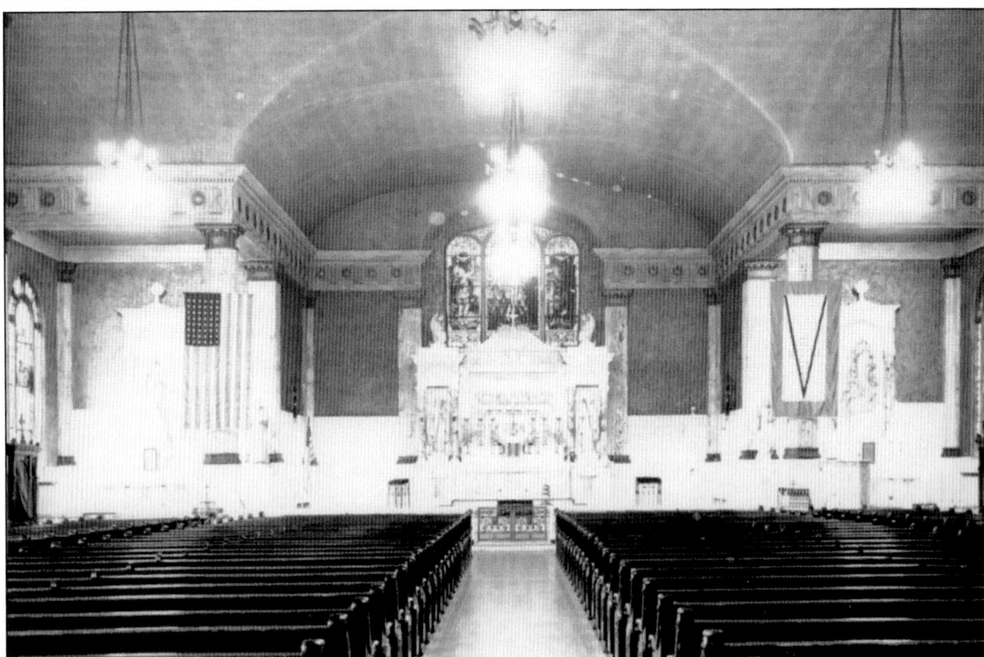

INSIDE THE 1905 CHURCH. The parish began rebuilding on the same site at Chestnut and Locust Streets in the spring of 1904. Bishop Francis Silas Chatard of Indianapolis dedicated the new church on October 2, 1905. Italian artists carved the beautiful altar, statuary, and other sculptures for which the church is well known beginning in 1924. This photograph from 1930 depicts the church with its new accouterments. (Photo: Dennis and Debbie Duffy)

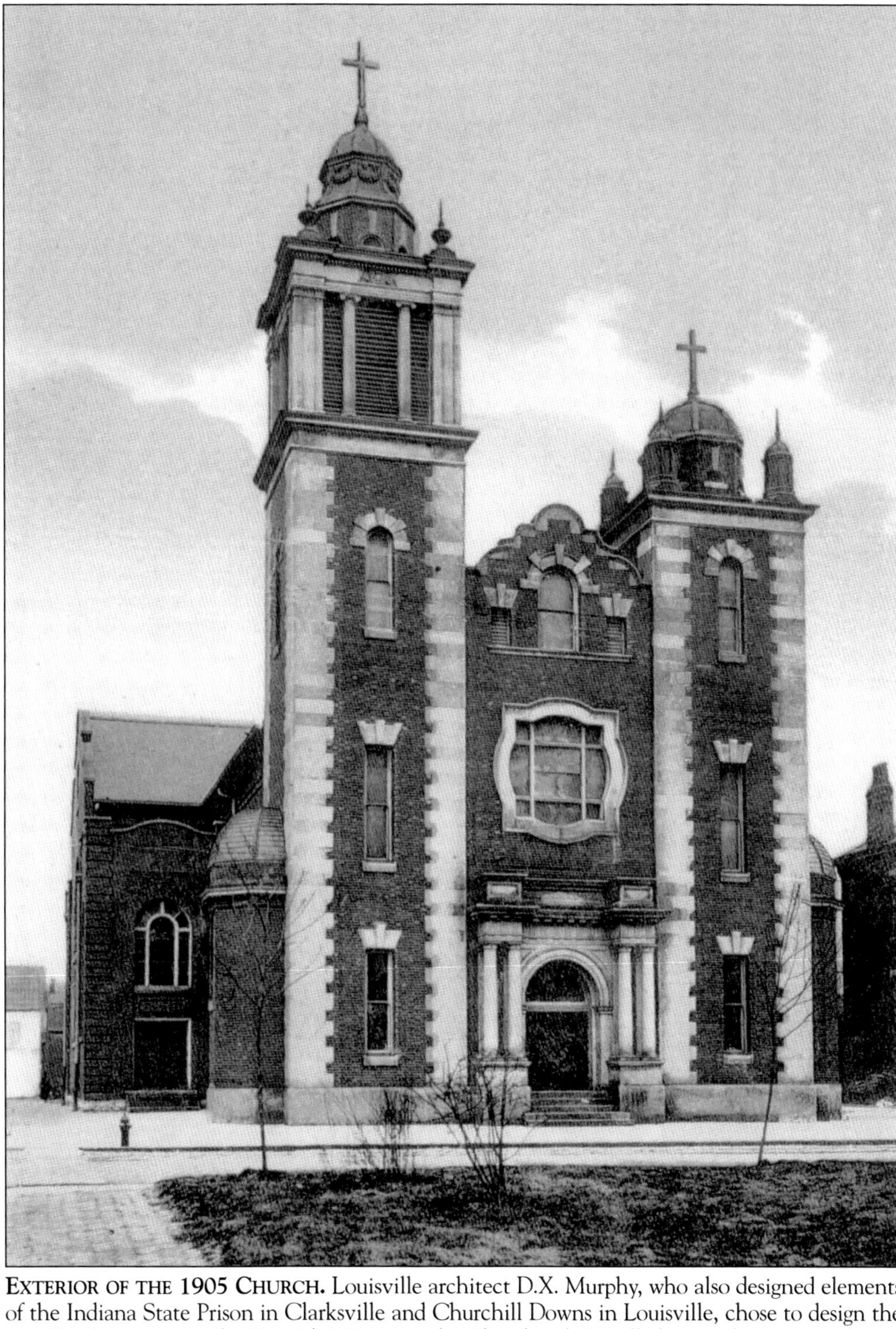

EXTERIOR OF THE 1905 CHURCH. Louisville architect D.X. Murphy, who also designed elements of the Indiana State Prison in Clarksville and Churchill Downs in Louisville, chose to design the new St. Augustine in the Spanish Mission style. The church installed magnificent stained glass windows imported from Germany in the 1920s, including one depicted on page 100 as a memorial to those who served and died in "The Great War." (Photo: Author's collection)

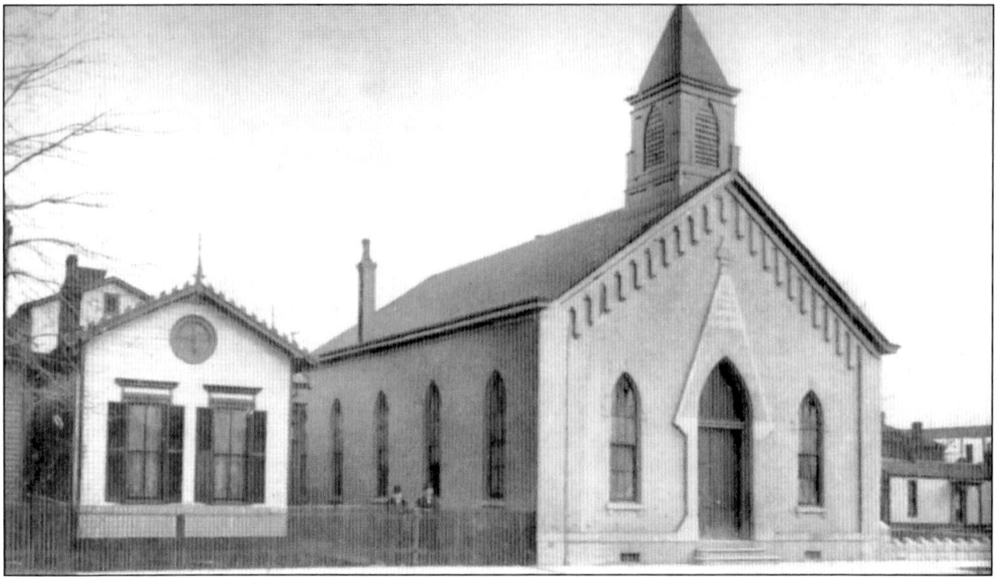

St. Luke's German Evangelical Reformed Church. A group of "German Protestants" met in June of 1860 and decided to establish their own congregation in Jeffersonville. A few weeks later, the new congregation purchased the old Presbyterian church on Market Street near Pearl for $1,200, into which they moved at the beginning of 1861. The new church, which had no official denominational affiliation, endured a time of internal doctrinal conflict, which it resolved by joining the Reformed Church Synod in 1870. The photograph above depicts the church and parsonage, built in the early 1870s. (Photo: Terry Stackhouse)

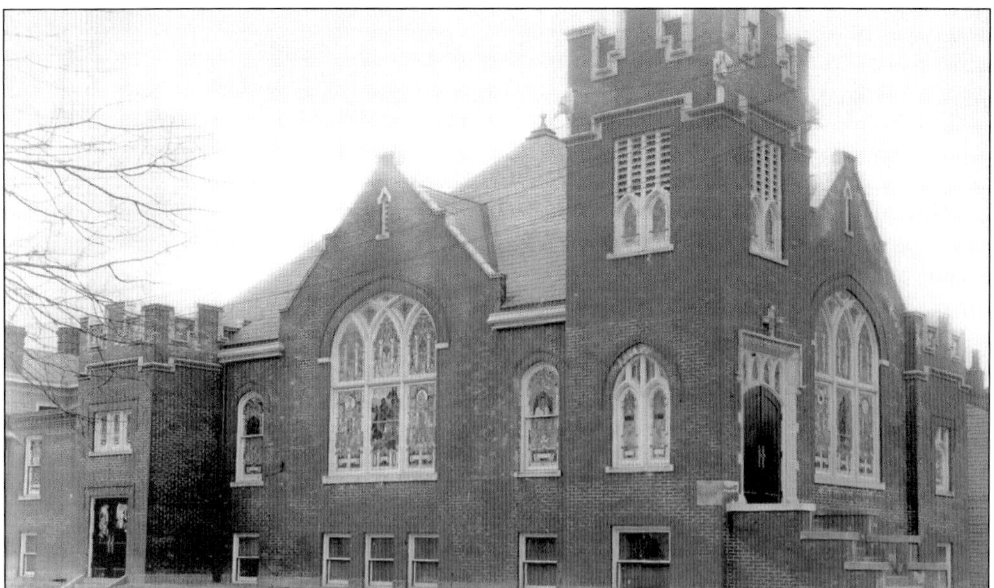

St. Luke's New Church on Maple Street. St. Luke's purchased land on Maple Street in 1909 for a new church, which it began building in May of 1914. The new church, depicted above, opened the following year for services. The congregation, known today as St. Luke's United Church of Christ, continues to worship in this facility. (Photo: St. Luke's United Church of Christ)

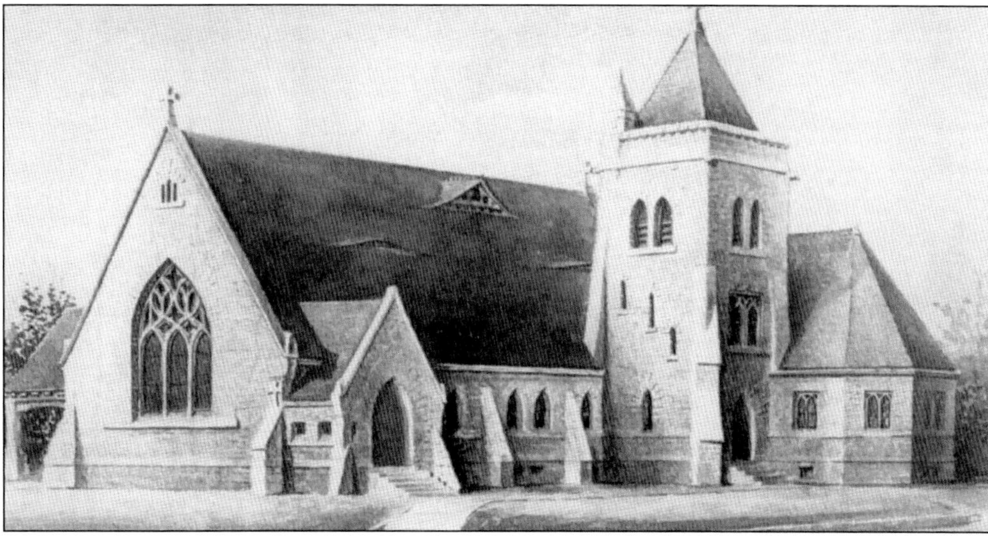

St. Paul's Episcopal Church. Jeffersonville's Episcopals organized the parish of St. Paul's on August 14, 1836, and built their first church on Spring Street in about 1840, which it later moved to a lot on Chestnut Street between Spring and Pearl Streets. In 1868, the church purchased the old chapel from the former Camp Joe Holt and moved it to that lot. In 1892, the congregation erected the present church, with plans donated by Arthur Loomis and funding provided in great part by shipbuilder Edmonds J. Howard. The illustration above depicts the church as architect Arthur Loomis designed it, but the bell tower never became a reality due to a shortage of funds. (Photo: Howard Steamboat Museum)

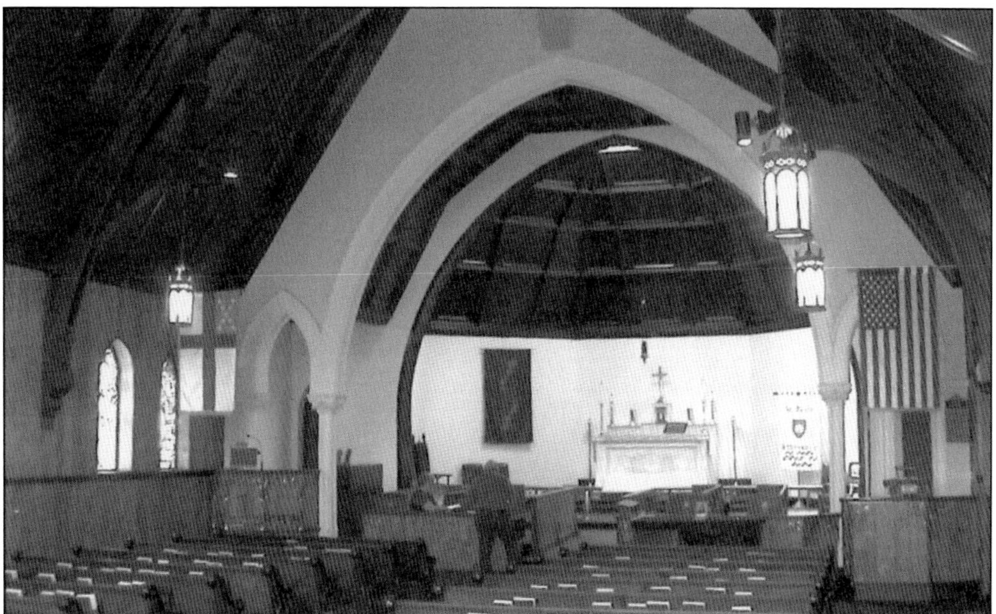

Howard Craftsmanship at St. Paul's. Captain Howard saved the church a great deal of money by providing and personally supervising workers from his shipyards to construct St. Paul's new church. Observers to this day can appreciate the workers' craftsmanship inside the church, whose ceiling resembles an upside-down boat hull. (Photo: Author's collection)

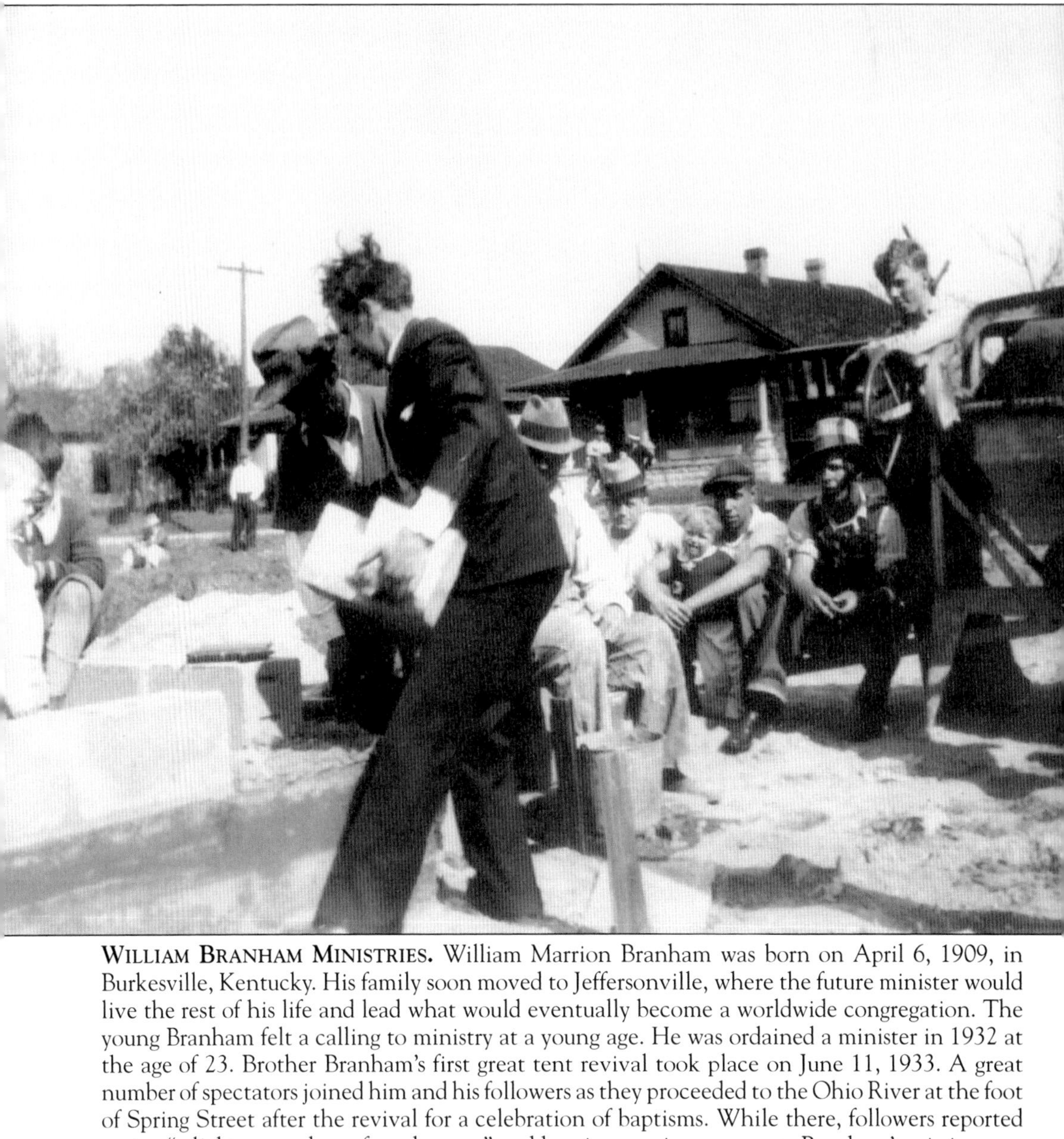

WILLIAM BRANHAM MINISTRIES. William Marrion Branham was born on April 6, 1909, in Burkesville, Kentucky. His family soon moved to Jeffersonville, where the future minister would live the rest of his life and lead what would eventually become a worldwide congregation. The young Branham felt a calling to ministry at a young age. He was ordained a minister in 1932 at the age of 23. Brother Branham's first great tent revival took place on June 11, 1933. A great number of spectators joined him and his followers as they proceeded to the Ohio River at the foot of Spring Street after the revival for a celebration of baptisms. While there, followers reported seeing "a light come down from heaven" and hearing a voice announce Branham's mission as a prophet. That same year Brother Branham (foreground, holding stone) laid the cornerstone for Branham Tabernacle at the corner of Penn and East Eighth Streets in a ceremony captured in the photograph above. Brother Branham preached across the country until his death in 1965 from injuries received in a tragic car accident in Texas. (Photo: William Branham Ministries)

Five

WORKING

BUSINESSES AND LABOR

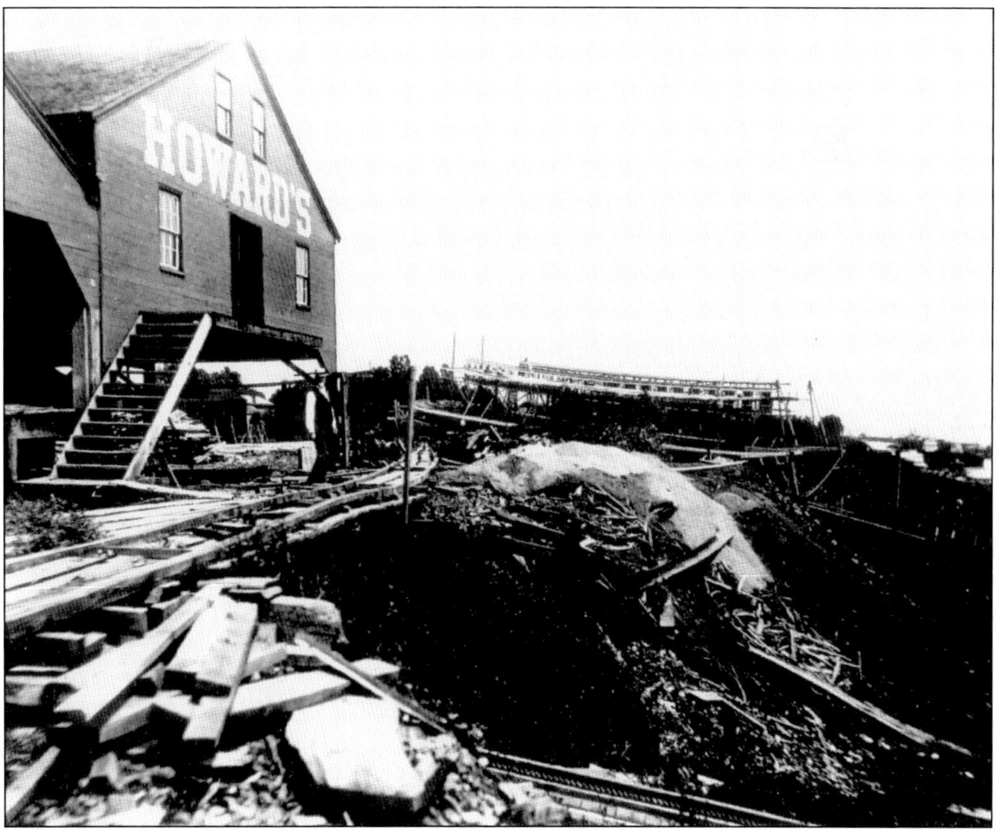

SHIPBUILDING IN JEFFERSONVILLE. Shipbuilding has played an important role in Jeffersonville's economy through most of the city's history. Companies run by the French brothers after 1829, Robert C. Green in the 1830s, Henry French and Peter Myers after 1847, David S. Barmore off and on from 1834 to 1885, and the Sweeney brothers from 1869 to 1938 would alone have drawn attention to the city and its immediate environs as a hub of shipbuilding. James Howard, however, who built his first steamer here in 1834, did more than any other to establish Jeffersonville as one of the nation's premiere shipbuilding centers. The photograph above depicts the circular and gang mill at the Howard Works. (Photo: Howard Steamboat Museum)

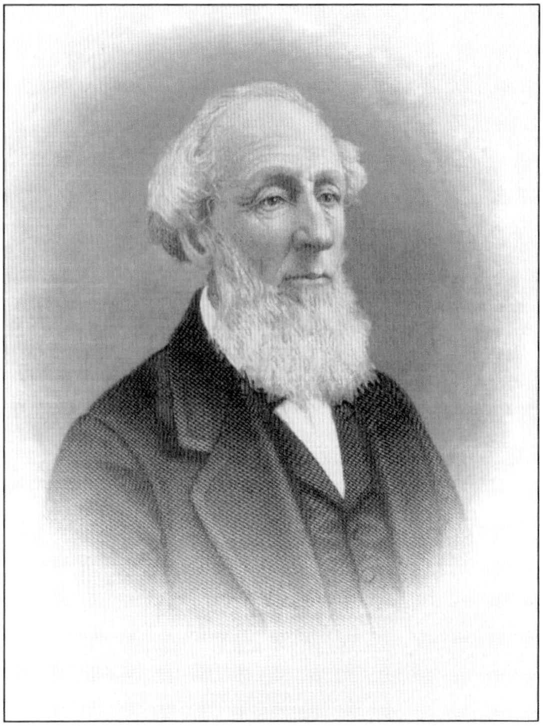

JAMES HOWARD. In 1819, at the age of five, James Howard emigrated to America from his native England with his parents and brother, locating eventually in Cincinnati, where the elder Howard established a wool mill. James Howard apprenticed with a steamboat builder in the city, where the young man learned the shipbuilding trade. Howard relocated to Jeffersonville and soon had a contract to manufacture his first boat, the *Hyperion*, in 1834. For the next 15 years, Howard lived upriver in Madison, served as an engineer and ship carpenter on the Ohio and Mississippi Rivers, and built a few boats at Shippingport in Kentucky. In 1849, he returned to the city and built up his famed shipyard here. Captain Howard died in a freak accident on October 14, 1876, when his carriage slipped off the back of the ferry to Louisville, drowning him in the Ohio River. (Photo: Howard Steamboat Museum)

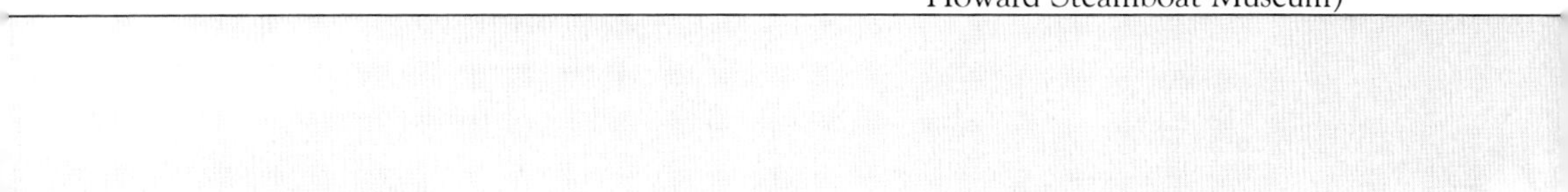

PANORAMA OF HOWARD SHIPYARDS. James Howard, who partnered with his brother Daniel in the firm's early days, located the firm on the river at the town of Port Fulton, adjacent to Jeffersonville and annexed by it in 1925. In the days of steamboat construction, separate contracts covered the construction of hulls and the fabrication of additions to it, such as the engine, boiler, and cabin. Hulls built by the Howards, for example, might have machinery

JAMES HOWARD HOME. Captain Howard lived in this home, built in 1856, at 1021 East Market Street until his death in 1876. Pictured here on April 25, 1893, from left to right, are the following: John F. Read (a prominent local businessman), Frank S. Armstrong (great-grandson of Col. John Armstrong and grandson of James Howard through his daughter Lucy at far right), William Baird (grandson of James Howard through his daughter Kate), Rebecca Ann Barmore Howard (James Howard's widow), and Lucy Howard Armstrong (daughter of James Howard). (Photo: Indiana Historical Society)

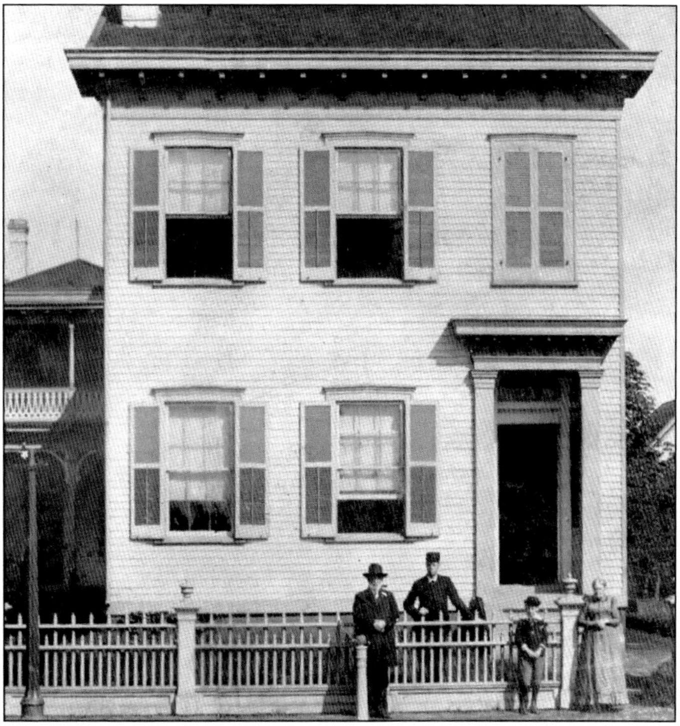

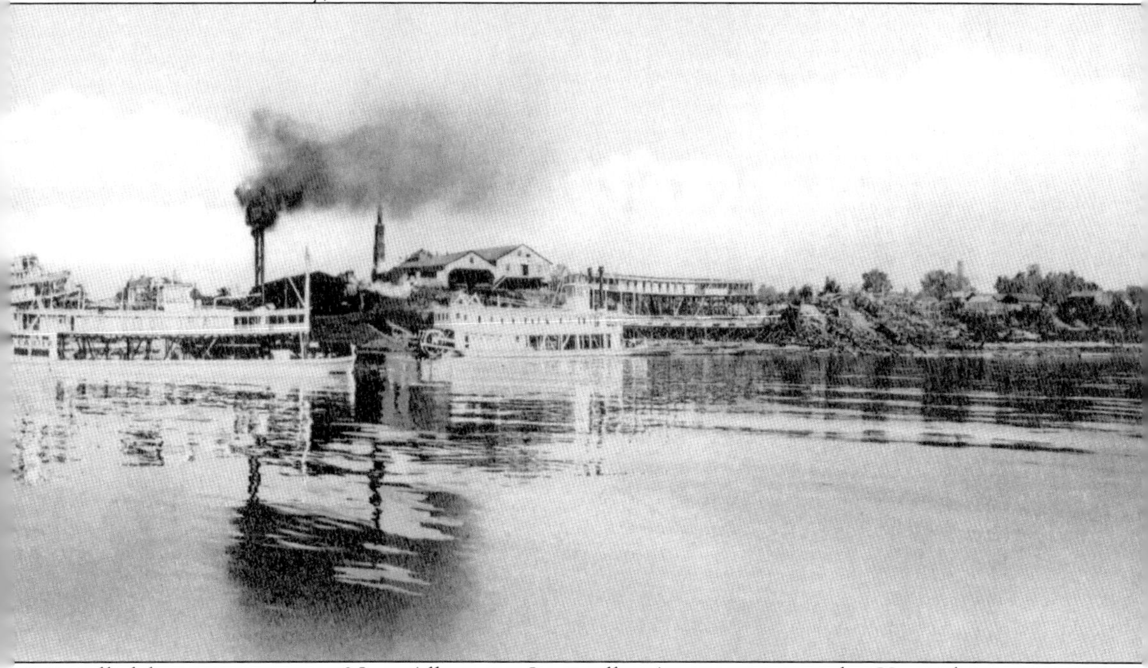

installed by a company in New Albany or Louisville. A testament to the Howards' great early success is the fact that in only their third year of operation, they were constructing 10 percent of all hulls launched on the western waters. The Howard Shipyards, in various corporate incarnations over its 93 year history after 1849, constructed a total of 1,123 hulls. (Photo: Charles R. Leap)

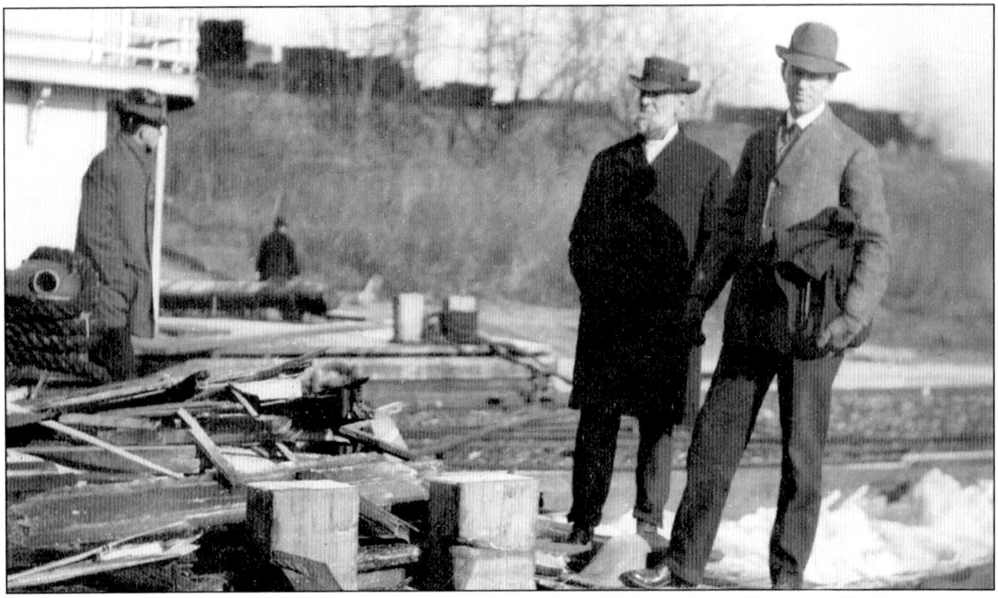

ED AND CLYDE HOWARD AT THE YARDS. James's son Edmonds J. Howard (left), assumed management of the company upon his father's death. The firm produced during his tenure many of the most famous steamers on the nation's rivers. "The largest and most elaborate steamboats in American history," according to author Charles P. Fishbaugh, "were built at the Howard Yard under his leadership." These "floating palaces" included the enormous masterpiece *J.M. White* and the speed record setting *City of Louisville*. Ed Howard's son Clyde (right) operated the company for a few years after his father's stroke in 1916. (Photo: Howard Steamboat Museum)

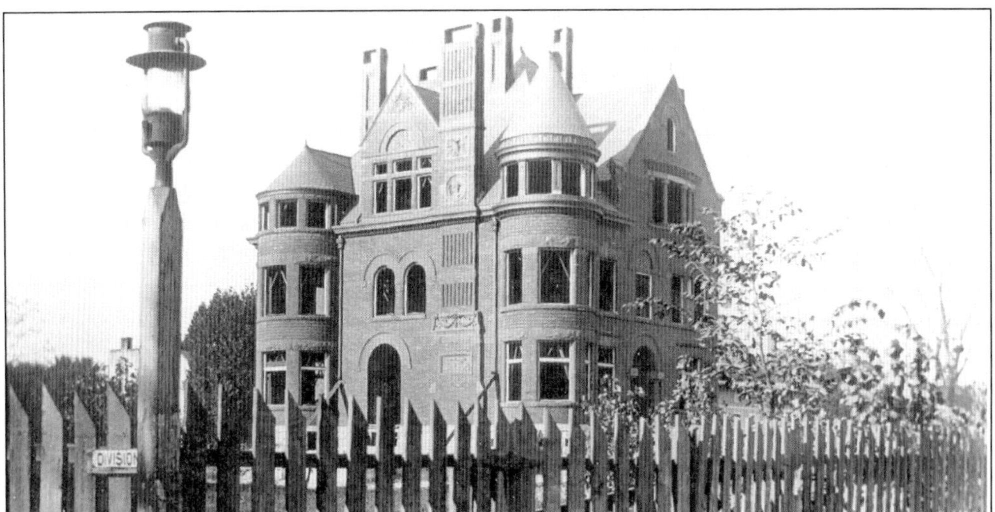

HOWARD MANSION. The wealth and prestige of the Howard Yards during Edmonds's tenure reflected in the new home he built for his family in the early 1890s, seen here under construction. Workers from the yards contributed their craftsmanship, honed at work on the floating palaces. The 22 room Romanesque Revival mansion, built of brick and limestone, features terra cotta adornments on the exterior and elaborate woodwork on the interior. The mansion, now on the National Register of Historic Places, has served as the Howard Steamboat Museum since 1958. (Photo: Howard Steamboat Museum)

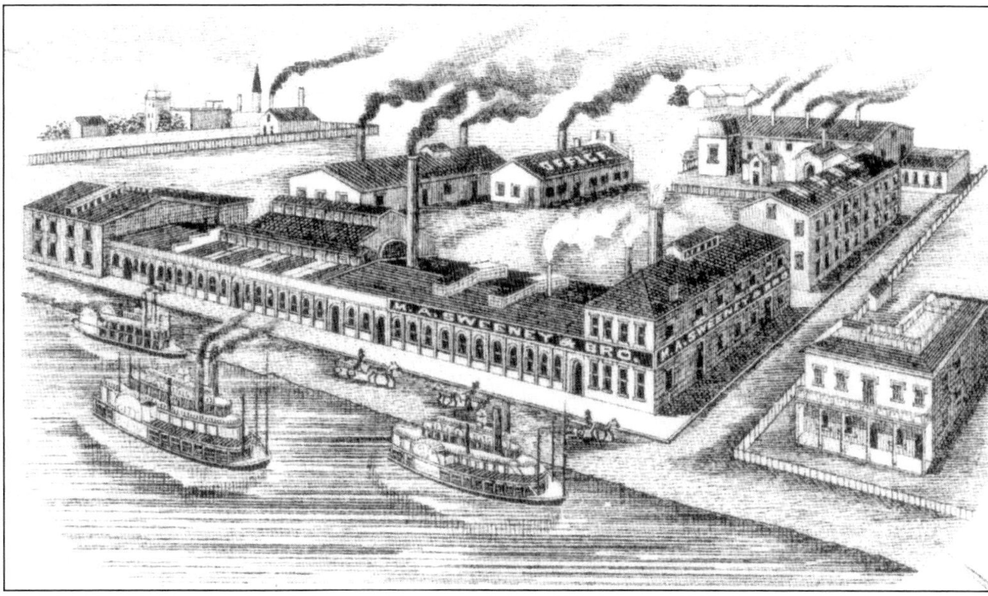

M.A. Sweeney and Bro. Foundry and Machine Works. Michael A. Sweeney operated a foundry in Jeffersonville after 1869 on Pearl Street and later in the location of today's Warder Park. His brother James W. joined the operation in 1876, and the firm relocated five years later to the riverfront just downstream of the Howard Yards. The new plant, depicted in this late-19th-century engraving, manufactured ship hulls and machinery in addition to structural and decorative iron and copper. (Photo: Author's collection)

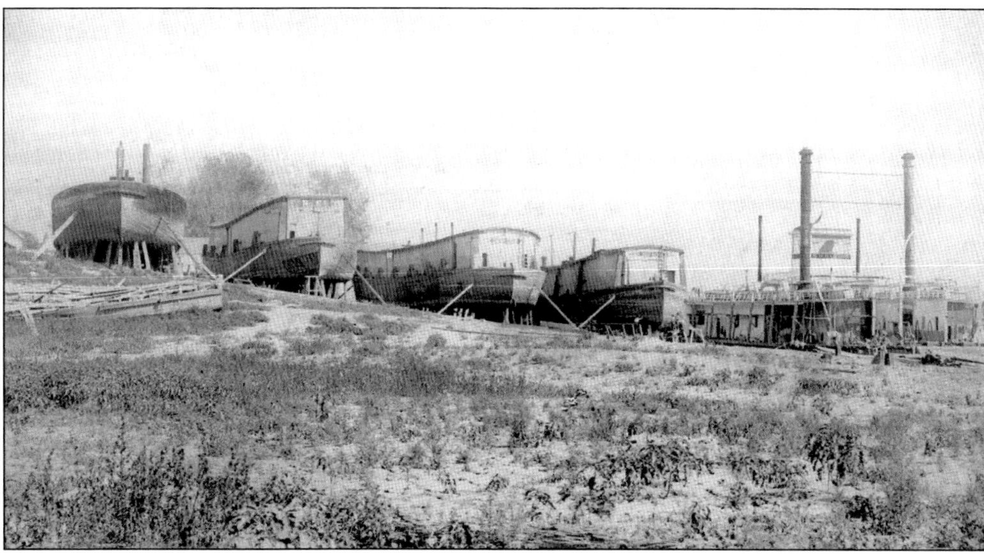

Steamers under Construction at the Sweeney Yards. The Sweeney Works operated until well into the 20th century. Its most famous product came down the ways in 1888 when it launched the hull for the government lighthouse tender *Golden Rod*, which was the first steel hull west of Pittsburgh. The photo above depicts the Sweeney Yards the following year on July 30 with several barges under construction and the steamer *S.D. Barlow* tied up at shore. The Sweeney family operated the shipyards until 1938, when the Inland Water Company purchased the company to create what would eventually become Jeffboat. (Photo: Howard Steamboat Museum)

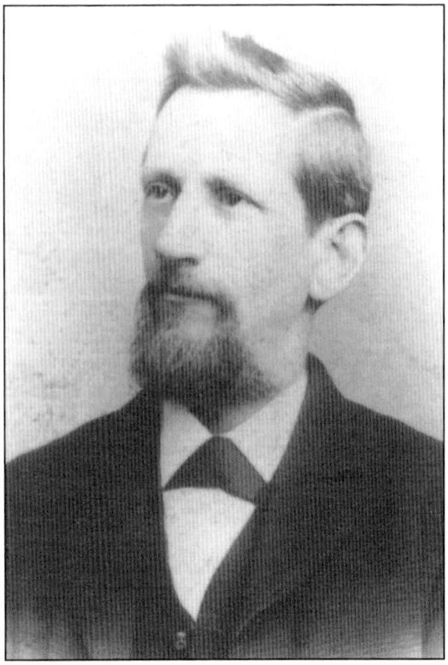

Gustav A. Schimpff Sr. Gustav Schimpff, whose family had been making candy in Louisville since the 1850s, opened his confectionery on Spring Street in 1891 at the suggestion of his brother, Charles, who owned a wallpaper and stationery store in the city. Five generations of the family have operated the business, which is one of the country's oldest, continuously operated family-owned candy businesses. Gus Sr. co-owned the business with his son, Gus Jr., until the elder's death in 1918. (Photo: Schimpff's Confectionery)

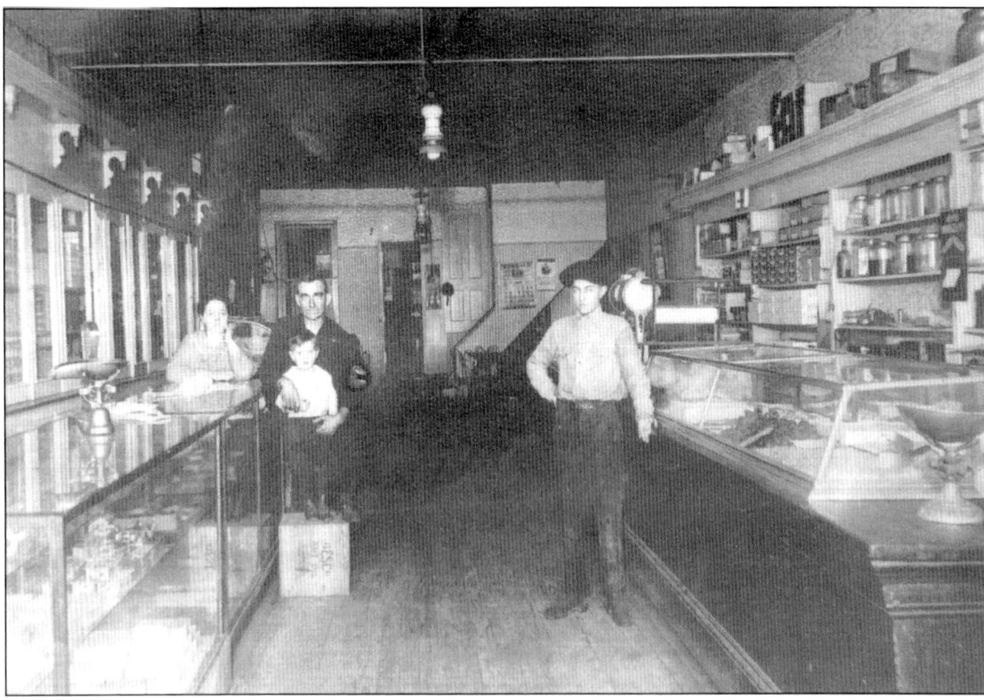

Inside Schimpff's Confectionery. Schimpff's Confectionery has operated at the same location, 347 Spring Street, since opening in 1891. Generations of customers have visited the store over the years to partake of its signature offerings, which include cinnamon red hots and caramel Modjeskas. This photo depicts the inside of the store in the early 1920s with Louisa and Gustav Jr., their son Charles, and store employee Johnny Kipper at right. Today's owners, Warren and Jill Schimpff, recently opened an enlarged candy making kitchen and museum in an adjacent storefront. (Photo: Schimpff's Confectionery)

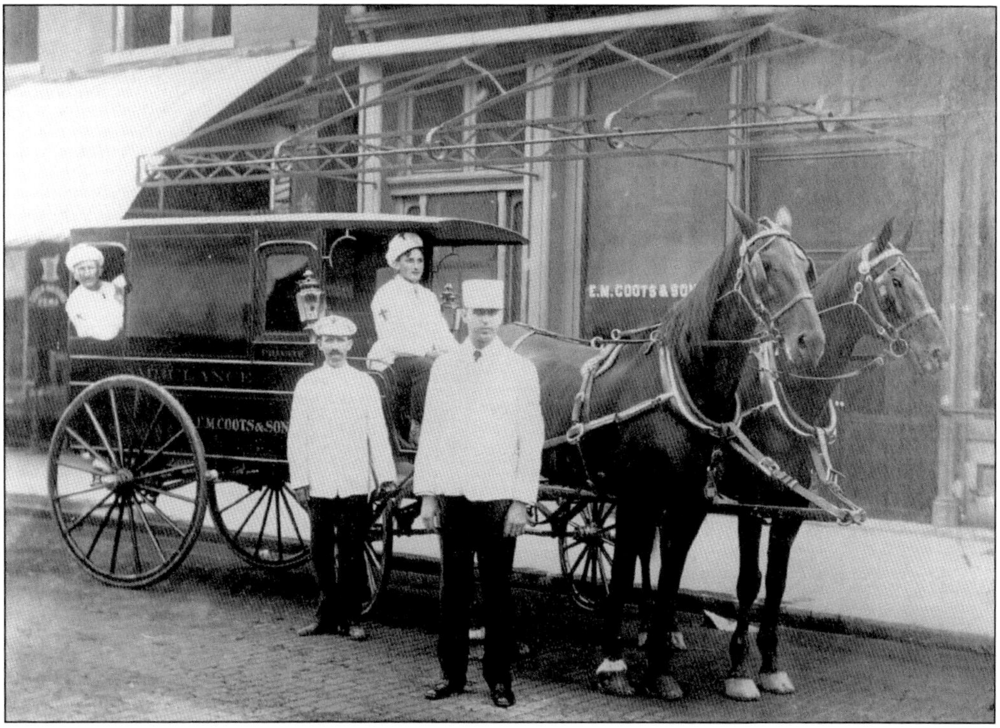

E.M. COOTS' SONS FUNERAL HOME. The Coots family had operated a funeral home in Shelbyville, Kentucky, for 30 years when Edwin M. Coots came to Jeffersonville in 1860 to open a funeral home here. The original funeral home operated on Chestnut Street, but by the 1890s had relocated to what is now the 400 block of Spring Street, where this photograph of a Coots ambulance and staff were taken. The business relocated to its present location at 120 West Maple Street in 1927 where it remains to this day. (Photo: E.M. Coots' Sons Funeral Home)

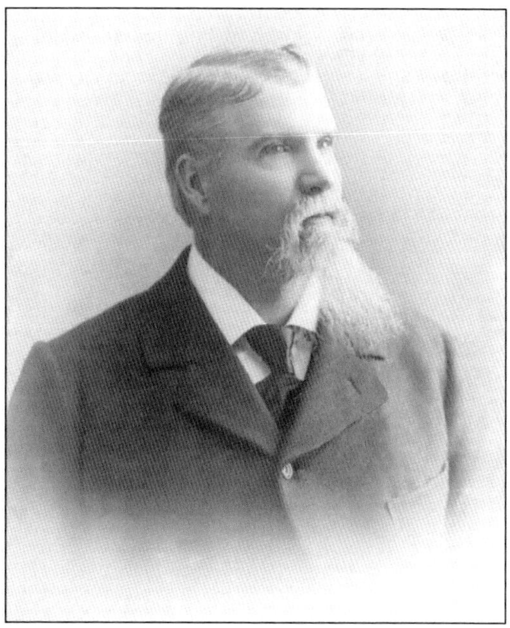

EDWIN M. COOTS. Founder Edwin M. Coots not only operated his funeral home business, he also served as county coroner beginning with his first election to the post in 1888. All five generations of his family have held this post to continue the family's tradition of service. Edwin M. Coots was a pioneer in funeral science, for he "was one of the first in the funeral profession to learn the art of embalming," according to an 1897 newspaper report. Coots died in 1907, leaving the business to his sons Glover and Froman. (Photo: E.M. Coots' Sons Funeral Home)

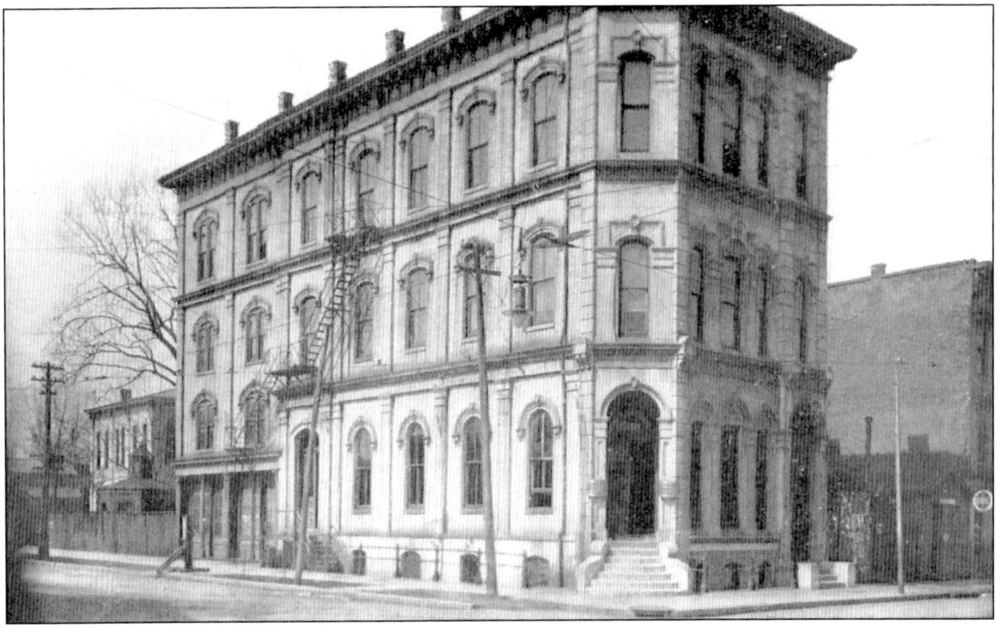

First National Bank of Jeffersonville. The First National Bank of Jeffersonville began operations in January of 1865 at a building on Spring Street north of Front Street (now Riverside Drive). It relocated in 1870 to a newly constructed brick and stone building, pictured above, at the northwest corner of Spring and Market Streets. The Great Depression struck the bank hard and Clark County State Bank took over First National's assets and business in September of 1931. (Photo: *Souvenir Jeffersonville, Ind.*)

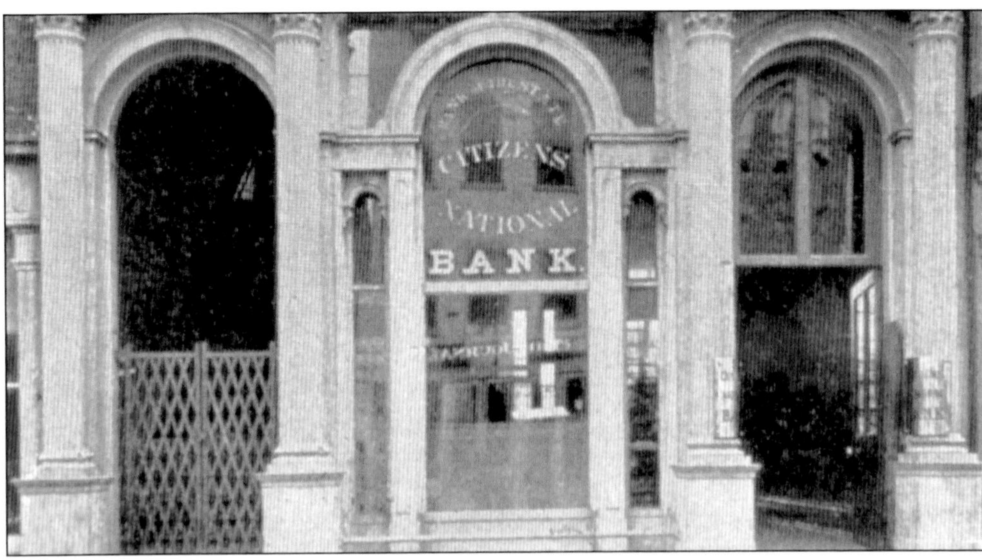

Citizens National Bank. The bank that would become Citizens National Bank began operations in 1855 as the Jeffersonville branch of the Third State Bank of Indiana with a capital of $100,000. It operated through the Civil War years at today's 300 block of Spring Street. Citizens National Bank, chartered on March 14, 1865, under new national banking laws, absorbed the Jeffersonville branch and operated in the same location until 1868, when it moved to the building at 219 Spring Street, whose façade is shown above. (Photo: Bank One)

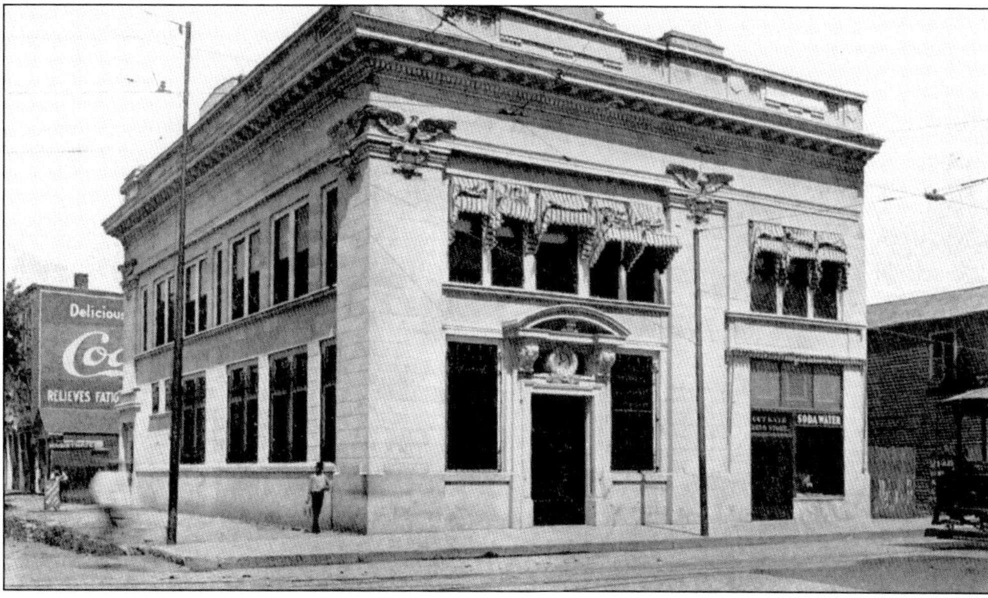

CITIZENS BUILDING AT COURT AND SPRING. Citizens National Bank continued to operate until 1914. Meanwhile, a new entity, Citizens Trust Company, was chartered on March 25, 1907. The new company started construction on a larger headquarters, depicted above, in 1907. It moved into the Arthur Loomis-designed neoclassical structure in 1908. Six years later, it consolidated with Citizens National Bank on a new state charter under the name Citizens Trust Company. The institution operated for more than six more decades until its merger with Clark County State Bank in 1984. (Photo: *Souvenir Jeffersonville, Ind.*)

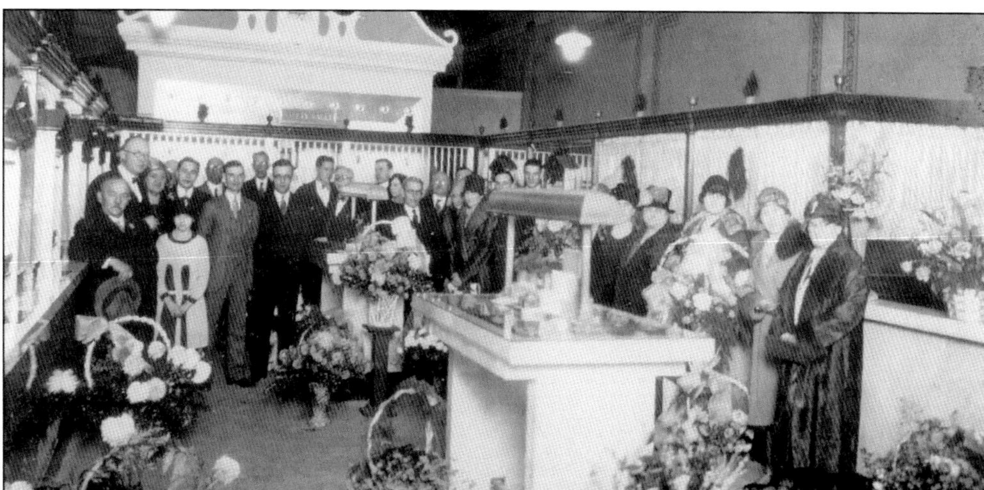

CLARK COUNTY STATE BANK. Clark County State Bank, chartered in November of 1917, once occupied a two-story neoclassical building at 443 Spring Street. This early interior photograph shows a number of people gathered in the bank for an unknown event. Visible in the rear is the bank' safety vault, in which a customer could rent a safety deposit box for 4¢ per week at one time. Clark County State Bank built newer facilities on the site and eventually merged with its cross-street competitor, Citizens, in 1984. The institution later disappeared in the frenzied world of bank mergers and acquisitions of the 1980s and 90s. (Photo: E.M. Coots' Sons Funeral Home)

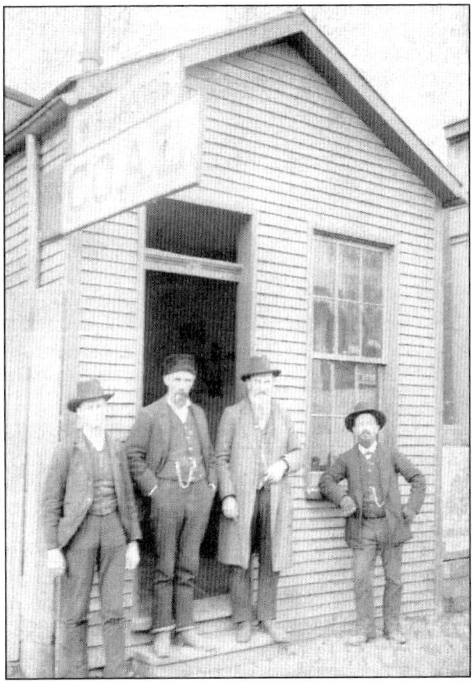

JACOBS COAL COMPANY. Jeffersonville plunged boiler-first into the heart of the industrial age in the second half of the 19th century. Coal fed the gaping furnaces of factories, steamers, locomotives, and other engines of progress and several local merchants controlled its supply. Pictured here is the coal business office of William S. Jacobs on Spring Street near Market Street (next door to the First National Bank building) before 1895, when the Jeffersonville Coal and Elevator Company purchased the company. (Photo: Charles R. Leap)

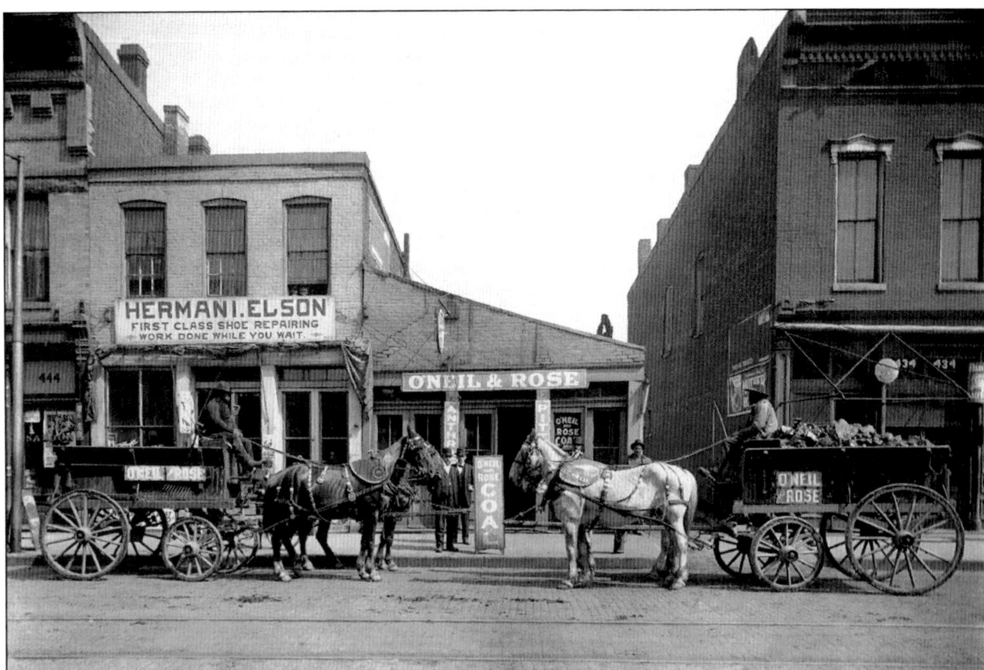

O'NEIL AND ROSE COAL COMPANY. Franklin M. Rose, who had learned the coal business under the tutelage of William S. Jacobs and had served as a manager at Jeffersonville Coal, formed a partnership with Thomas O'Neil in 1904 and opened an office at 438 Spring Street. Frank Rose stands at center left behind two of his delivery wagons. Rose bought out his partner in 1911, and the company and its coal yard at Eighth and Wall Streets continued under his and his son's management until the mid 1960s, when coal ceased as a viable business. (Photo: Charles R. Leap)

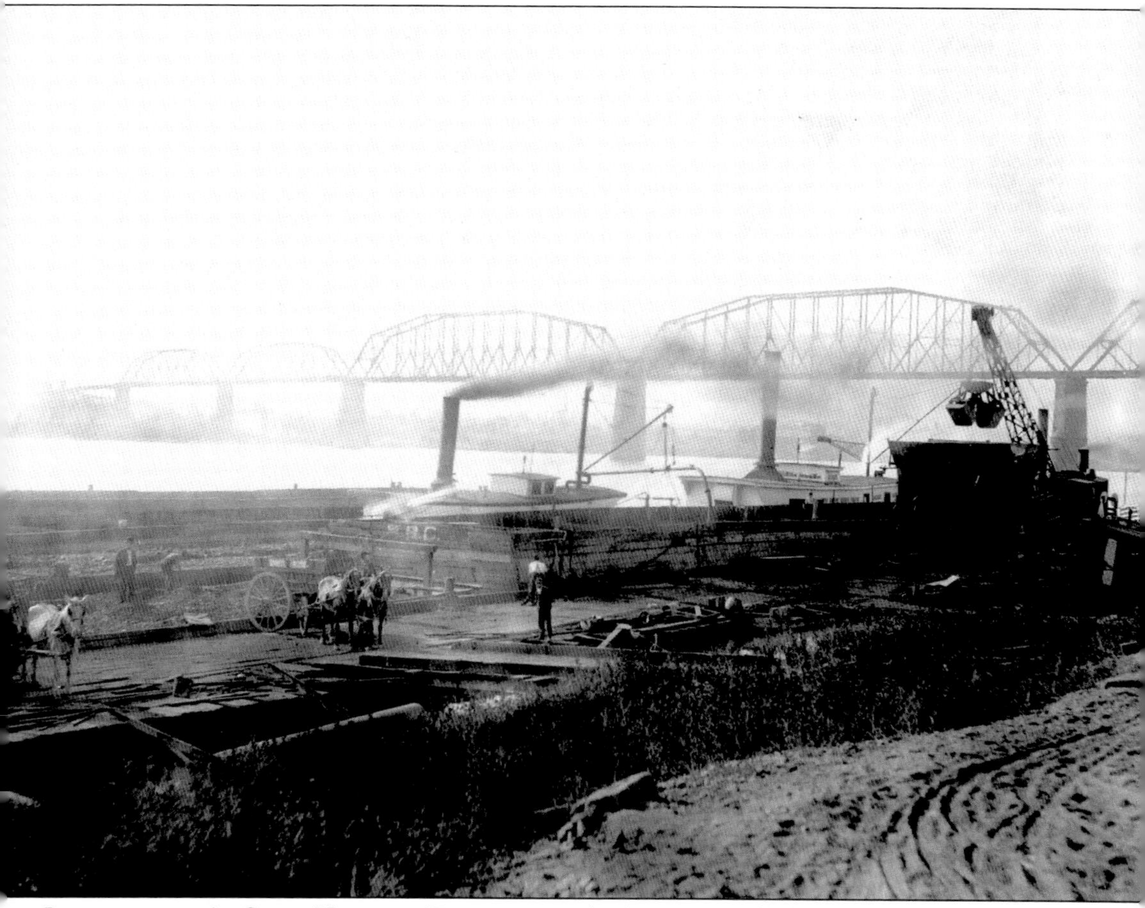

Jeffersonville's Coal Harbor. Transportation by barge proved the cheapest method of transferring coal from the mines of Pennsylvania, West Virginia, and Kentucky to towns along the Ohio River, as the coal barges that float by the city confirm today. Jeffersonville's coal harbor received new supplies near the foot of Spring Street for transfer by wagon into the coal yards of the city. Here, wagons of the Rose Coal Company await their loads before climbing the hill to town. The Big Four Bridge stretches across the river in the background. (Photo: Charles R. Leap)

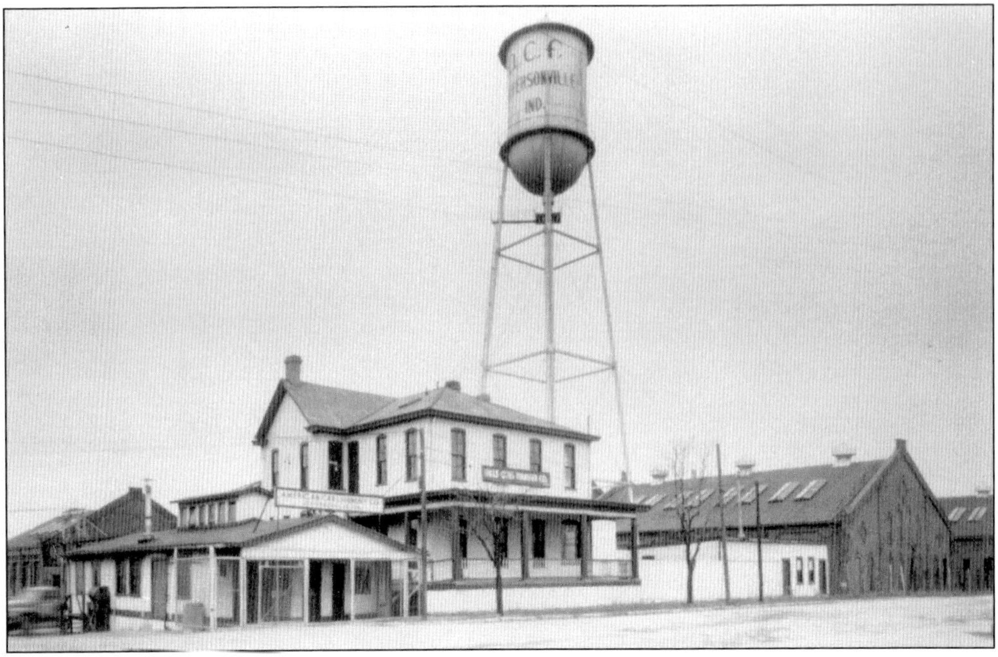

AMERICAN CAR AND FOUNDRY COMPANY. The Ohio Falls Car and Locomotive Company began operating on June 1, 1864, at its factory west of Missouri Avenue (most of which is actually in Clarksville). The company had a slow first two years until Joseph W. Sprague assumed control of the company, increasing orders for the company's railcars. A fire in 1872 and the financial panic of 1873 struck the company hard but it rebuilt and reorganized. In 1899, it formed part of a group of about 13 companies that combined to form American Car and Foundry Company. The Great Depression finally shuttered the plant in 1933, but its buildings remain where they have undergone creative restoration for reuse by businesses. (Photo: Cornerstone Group)

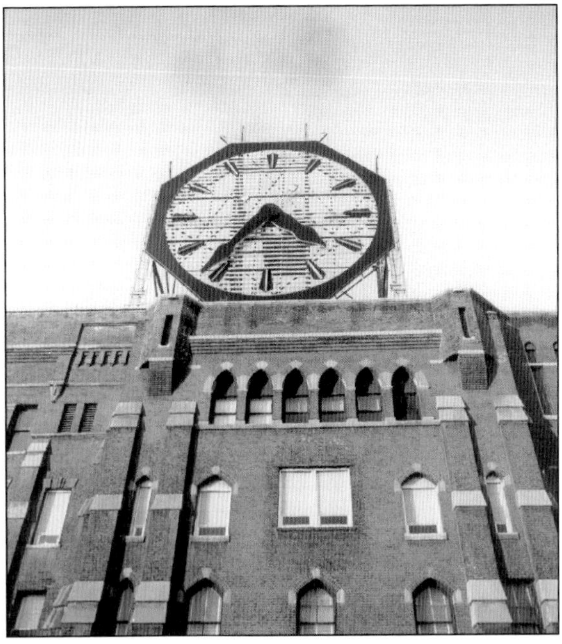

COLGATE-PALMOLIVE-PEET CO. The Colgate-Palmolive-Peet Company, facing increased demand after the Great War, sought to expand its facilities in the Midwest, when it learned that the state of Indiana sought to relocate the state prison from Clarksville. The company negotiated purchase of the plant and prisoners still occupied cells there while the company reconstructed portions of the physical plant. The factory, known as the "Jeffersonville Plant," opened in Clarksville officially on November 17, 1924, with the lighting of its 40-foot diameter clock, which has become the company's and southern Indiana's landmark. (Photo: Bank One)

GEORGE PFAU SR. George Pfau Sr. started his animal oils business in a building on Front Street (now Riverside Drive) in 1869. Four generations of his family have continued the business despite numerous floods and a devastating fire in 1944 that destroyed the company's riverfront building (see page 116). The company has become a leading processor of animal fats and oils from its modern processing facility on Wall Street. (Photo: Geo. Pfau's Sons Oil Co.)

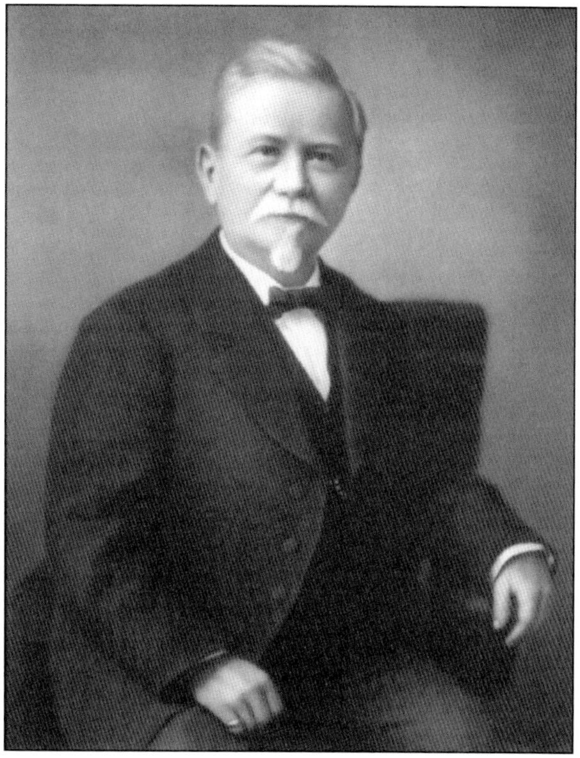

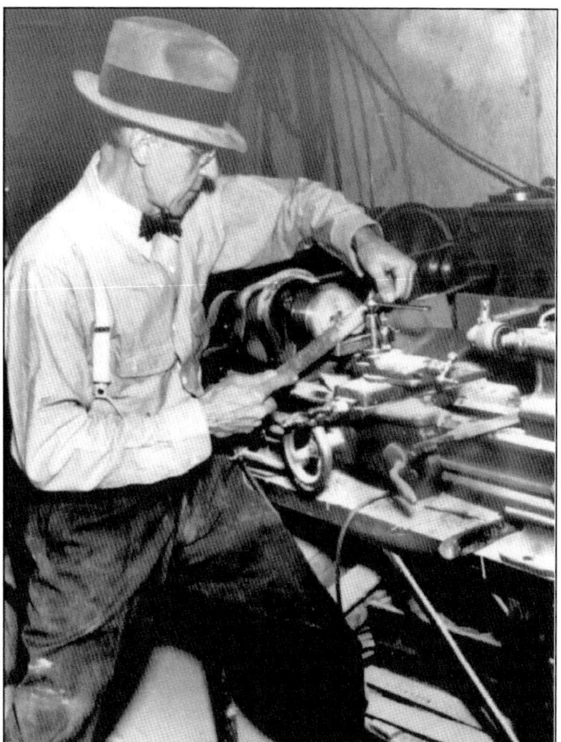

GORSUCH FOUNDRY. James A. Gorsuch Jr. came to Jeffersonville from his native Ohio at the age of 20, starting a foundry business here in the 1920s. Gorsuch, seen here hard at work in his shop, served as president of the company until his death in 1960. The company was purchased in the early 1980s, and Robinson Foundries now owns the old foundry's property at 120 East Market Street. (Photo: Scott Funeral Home)

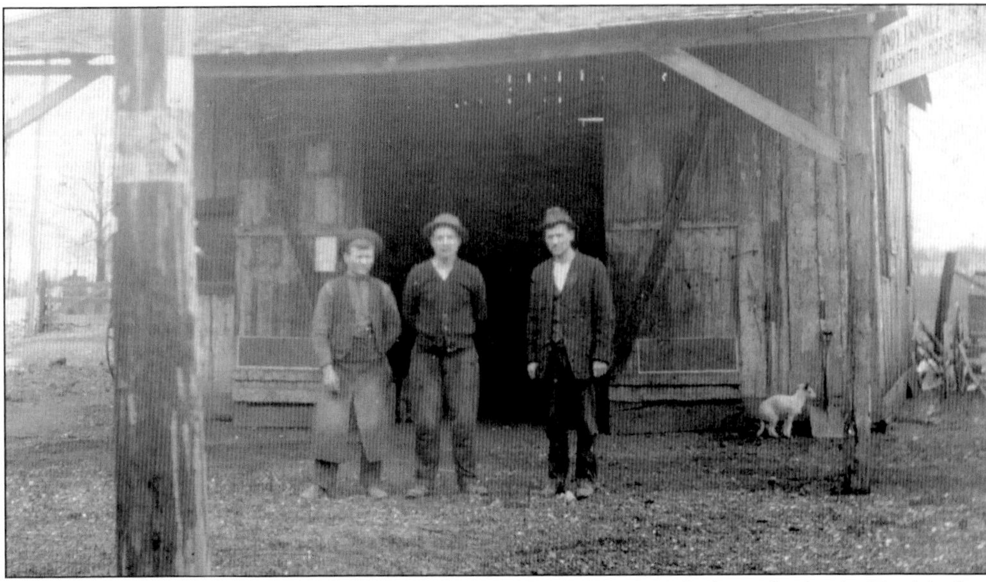

TRINKLE BLACKSMITH AND SADLER SHOP IN CLAYSBURG. Blacksmith Andy Trinkle had worked at the Ohio Falls Car Works for many years before starting his own shop in Claysburg. A number of blacksmiths operated in and around Jeffersonville, providing horseshoes and other implements needed in the days of horse-drawn transportation, but their business died out with the rise of the automobile. (Photo: Jeffersonville Township Public Library)

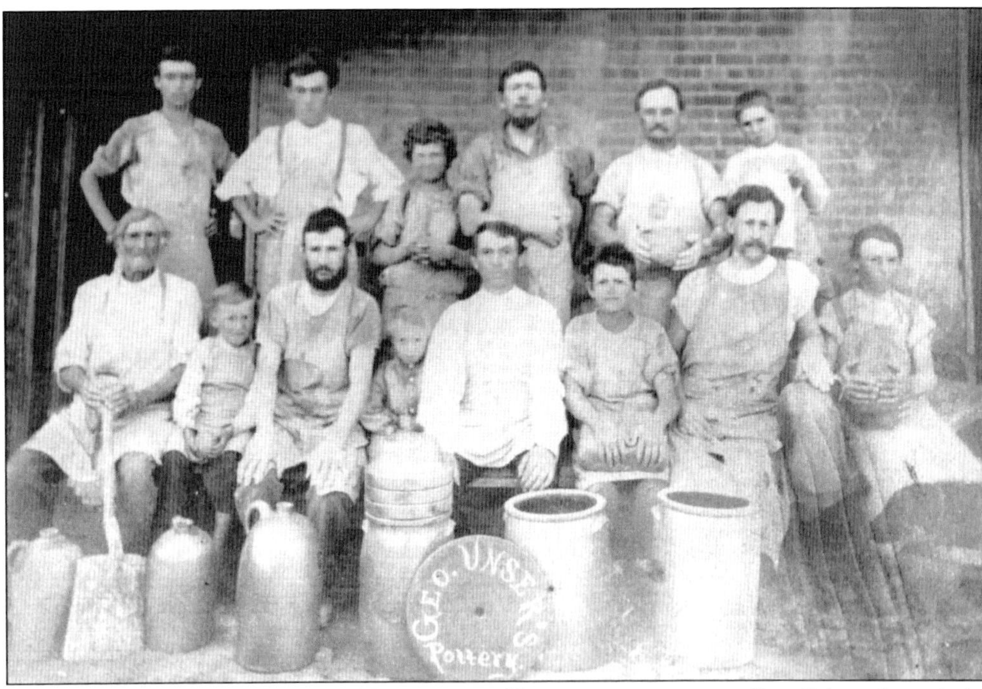

GEORGE UNSER POTTERY. George Unser operated his pottery company in Port Fulton through the second half of the 19th century. Master potter John Bauer, a Jeffersonville native and employee of Unser, left the company in 1879 to found his own business in Louisville, what would eventually become Louisville Stoneware Company. (Photo: Jeffersonville Township Public Library)

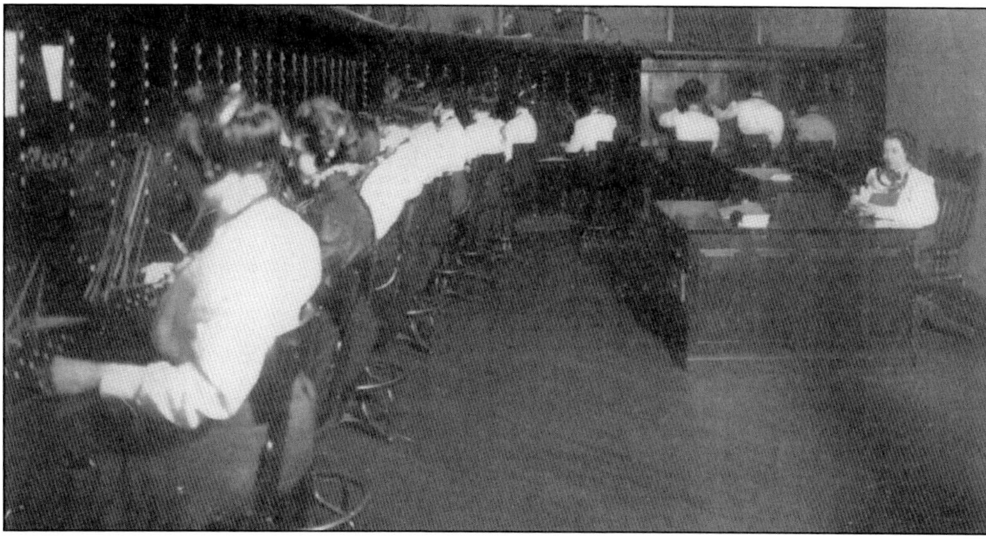

CUMBERLAND TELEPHONE AND TELEGRAPH COMPANY. Jeffersonville received its first telephone service in 1883 when the Ohio Valley Telephone Company, a Bell licensee, extended service from New Albany. For a time, the telephone exchange operated on Spring Street out of the second floor of a business with a bay window, "which was of great convenience to the operator in spying out persons who were wanted at the 'phone," according to Lewis Baird. The Cumberland Telephone and Telegraph Company, whose operators are depicted above, acquired the former company and had about 1,400 subscribers in the Jeffersonville exchange in 1909. (Photo: *Souvenir Jeffersonville, Ind.*)

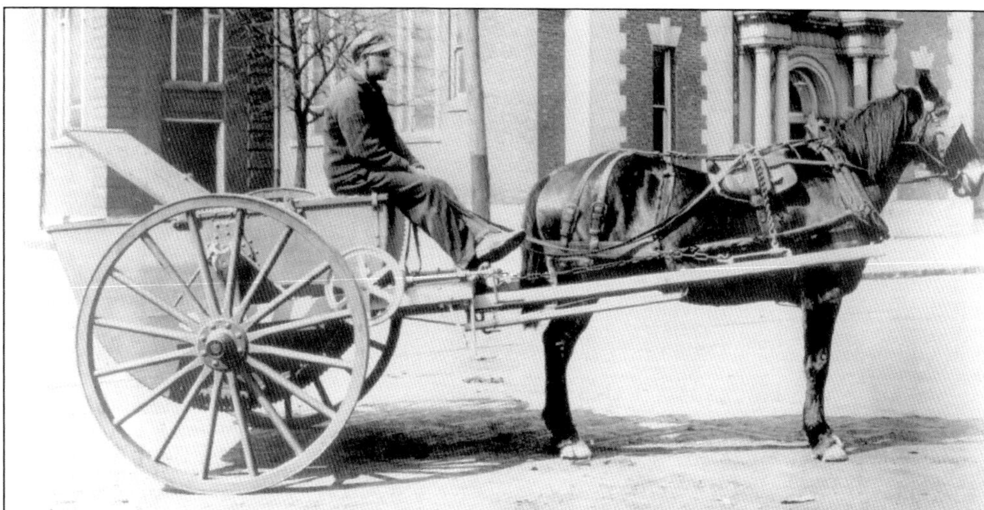

GEORGE H. HOLZBOG AND BROTHER CARRIAGE WORKS. George J. Holzbog, a skilled carriage-maker who emigrated from Germany in the early 1850s, started his business at the southwest corner of Locust and Chestnut Streets in Jeffersonville in 1854. His sons carried on the family business as George H. Holzbog and Brother. The company continued to manufacture wagons and carriages well into the 20th century, as shown in this 1917 builder's photograph of a street-cleaning wagon it sold to the U.S. Government (note St. Augustine Church in the background). The company went out of business after the automobile displaced horse-drawn transportation. (Photo: National Archives, Kansas City Branch)

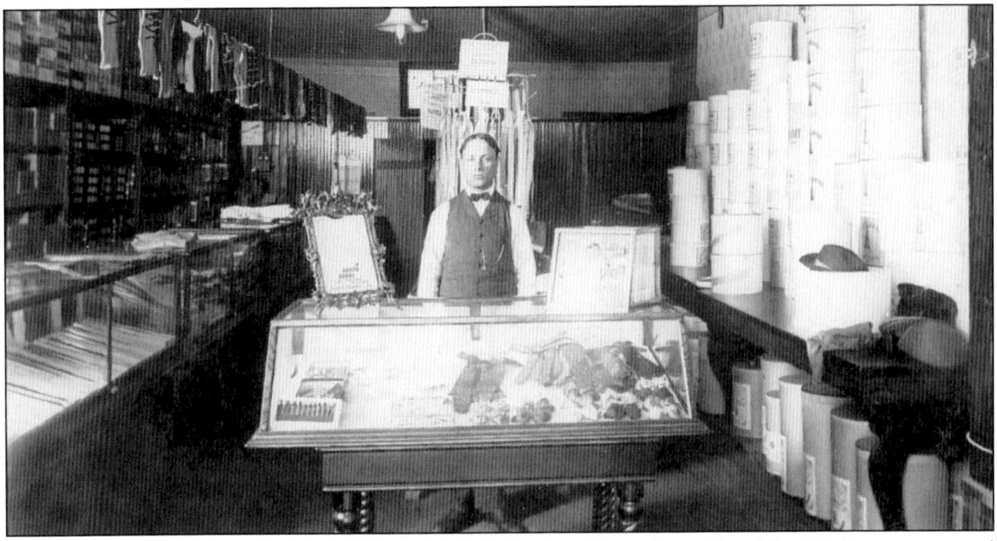

INTERIOR OF D.H. ROSE. David H. Rose, brother of coal merchant Franklin M. Rose, operated this variety store at Seventh and Mechanic Streets before World War I. This interior photo shows a clerk surrounded by some of the store's clothing wares, including socks, hats, gloves, suspenders, and cravats. An external photograph from the same era advertises the store's "notions, fruits and vegetables, groceries, and hardware." (Photo: Charles R. Leap)

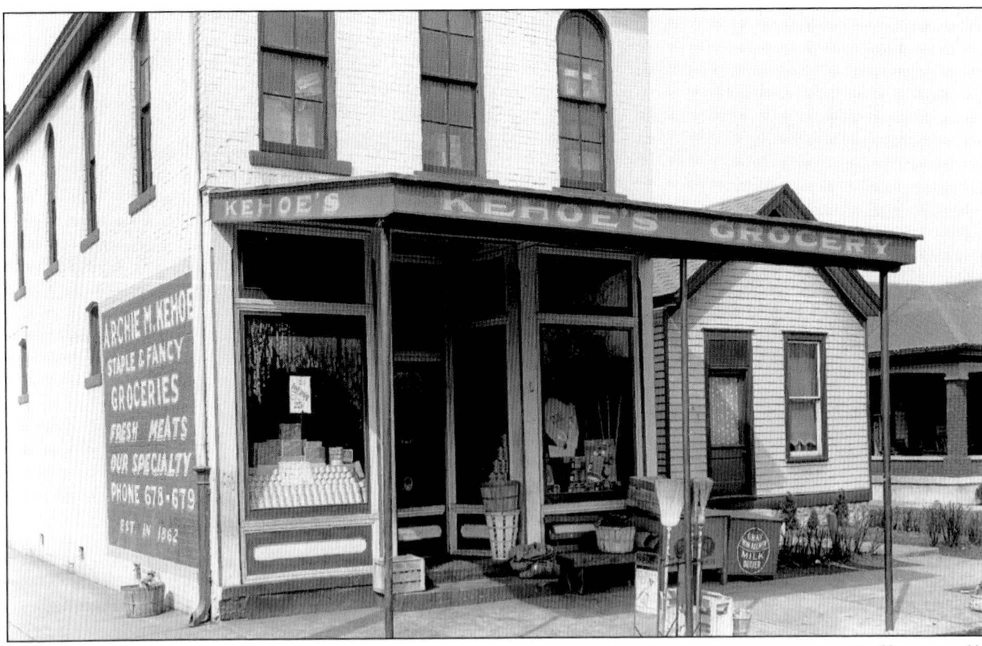

KEHOE'S GROCERY IN 1930. The Kehoe family opened their first grocery store in Jeffersonville in 1862. By 1930, when this photograph was taken of the store at 701 Ohio Avenue, Arch Kehoe was proprietor. An ingenious gambler in the city at about this time realized that the digits in Kehoe's phone number, 678, totaled 21, leading gamblers at the tables to call out "Kehoe's!" when they reached that magical number at Blackjack. Several Kehoes operated stores in the city, including Doc Kehoe seen with his baseball team outside his store on page 24. (Photo: University of Louisville Photographic Archives)

SAMUEL G. SHANNON. Sam Shannon opened his dairy business on West Maple Street in 1918 and operated it until he sold the business to Kannapel's in 1961. Shannon took a key interest in community service and even served as mayor of Jeffersonville from 1942 to 1951. He died in 1975. (Photo: Bruce "Corky" Scales)

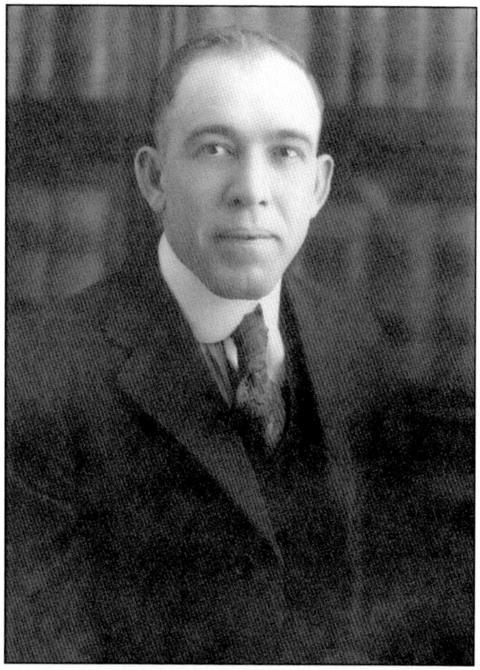

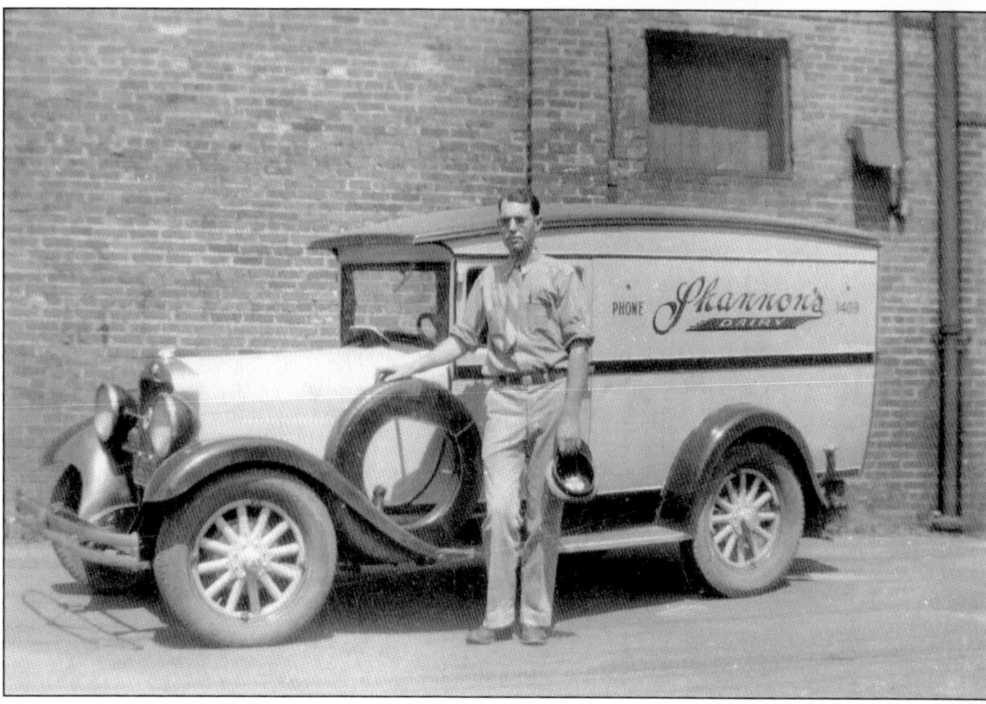

SHANNON'S DAIRY AND MILK ON THE DOORSTEP. Shannon's Dairy, like the rest of the industry, delivered milk fresh to the door, with horse-drawn wagons in the early days. The company shared a horse barn on Pearl Street with E.M. Coots Sons Funeral Home. Shannon's continued to deliver milk to customers after it mechanized its mode of transportation. This photograph shows dairy employee Slim Edwards in front of one of the company's delivery trucks. (Photo: Bruce "Corky" Scales)

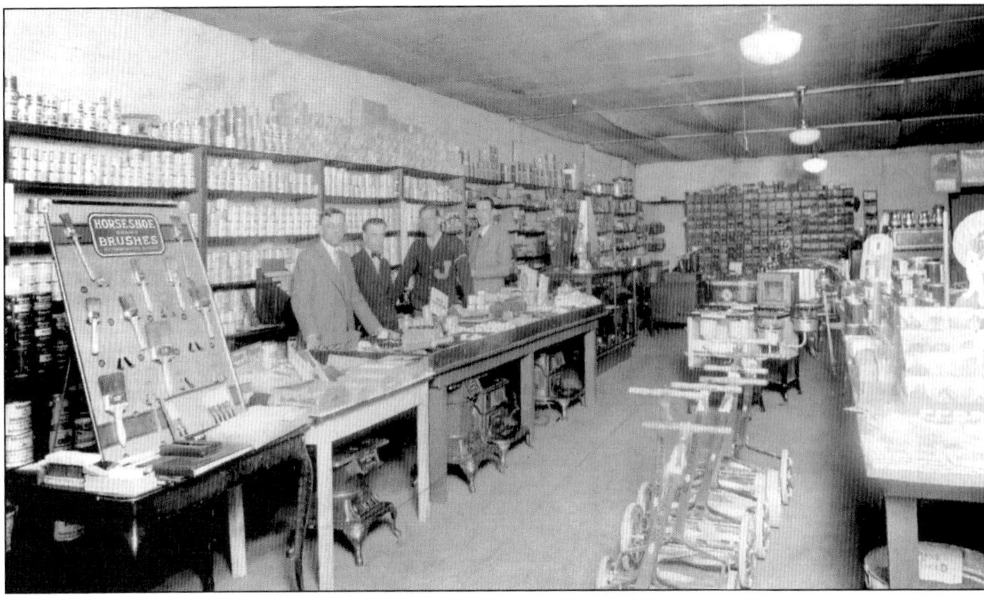

HEUSER HARDWARE. James R. Heuser, a former employee of Belknap Hardware in Louisville, joined with Frank Stutzenberger and John Kenny to open Heuser Hardware in Jeffersonville in 1923. Pictured here at the store's first location, Eighth and Main Streets, from left to right are Heuser, Stutzenberger, employee Millard Thorpe, and J. Willard Heuser (James's brother). The business moved to its present location at 523 Spring Street in 1930. (Photo: Bob Weber)

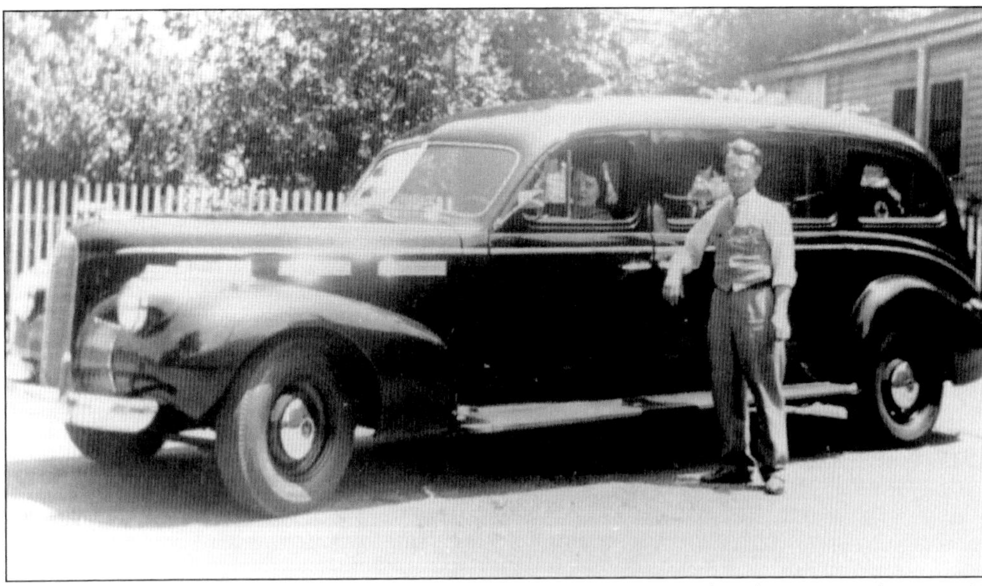

COMBS AND SCOTT FUNERAL HOME. William M. Scott partnered with Asa Combs in 1930 to open a funeral chapel at 211 East Maple Street. The business thrived for just over a decade when World War II came along and the partnership dissolved. Scott reentered the business in 1946 with Scott Funeral Home and the fourth generation of the Scott family has joined management of the company. The photograph above depicts Combs and Scott employee Emil Wulf standing next to the funeral home's 1936 LaSalle ambulance near the company's chapel on East Maple Street. (Photo: Scott Funeral Home)

Six

SERVING

THE MILITARY

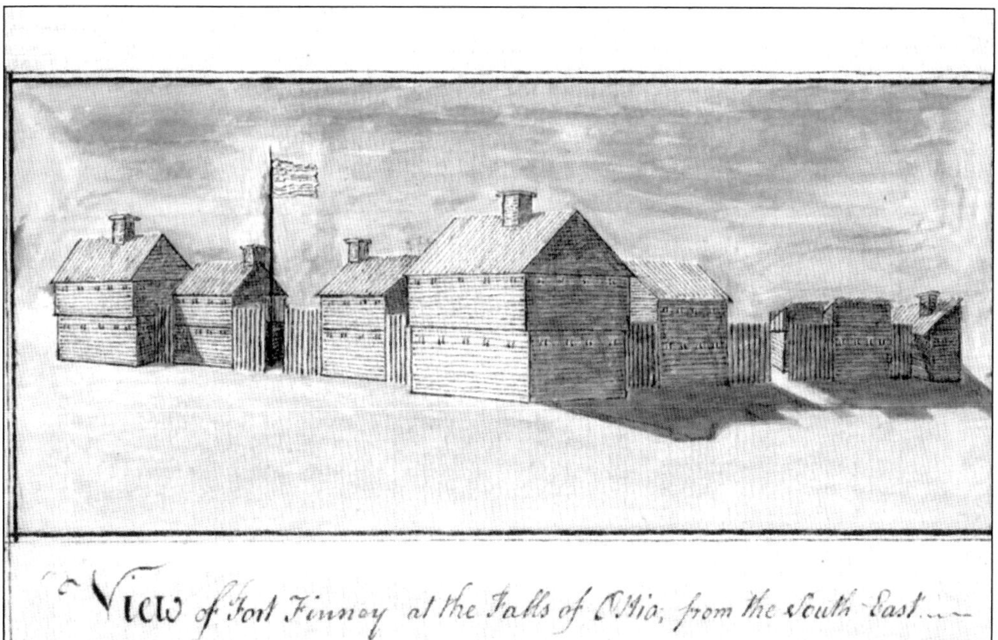

FORT FINNEY. The U.S. Army constructed a series of forts along the Ohio River to protect settlers from the threat of Indians. Planners recognized the strategic advantage of the good view offered by the bend in the river near the site of today's Fort Street and so located a fort there in 1786. Major Finney, for whom the local garrison was named, constructed this and a number of the other forts. Lt. Erskurius Beatty wrote in 1787 that the fort sat on a "beautiful bank about half a mile above the beginning of the rapids on the Indiana shore...a very strong defensible fort built of block houses and pickets about ninety yards from the river." This pen and ink drawing by Capt. Jonathan Heart shows Fort Finney from the southeast. (Photo: Indiana Historical Society)

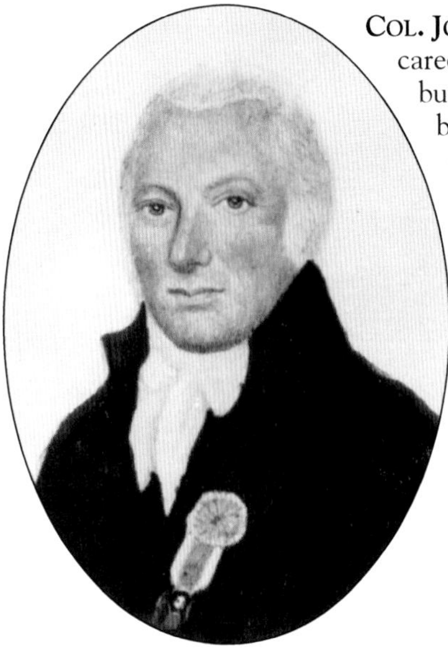

Col. John Armstrong. Colonel Armstrong began his military career in the Revolutionary War as a private in Philadelphia, but soon worked himself up as a commissioned officer by the end of the war. He continued in the service as commandant of several forts, including Fort Finney from 1786 to 1790. Colonel Armstrong retired in 1793 and later served as treasurer of the Northwest Territory. He lived in Ohio from 1793 to 1814, but returned to Clark County where he lived two more years, dying near Charlestown. His son, William G. Armstrong, served as first president of the Jeffersonville Railroad (see page 31). (Photo: Indiana Historical Society)

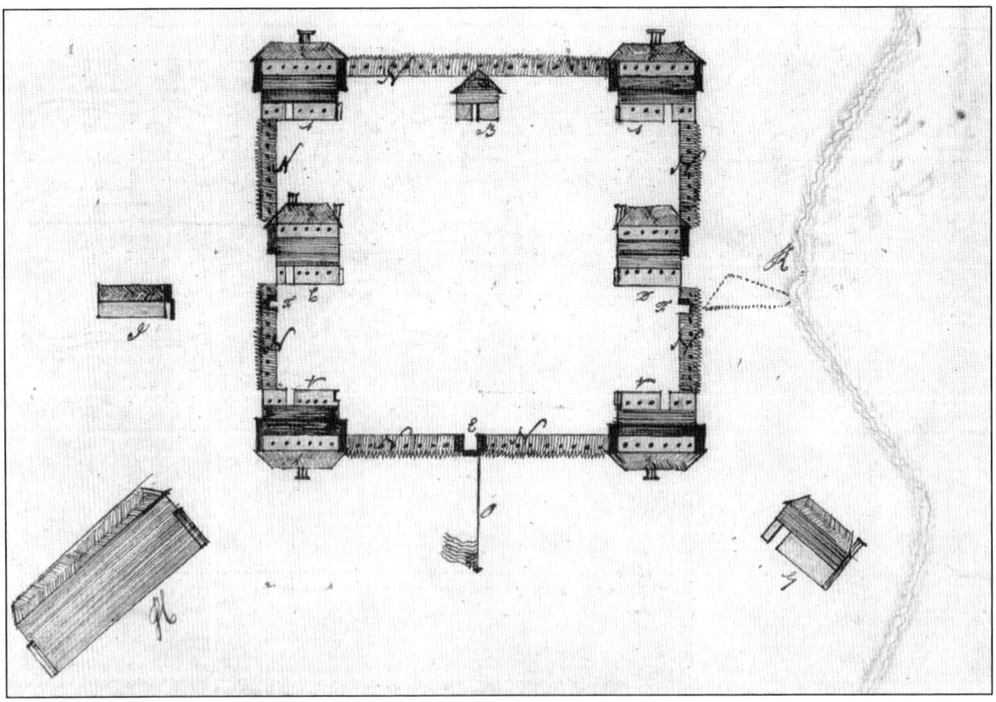

Fort Finney from Above. This pen and ink diagram by Capt. Jonathan Heart places Fort Finney and its outbuildings onto the landscape. The Ohio River is shown "150 yards distant at low water" at bottom and a stream called the "Miami" is shown emptying into the Ohio "about one mile distant" at right. Four block houses occupy the corners, two large structures face east and west protecting the sally ports, and a nine-foot palisade joins them all together. Unattached structures include the magazine inside of the fort opposite the main gate that faced the river, the kitchen outside at lower right, and a "council house" at lower left. The outpost was renamed Fort Steuben in 1789 and had a garrison of 61 soldiers in 1791, but it faded into obscurity after that date. (Photo: Indiana Historical Society)

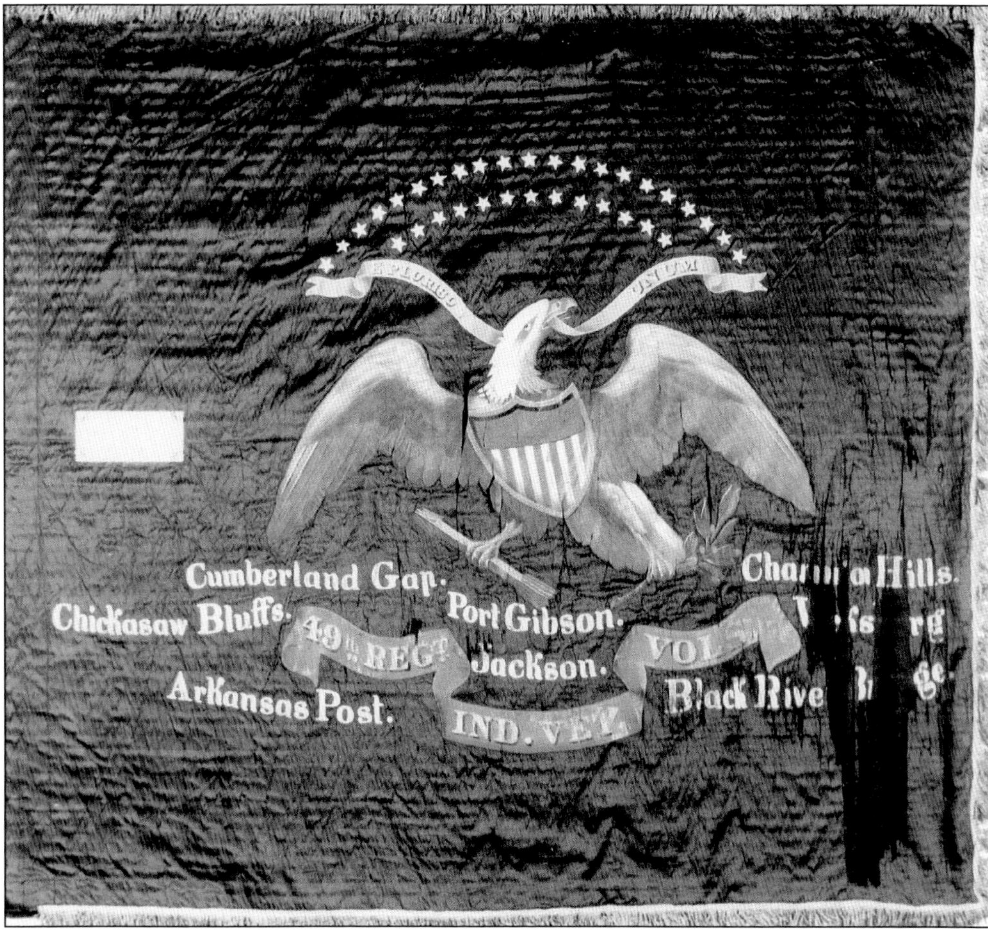

THE 49TH INDIANA INFANTRY REGIMENT. Many men from Jeffersonville served in the Union army, but the 49th was Clark County's, and to a great extent Jeffersonville's, only regiment raised and entirely organized here. When the men first mustered in to the service at Clarksville's Camp Joe Holt in November of 1861, according to an anecdote related by historian Lewis Baird, they arrived wearing their oldest and worst clothes, having been told by friends that they could dispose of these rags after receiving their new uniforms. A delay led to the men wearing their rags for an entire week, much to the dismay of the ladies who organized a reception in their honor in Jeffersonville! The ragged unit soon cleaned up, received its training, and headed south. The unit saw action at a number of locales (added later to their regimental flag seen here), but it earned its greatest glory at Port Gibson, a noteworthy U.S. victory that secured a Union foothold for the assault on Vicksburg. The men executed a bayonet charge against a Virginia artillery battery holed up in and near a strategic farmhouse and a Missouri infantry regiment maneuvering behind. After the 49th had routed the rebels, General Osterhouse rode up and said, "Put that 49th flag on the top of the house; no other shall go there." Even General Grant acknowledged the unit's contribution, telling them, "Men, I thank you for what you have just accomplished." The Indiana War Memorials Commission has preserved this and all of Indiana's battle flags in Indianapolis to this day. (Photo: Indiana War Memorials Commission)

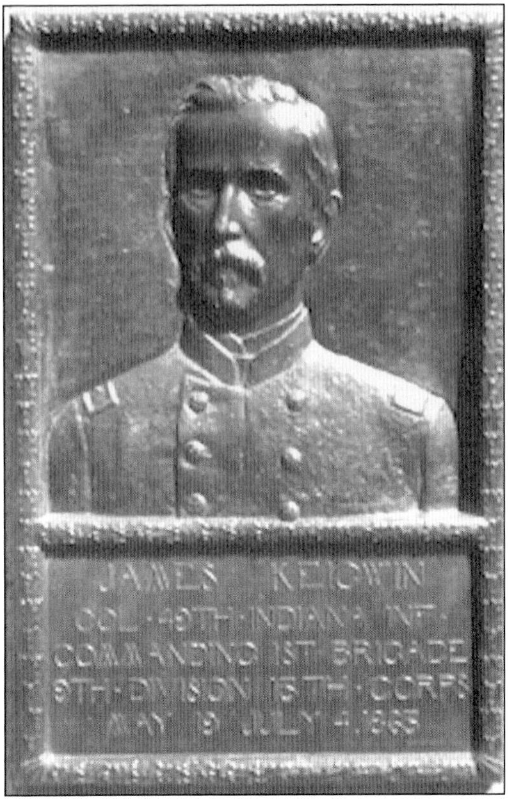

COL. JAMES KEIGWIN. Jeffersonville-born James Keigwin began his Civil War service as colonel of the 8th Regiment, but soon resigned to become lieutenant colonel of the 49th upon its formation later in 1861. A year later he assumed command of the regiment as colonel. Keigwin led his men through many of their most famous exploits, including the bayonet charge at Port Gibson. Keigwin received serious injuries once while escorting some Confederates under a flag of truce, when men of the 49th mistakenly opened fire on the group, wounding his horse and throwing him to the ground. This monument at Vicksburg honors Keigwin's service as a brigade commander. Keigwin later served for a time in the state senate and died in 1904. (Photo: Vicksburg National Military Park)

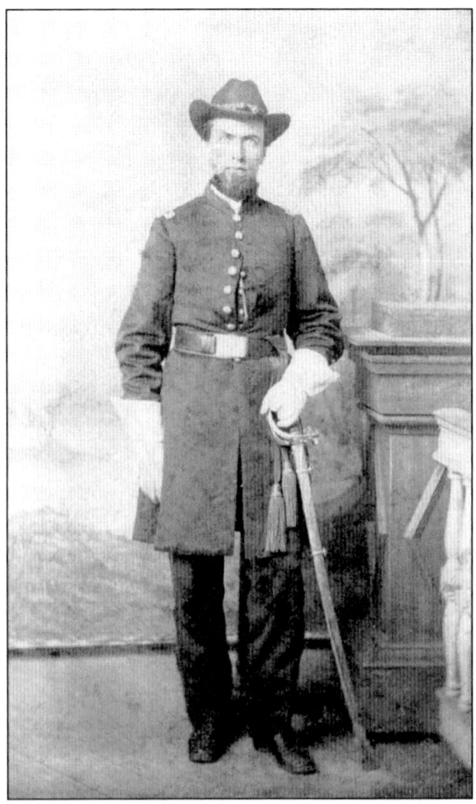

CAPT. JAMES W. THOMSON. As a boy, James Thomson moved to Jeffersonville with his family from his native St. Louis. He served as captain of the 49th's Company B, and while in the vicinity of Big Creek Gap, Tennessee, in 1862, he and his company skirmished with the 1st Tennessee Confederate Calvalry, capturing that unit's regimental banner and assisting in the capture of 2 officers and 32 enlisted men. After the war, Thomson served Jeffersonville as city clerk from 1880 to 1883. He also worked as a clerk in the Treasury Department in Washington D.C. Thomson died in Jeffersonville in 1911. (Photo: Filson Historical Society)

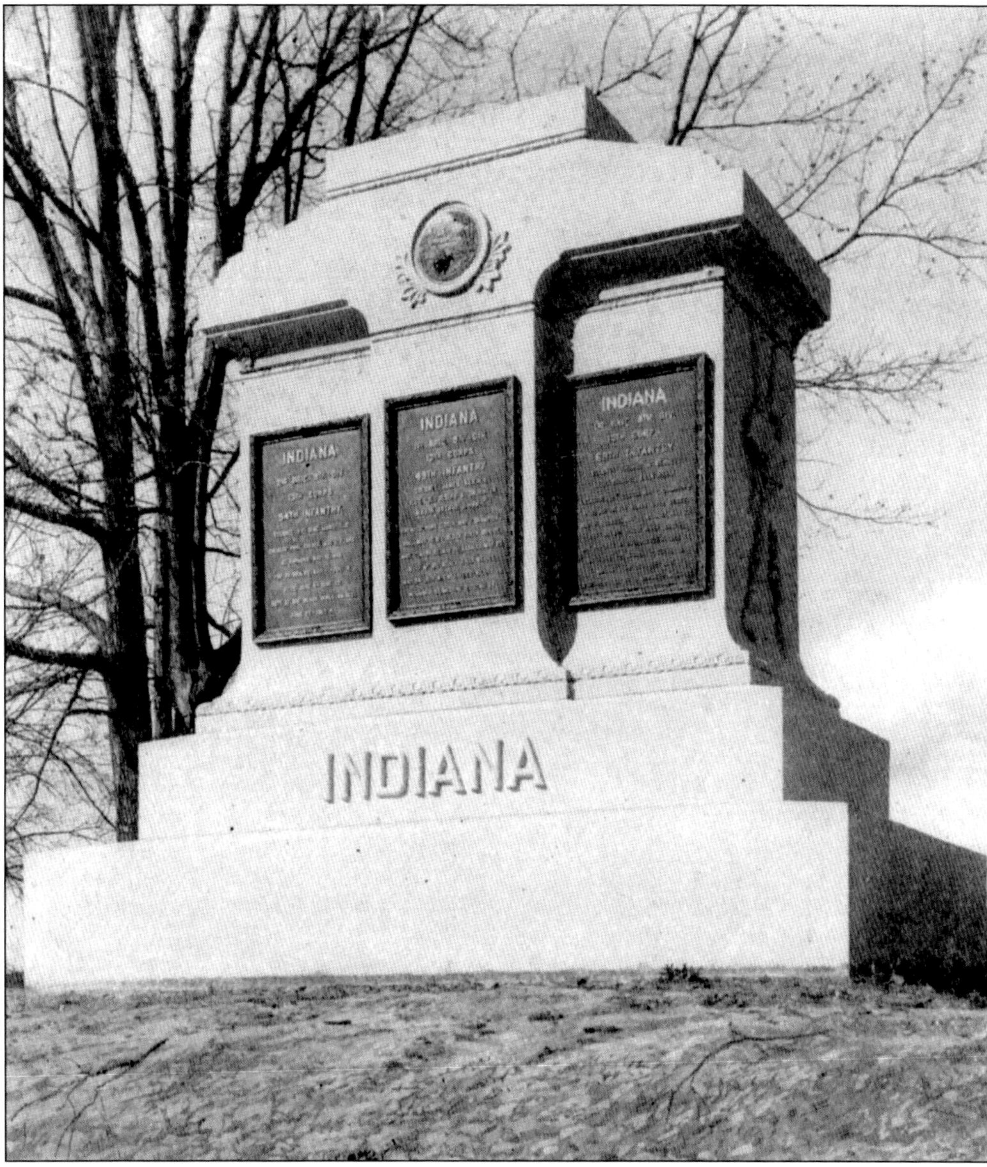

THE 49TH AT VICKSBURG. The 49th took part in one of the western campaign's most famous and pivotal engagements, the siege and capture of Vicksburg. On the morning of May 17, 1863, Keigwin and his regiment with the other Federals breached the works surrounding the besieged Confederate city, taking numerous prisoners and 17 artillery pieces, which some of the 49th turned back toward the rebels now fleeing toward the city. The next morning the regiment crossed a pontoon bridge across the Big Black River, marched 10 miles, and sighted the city and its fortifications for the first time. The regiment took part in the bloody, but ultimately unsuccessful assaults on the city on May 19 and 22. "God what a charge it was!" remembered one Union general of the first assault. "We had to walk in on foot, over tangled abattis, up precipitous hills, and against ramparts bristling with cannon and rifle." Despite these setbacks, General Grant won his victory on July 4 with the surrender of the 29,500 rebels defending Vicksburg. The monument above at the Vicksburg National Military Park commemorates the 49th and two other Hoosier regiments' bravery there. (Photo: *Indiana at Vicksburg*)

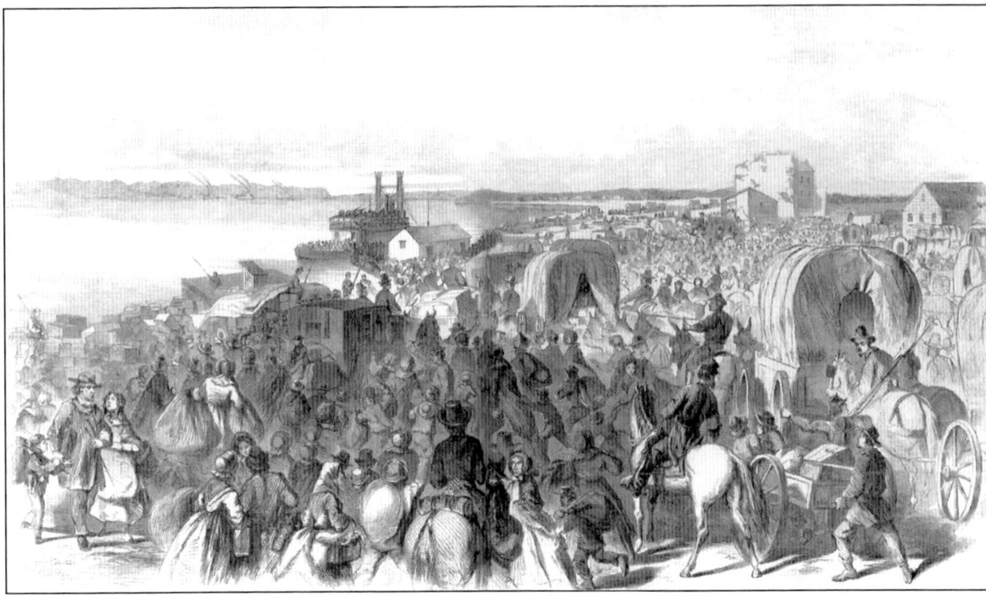

Evacuation of Louisvillians to Jeffersonville. Two Confederate armies under Gens. Braxton Bragg and E. Kirby Smith closed in on Louisville, a key strategic prize, in September and October of 1862. Gen. William "Bull" Nelson ordered women and children to leave the city. Louisville's wharf became a bedlam and so many fled across the river to Jeffersonville, as depicted in this engraving, that the city's hotels and rooming houses filled to capacity. Gen. Don Carlos Buell and his men barely reached the city ahead of the Confederates on September 24 and the now 100,000 federals defending Louisville forestalled any invasion. (Photo: *Frank Leslie's Illustrated Newspaper*, courtesy Indiana University—Bloomington)

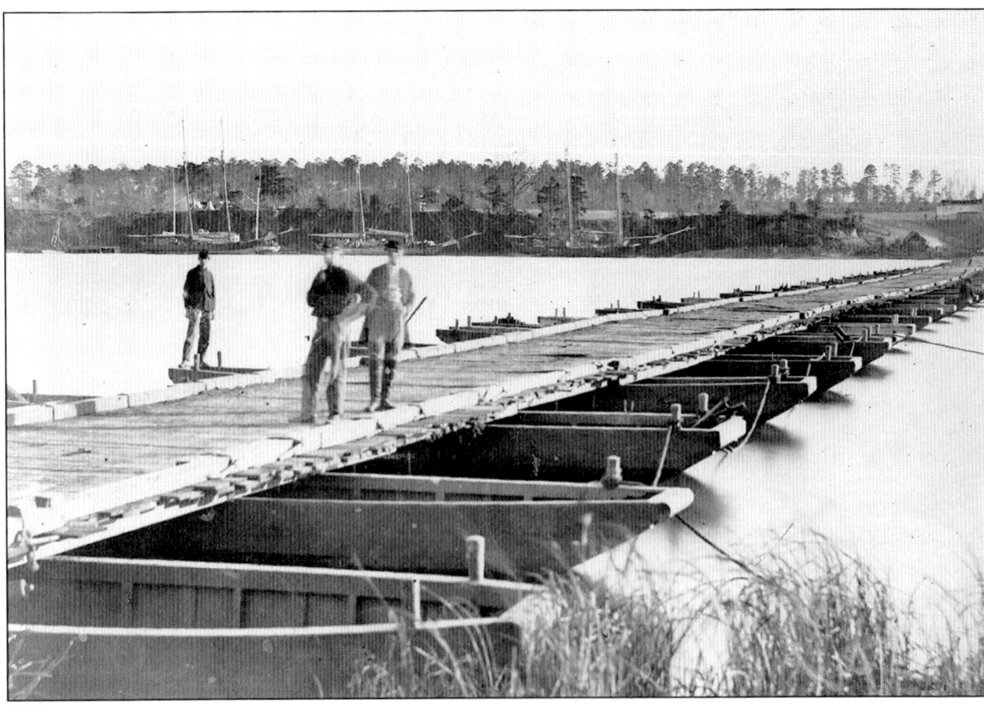

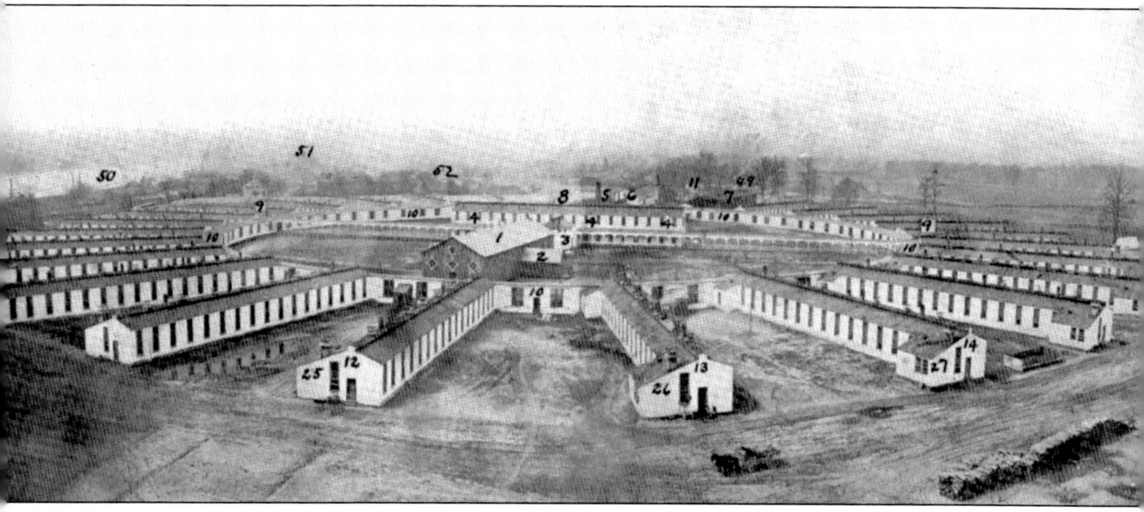

JEFFERSON GENERAL HOSPITAL. Jeffersonville sent many soldiers and much materiel south for the war effort, but it received a sad dividend in the thousands of wounded and dying men shipped north for medical care. The first wounded received care at Clarksville's Camp Joe Holt, but it became clear that the army needed a new facility to receive so many soldiers. Jefferson General Hospital, the third largest hospital in the United States during the war, opened in 1864 a short distance upriver of Jeffersonville, near today's Park Place. The government built the hospital on land seized from U.S. Senator Jesse D. Bright, who had turned his allegiance to the South. It offered a good landing for steamers and easy access to the Jeffersonville Railroad. The hospital cared for 16,120 patients from 1864 to 1866. This photograph, looking west toward the half-mile in circumference facility, shows how 27 buildings radiated outward from the center like spokes from a hub. The building marked "1" served as the facility's chapel and reading room. That marked "2" was the chaplain's office while "3" served as the operating room. Headquarters, marked "4," stretched behind this cluster. Hospital matron Elvira Powers wrote a book after the war in which she chronicled her experiences at Jefferson General. Her entry for Christmas Eve 1864 reveals the grimness of attending to the dying: "The second death in the ward. It was that of a young, noble-looking man—Prevo, of the 40th Indiana. He died of a gunshot wound, the ball entering the lungs. . . . A lock of hair and a few words of condolence will go to one more mourning family in place of the dear, noble boy." (Photo: Indiana Historical Society)

Opposite: **UNION ARMY'S PONTOON BRIDGE FROM JEFFERSONVILLE TO LOUISVILLE.** Jeffersonville served as the southern terminus of the Jeffersonville Railroad and the city had a number of Union supply operations. General Nelson recognized the strategic importance of improving the link to southern Indiana, so he militarized the Jeffersonville ferry and ordered that the army construct two pontoon bridges across the Ohio River at Jeffersonville and New Albany. Engineers anchored the Jeffersonville bridge at the foot of Fort Street and completed it by September 28, 1862. It remained for approximately 15 months. This photograph of a Virginia bridge illustrates the army's method of constructing such a span. (Photo: Library of Congress)

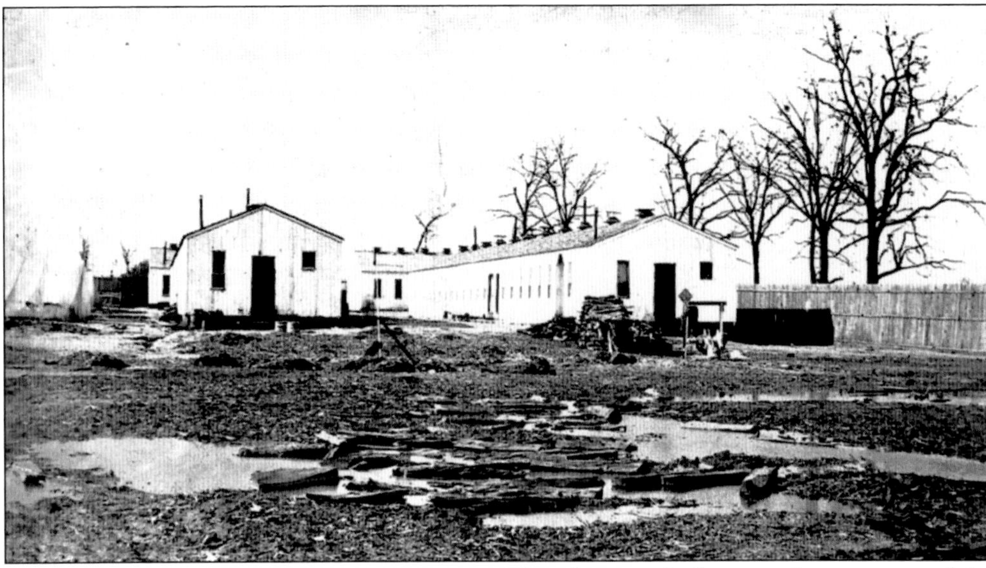

Barrack at Jefferson General Hospital. This photograph shows a close-up view of the guard barracks, which provided quarters for the soldiers guarding and policing the installation. (Photo: Indiana Historical Society)

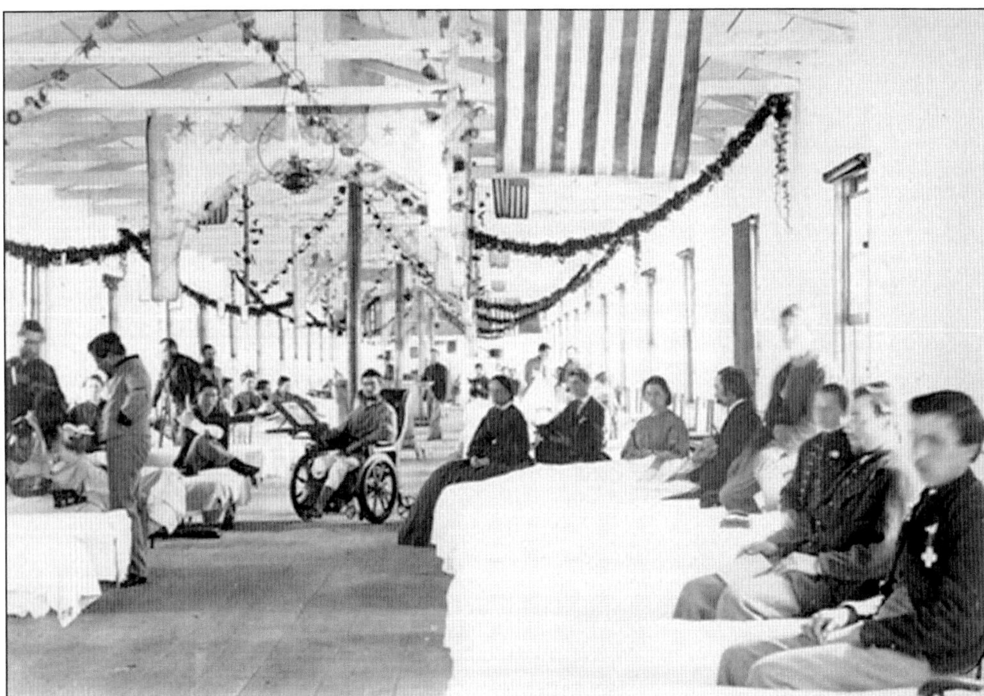

Interior of a Civil War Hospital. No known photograph exists of Jefferson General Hospital's interior, but this photograph of a Washington D.C. hospital suggests what it may have resembled. The wards at Jefferson General, like the one pictured here, had high ribbed ceilings open under the combs for ventilation. One window between every two beds allowed sunlight to cheer and warm occupants. (Photo: Library of Congress)

Jefferson General Hospital Laundry and Engine House. The hospital's laundry house, at left, had a fresh supply of water from the Ohio River for it sat close to the river bank. The building with the smokestack to the right served as an engine house, possibly for the heating or pumping of water. (Photo: Indiana Historical Society)

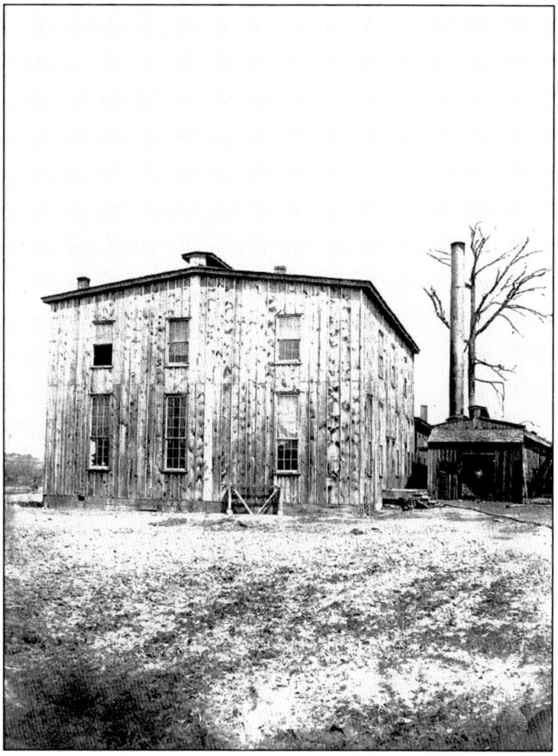

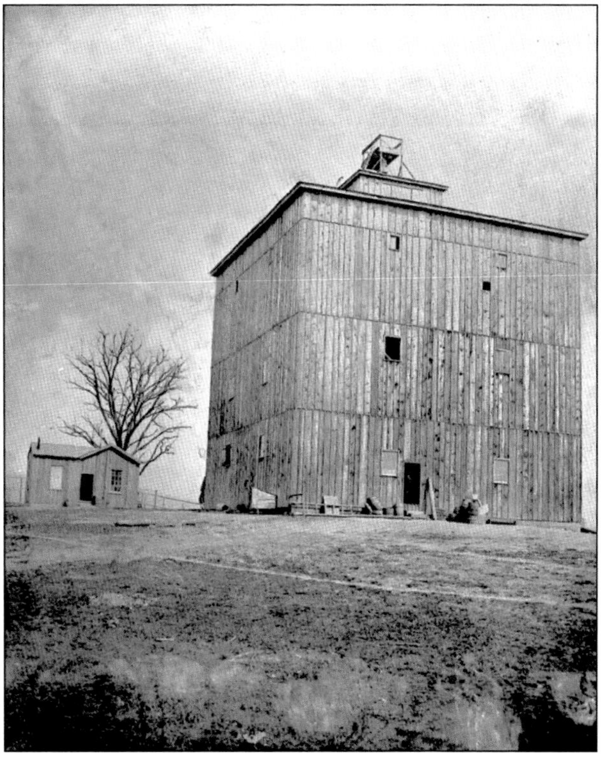

The Hospital's Tank House and Band House. The hospital's tank house for storing water, at right, towers next to the facility's band house, at left. (Photo: Indiana Historical Society)

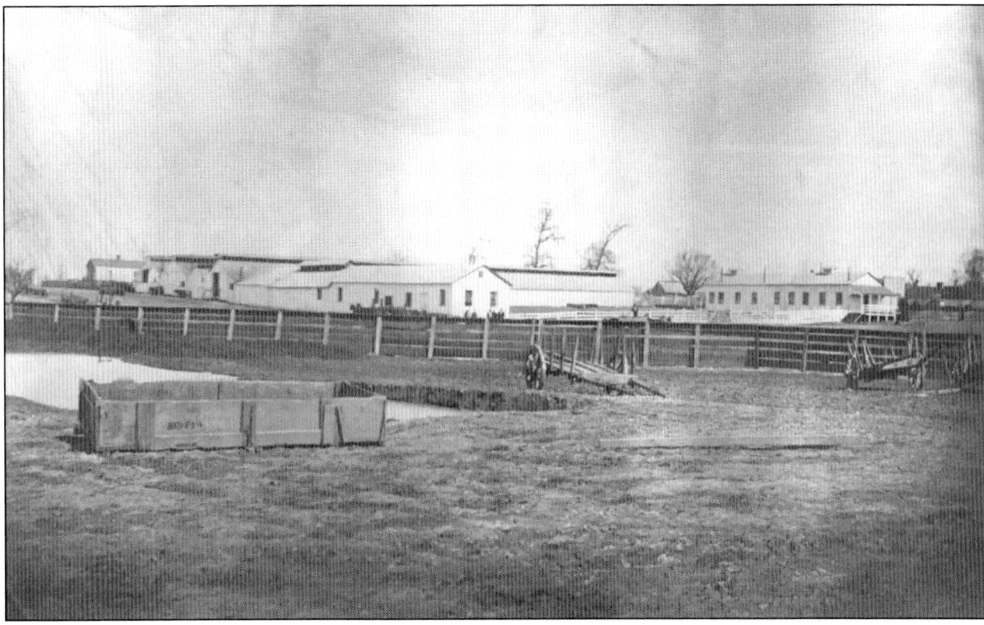

U.S. GOVERNMENT STABLES ABOVE CANAL STREET. Jeffersonville hosted a number of military installations throughout the Civil War, as the city occupied a strategic logistical location. Locomotives conveyed men and material by rail and steamers by water, but horse-drawn vehicles met short-haul transportation needs. This photograph depicts the government's stables on Canal Street (now Meigs Avenue) between Seventh and Eighth Streets. (Photo: Indiana Historical Society)

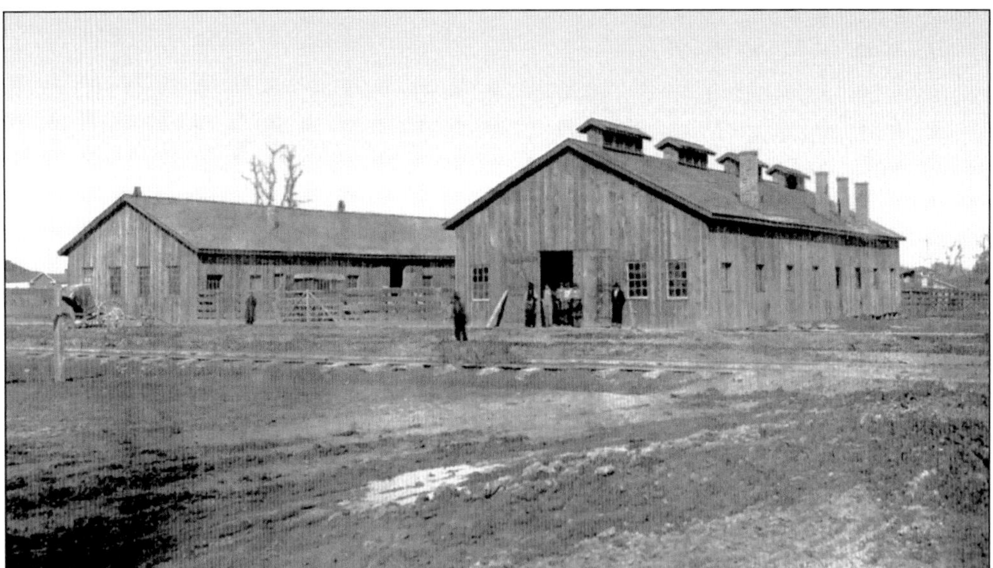

BLACKSMITH AND WAGON REPAIR SHOP. Blacksmiths (right building) and mechanics (left building) worked at this location, the site of today's courthouse. Just visible stretching past the front of the buildings are the temporary railroad tracks laid in New Market Street (now Court Avenue) that ran to the Jeffersonville Railroad depot, which occupied the blocks where today's library and post office stand. (Photo: Indiana Historical Society)

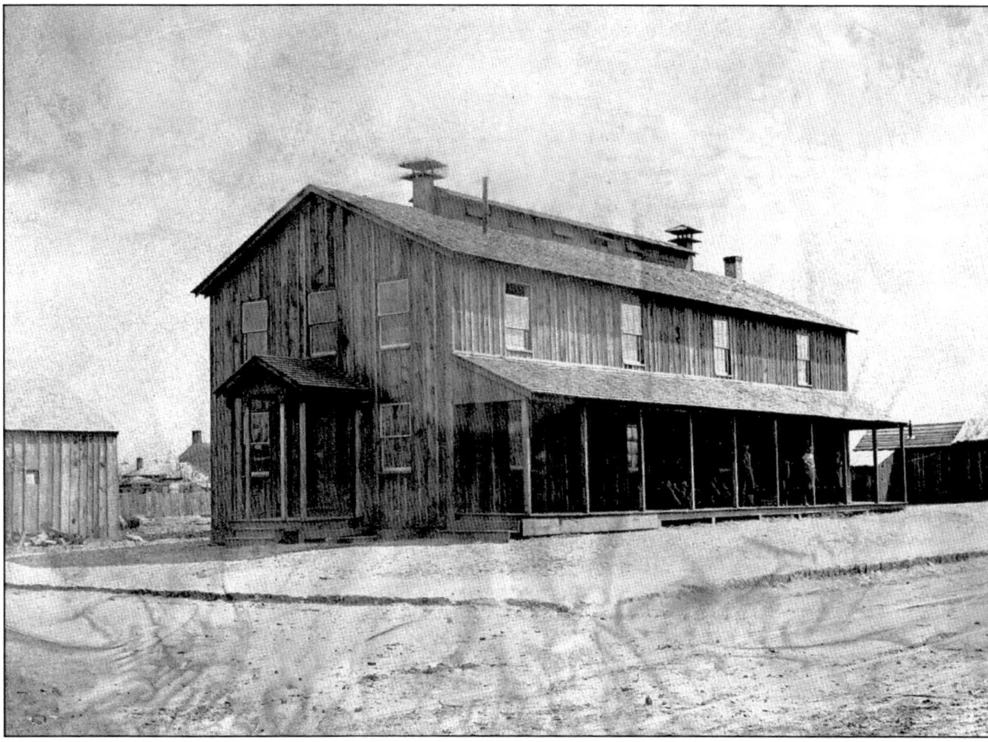

BARRACK FOR COMPANY OF INFANTRY. This barrack at the corner of Maple and Wall Streets provided quarters for a company of infantry in the early months of the war. St. Anthony of Padua would build its new church at the site in 1876. (Photo: Indiana Historical Society)

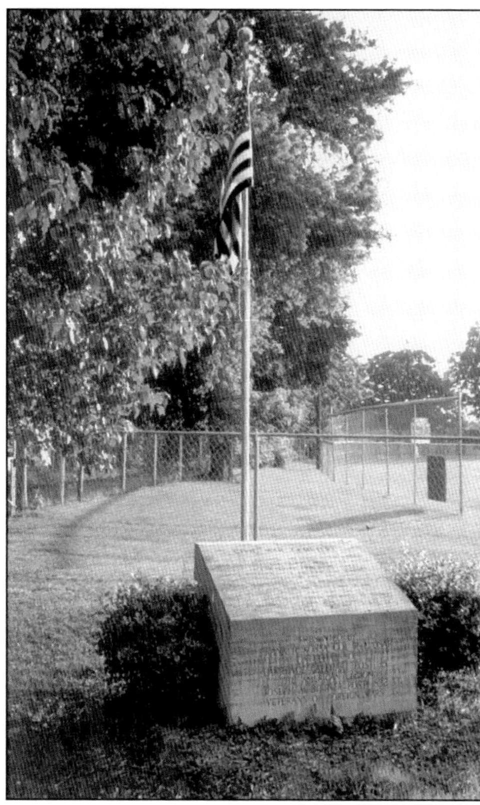

JEFFERSONVILLE'S CIVIL WAR CEMETERY. A Civil War cemetery lies buried under a ball field in Jeffersonville to this day, memorialized now by a flagpole and marker. The marker's inscription tells the story. "On this site, 1861–1865, are buried several hundred Union and Confederate soldiers, killed in the western campaign. Lack of interest from distant families allowed deterioration of the wood grave markers and heavy overgrowth. In 1927, the Jeffersonville council determined 'better the sound of children's footsteps at play than the silent stride of the nearly forgotten great spirit army here at rest.' The only intact stone marker was moved to Walnut Ridge Cemetery. No bodies were exhumed." (Photo: Author's collection)

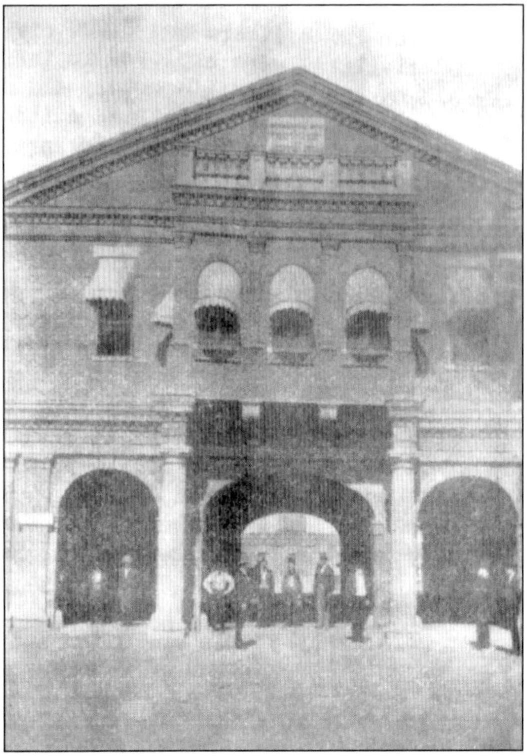

QUARTERMASTER DEPOT ENTRANCE AND ADMINISTRATIVE OFFICES. In 1871, the U.S. Army began construction of the U.S. Quartermaster Depot in Jeffersonville, consolidating into four square blocks, operations which had been scattered through the city since the Civil War. Quartermaster General Montgomery C. Meigs, for whom Canal Street was renamed, designed this imposing structure, which opened in 1874. This early photograph depicts the building's main entrance over which the installation's administrative offices were headquartered. (Photo: Jeffersonville Township Public Library)

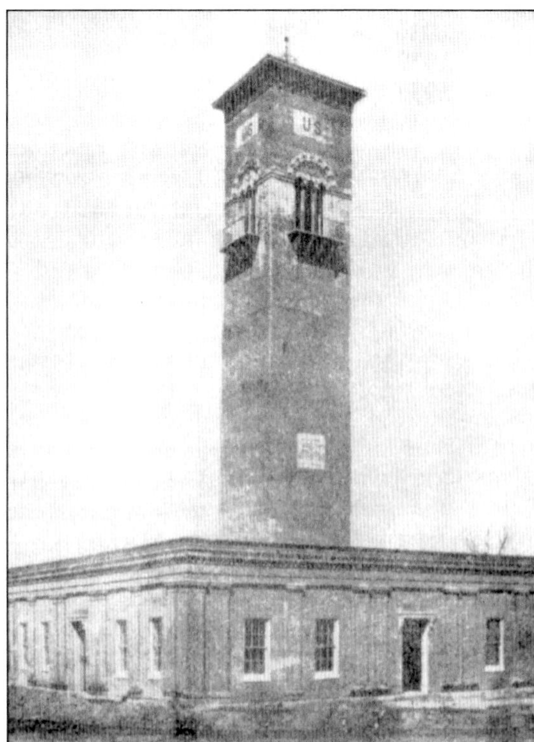

WATCH TOWER AND POWER PLANT. A combination watch and water tower soared 100 feet over the facility's squat power plant as seen in this photograph. The tower, according to one source, was "one of the most conspicuous structures about the falls of the Ohio." It provided a high vantage point for guards to watch for fires or disturbances. The army razed the tower after 1900 and used its brick to build the power plant into a two story administration building. (Photo: Jeffersonville Township Public Library)

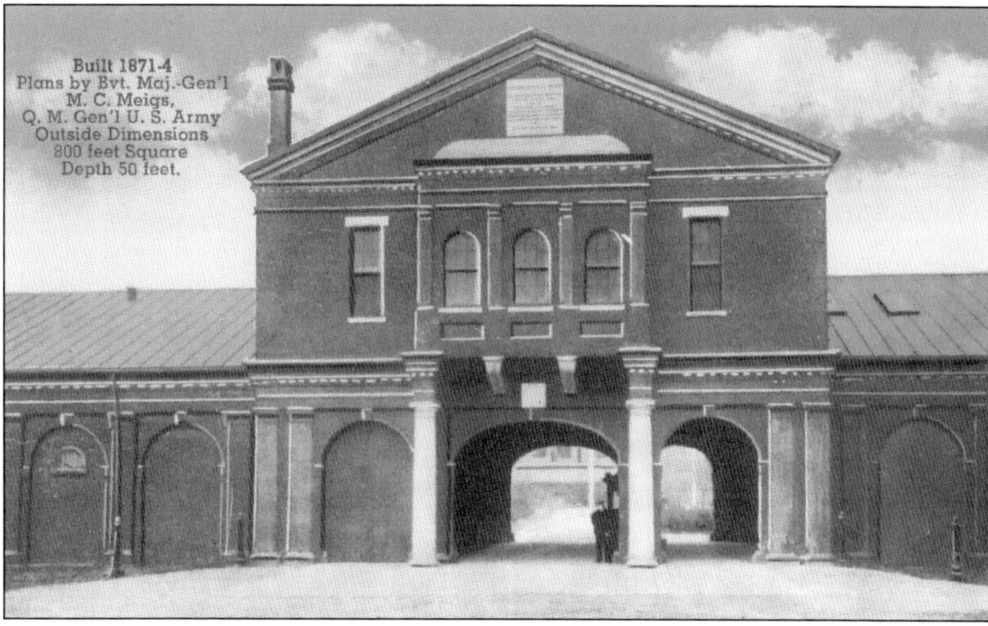

QUARTERMASTER DEPOT ENTRANCE IN THE EARLY 20TH CENTURY. Erecting the administration building at the center of the installation's quadrangle allowed its cramped staff to leave its obsolete offices over the main entrance, depicted here in the early 20th century. The old office was transformed into a record storage area. Visitors to the front of the former depot, now a shopping center slated for redevelopment, can still see the dedicatory stone set into the pediment. (Photo: Jeffersonville Township Public Library)

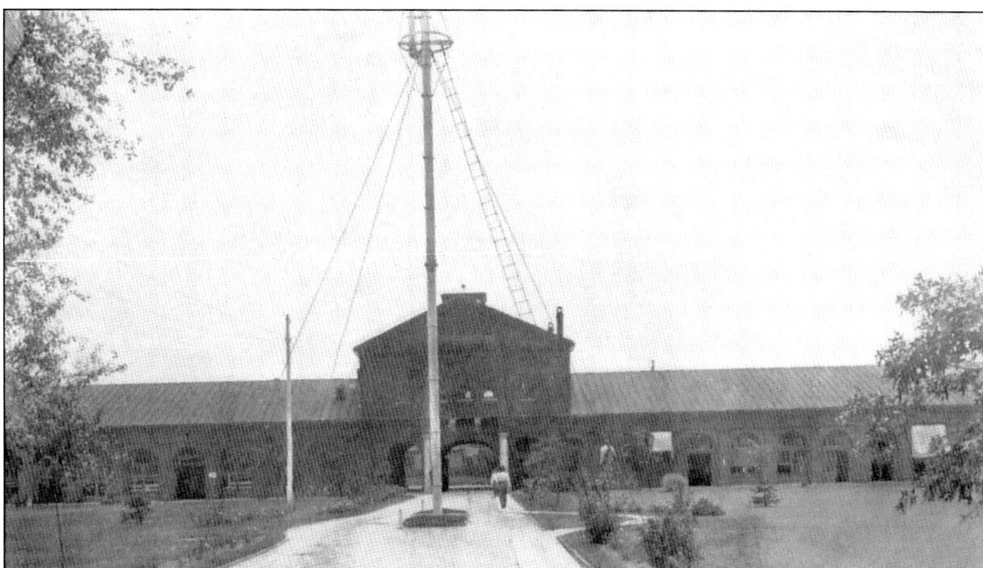

QUARTERMASTER DEPOT GROUNDS. The depot's imposing, quadrangle-style building surrounds a central courtyard, for which famed landscape architect Frederick Law Olmstead provided a formal plan. There is no evidence, according to historian Carl Kramer, that the depot ever implemented Olmstead's plan. In any case, the army built new structures on the land inside the quadrangle as the depot increased its presence in the city. (Photo: *Souvenir Jeffersonville, Ind.*)

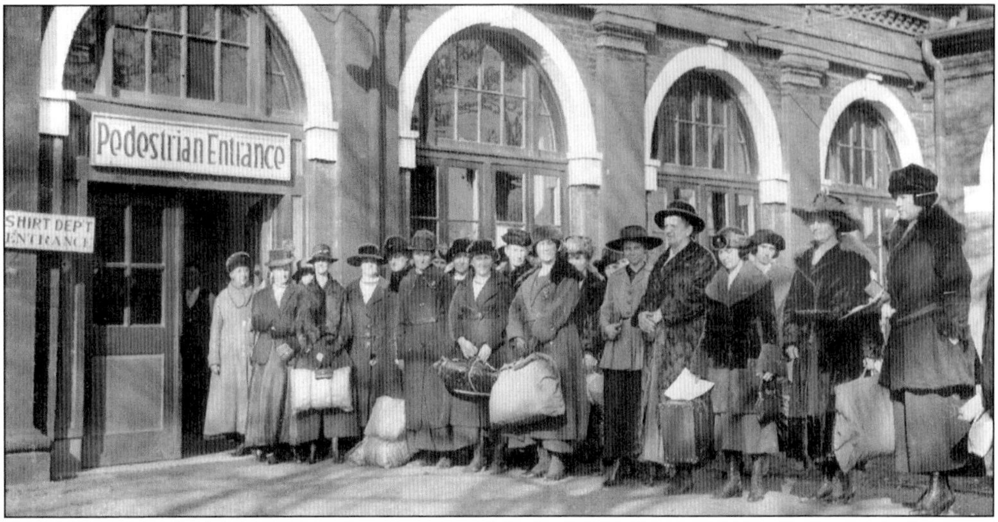

AMERICA'S LARGEST SHIRT FACTORY. On the eve of World War I, the depot produced and supplied a wide range of items from saddles and harness to stoves and kitchen utensils. Its most famous product however, was uniform garments for soldiers. The depot turned out 100,000 shirts per month during the Spanish-American War, but that total pales in comparison to the approximately 700,000 shirts produced per month during the Great War, earning the depot the nickname "America's largest shirt factory." The depot employed numerous home workers, who picked up raw materials, sewed them together at home, and returned the finished product. A group of these seamstresses pose with their bundles outside the shirt department entrance in 1917. (Photo: Jeffersonville Township Public Library)

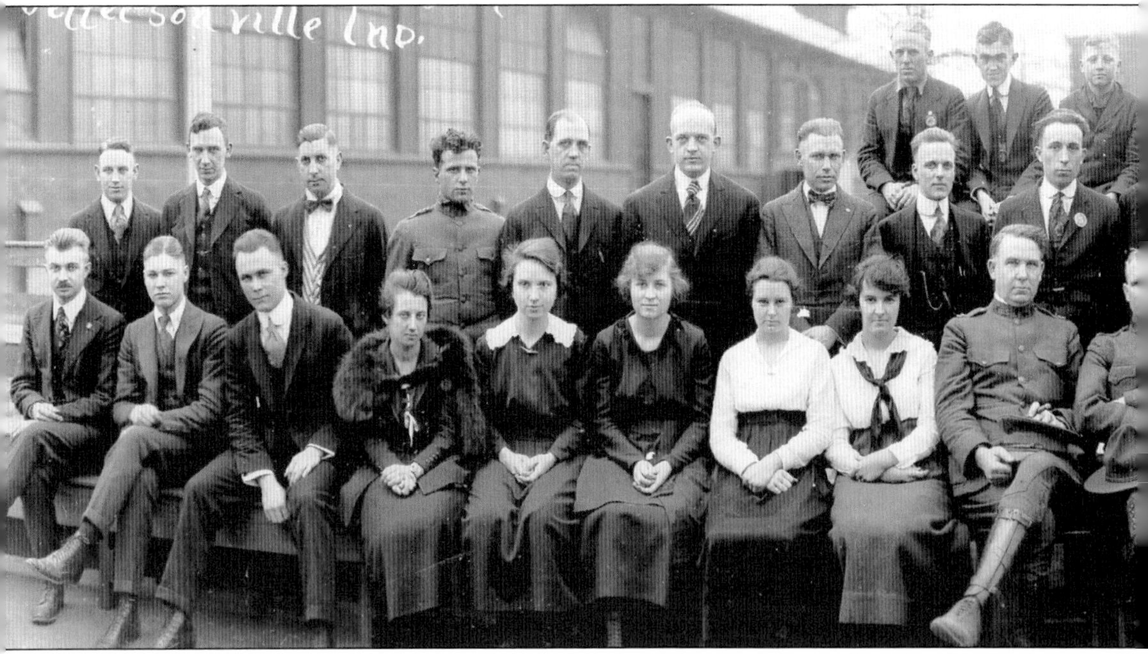

CIVILIAN AND MILITARY COLLABORATION AT THE QUARTERMASTER DEPOT. This panoramic photograph of the depot's plant maintenance division, taken shortly after the war on January 22, 1919, symbolizes how civilian and military staff always worked side-by-side through

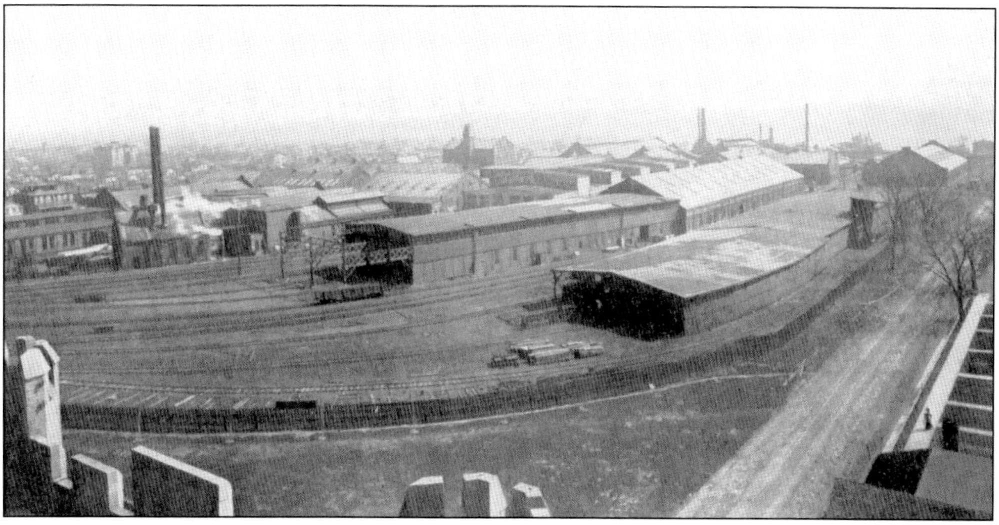

American Car and Foundry in the War Effort. The American Car and Foundry Company's local plant also contributed greatly to the world war effort. The U.S. Army Ordnance Department charged New York-based A.C.F. and its other civilian suppliers with "the task of forging and forming from the fire and steel of united American industry a weapon suitable for the successful wielding of the American fighting giant of three million manpower," according to the Army's chief of ordnance. The Jeffersonville plant manufactured a wide variety of products ranging from components for over 228,000 artillery shells to 18,156 cake turners. Wartime employees received handsome medals "for service faithfully rendered." (Photo: *Souvenir Jeffersonville, Ind.*)

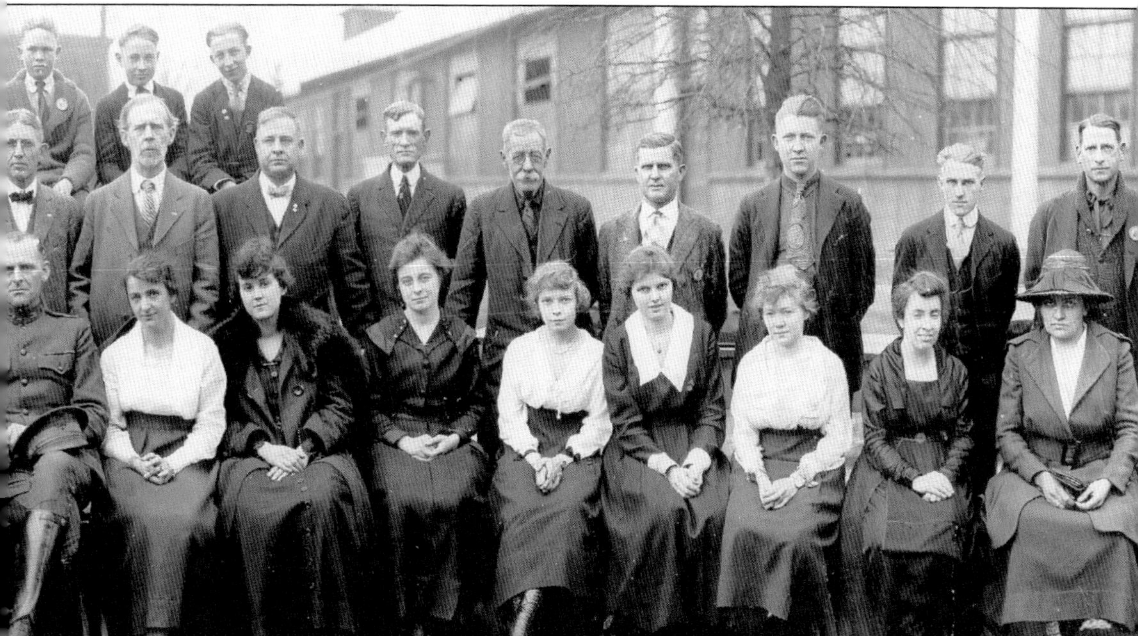

the depot's years of operation. Just a few years after the Great War, civilian employment fell to 445 and the military presence dropped to ten officers and two enlisted as the U.S. geared down from the massive war effort. (Photo: Filson Historical Society)

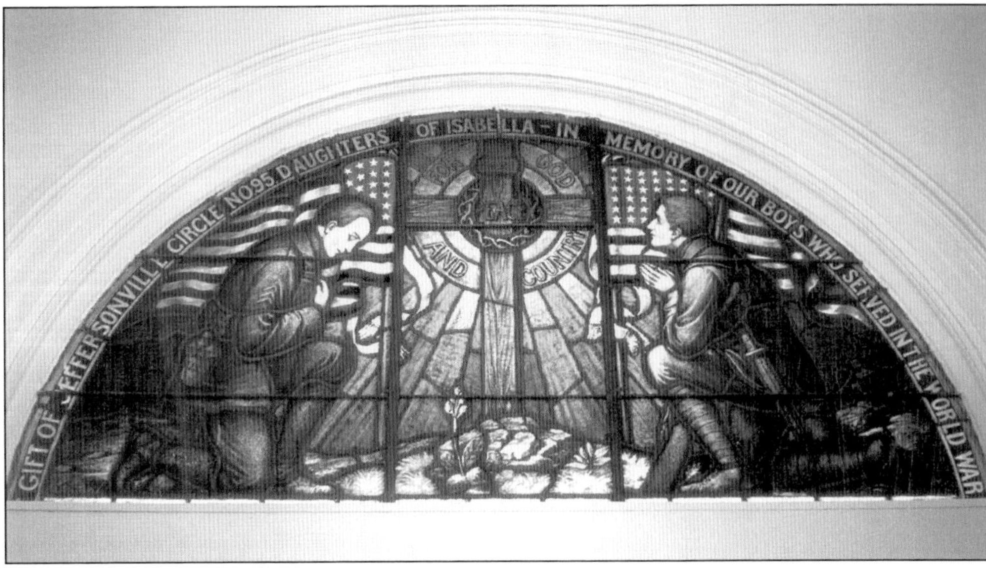

REMEMBERING THE GREAT WAR. Jeffersonville contributed so much to the war effort from the home front, but like countless cities and towns across the country it also sent its boys to fight, and die, in "the corner of some foreign field." Clark County saw 40 (42 by another account) of its own die in the Great War, including one woman, a Red Cross nurse. This stained glass window over the main doorway at St. Augustine's Roman Catholic Church commemorates their sacrifice "for God and country." (Photo: Author's collection)

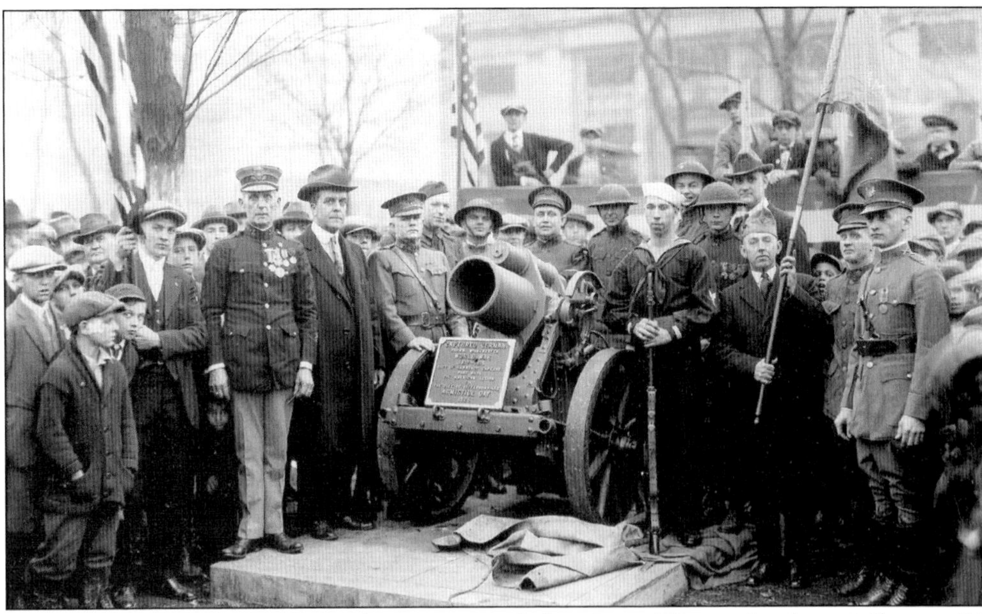

ARMISTICE DAY CEREMONIES. The memory of the Great War endured in Jeffersonville's consciousness long after the war's end. A crowd of two to three thousand gathered for an Armistice Day ceremony in Warder Park in 1925, seen here in this photograph, in which Jeffersonville's American Legion post presented a captured German cannon to the city. Mayor Joseph H. Warder, in civilian dress just left of the cannon, stated that he hoped the memorial would remind those passing by "of the awfulness of war and the sweetness of peace." (Photo: American Legion Post 35)

LAWRENCE CAPEHART. Jeffersonville's American Legion post honored Clark County's first soldier to die in the war by adopting his name for theirs. Lawrence Capehart was born in New Albany in 1892 and moved with his family to Jeffersonville in 1899. He joined the U.S. Marine Corps as a private on January 14, 1918, and soon found himself "over there." Capehart fought bravely, but received wounds in battle that led ultimately to his death in a military hospital in Paris in August of 1918. His mother had his body reburied in the national military cemetery in New Albany. (Photo: American Legion Post 35)

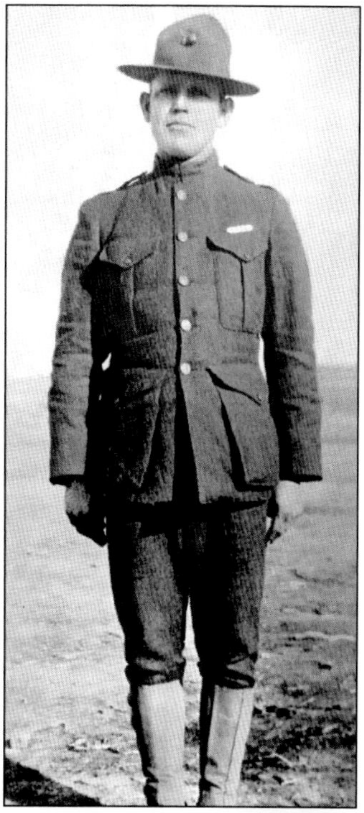

AMERICAN LEGION. Veterans of the American Expeditionary Force founded the American Legion in Paris in 1919 and posts soon organized across America, including early Post 35 in Jeffersonville. This photograph, taken sometime before World War II, shows the post's band on the steps of the Masonic Temple across from Warder Park. Jeffersonville's Veterans of Foreign Wars post has also served as a uniting and comforting force advocating for veterans in this community. (Photo: American Legion Post 35)

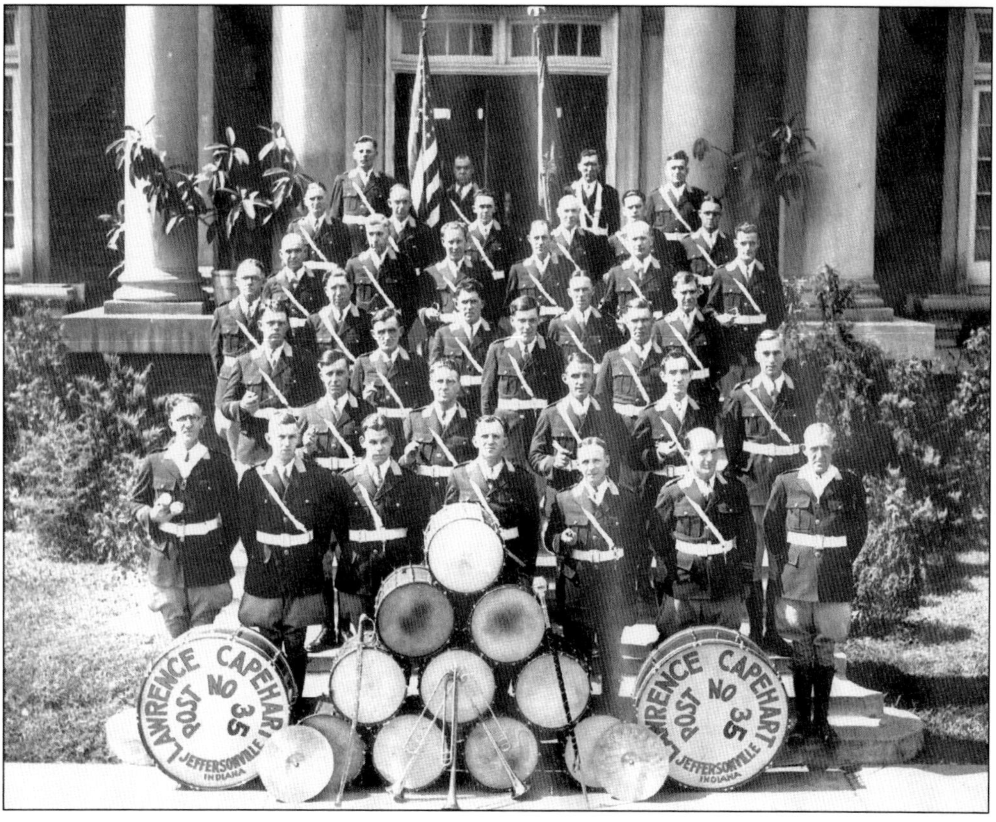

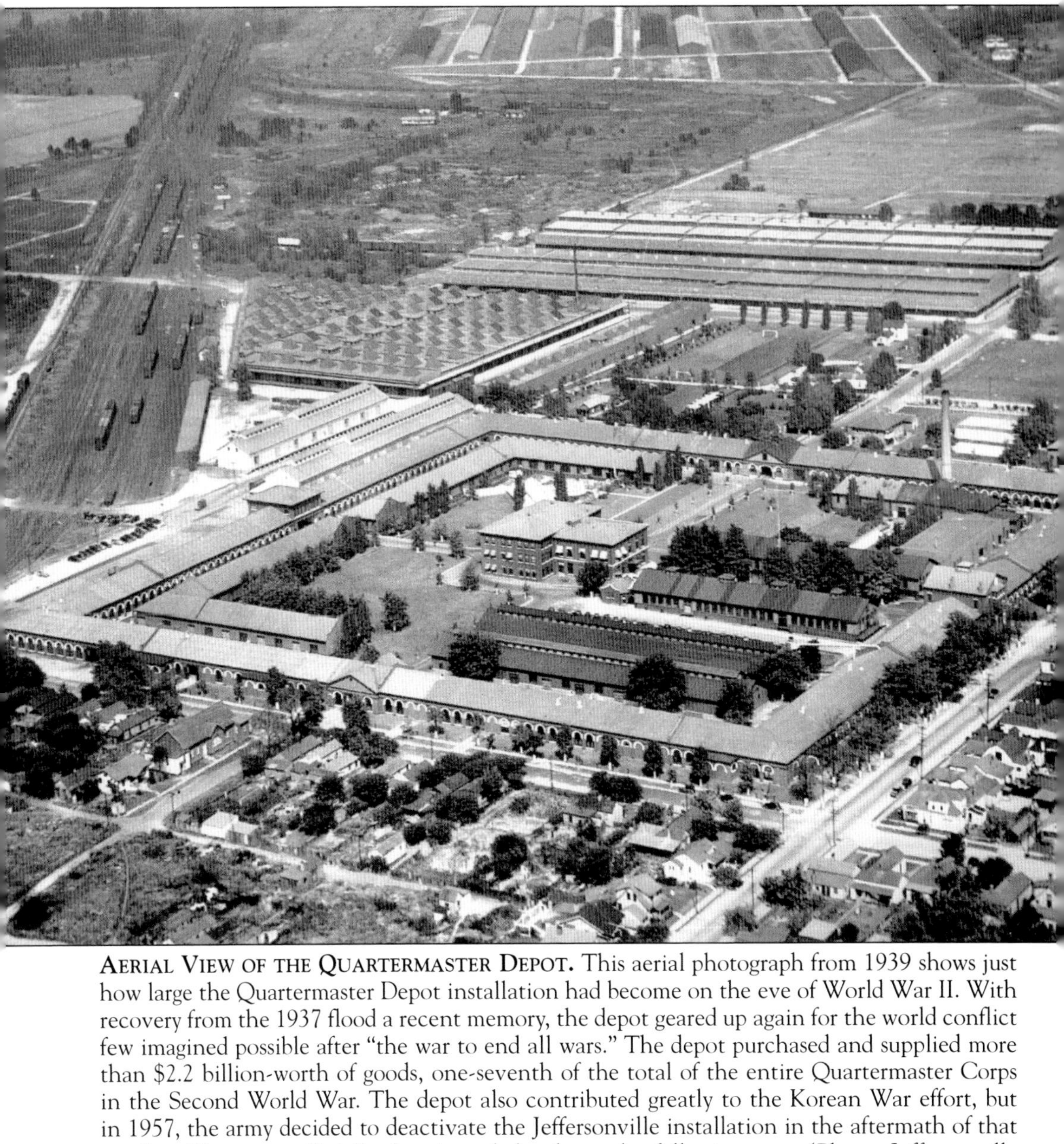

AERIAL VIEW OF THE QUARTERMASTER DEPOT. This aerial photograph from 1939 shows just how large the Quartermaster Depot installation had become on the eve of World War II. With recovery from the 1937 flood a recent memory, the depot geared up again for the world conflict few imagined possible after "the war to end all wars." The depot purchased and supplied more than $2.2 billion-worth of goods, one-seventh of the total of the entire Quartermaster Corps in the Second World War. The depot also contributed greatly to the Korean War effort, but in 1957, the army decided to deactivate the Jeffersonville installation in the aftermath of that conflict. The army officially deactivated the depot the following year. (Photo: Jeffersonville Township Public Library)

Seven

SUFFERING

OHIO RIVER FLOODS

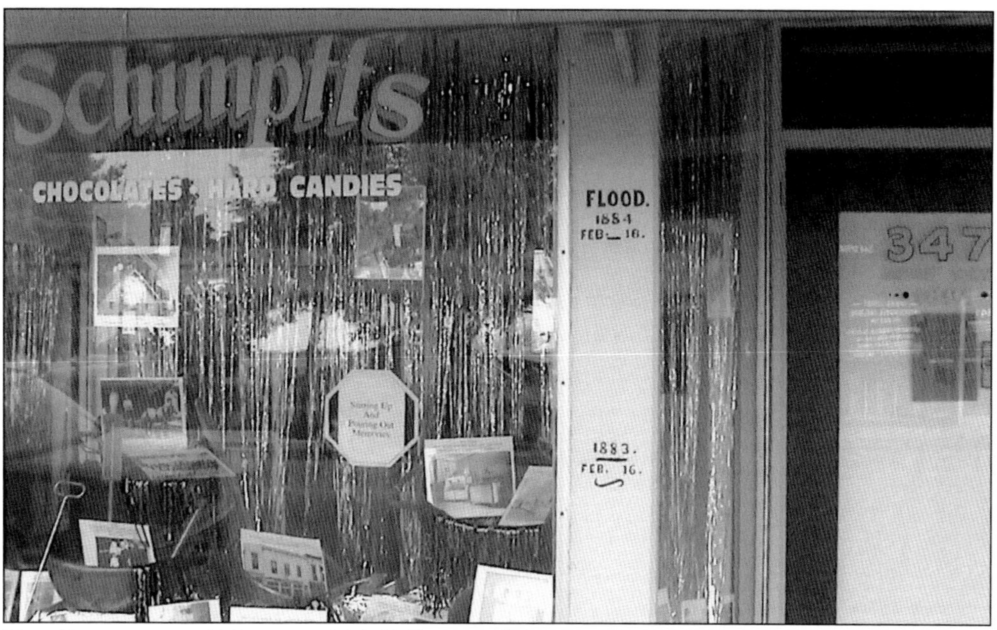

THE FLOODS OF 1883 AND 1884. Jeffersonville's proximity to a major artery like the Ohio River provides the city with many commercial assets, but that proximity can be a liability when the cold waters of winter and spring reach into the city. Jeffersonville experienced its worst flood in 50 years when the river rose to 44.8 feet in February of 1883. Incredibly, just one year later, the river inundated the city again, reaching a height of 47.4 feet. This modern photograph shows the high water marks carved into the wall outside of Schimpff's Confectionery on Spring Street. (Photo: Author's collection)

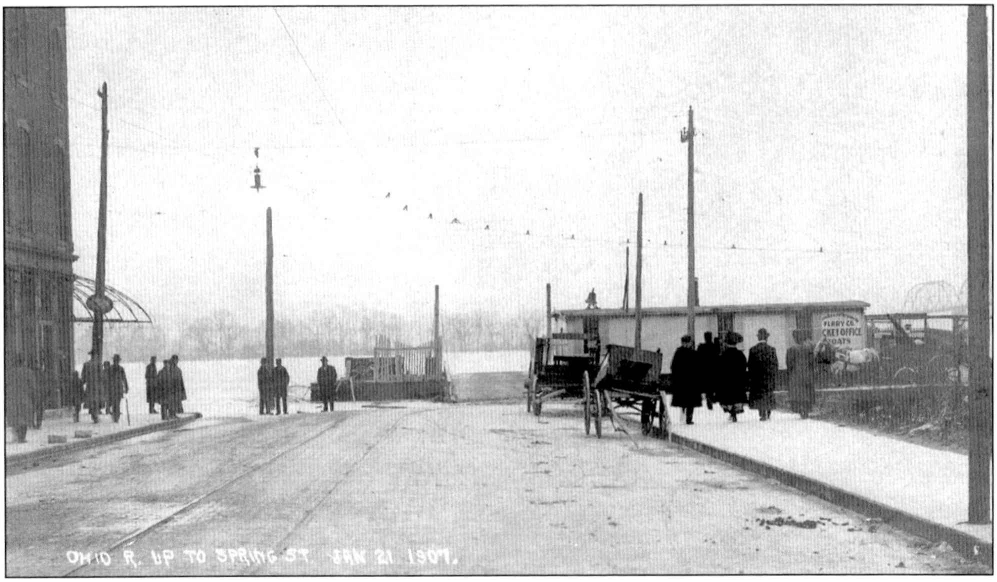

FLOOD WATERS OF 1907 THREATEN JEFFERSONVILLE. The federal government constructed a levee shortly after the 1884 disaster in an effort to prevent another such catastrophe. Inevitably, the river would rise again to test the city's resolve. The Ohio reached flood stage again in 1907, but the levee held, leading historian Lewis Baird to remark two years later in a fit of hubris, "Jeffersonville is today the safest and dryest river town from Pittsburg [*sic*] to Cairo." This image from January 21, 1907, shows the Ohio rushing past the foot of Spring Street to such a height that the ferry dock may be seen at eye level. (Photo: Charles R. Leap)

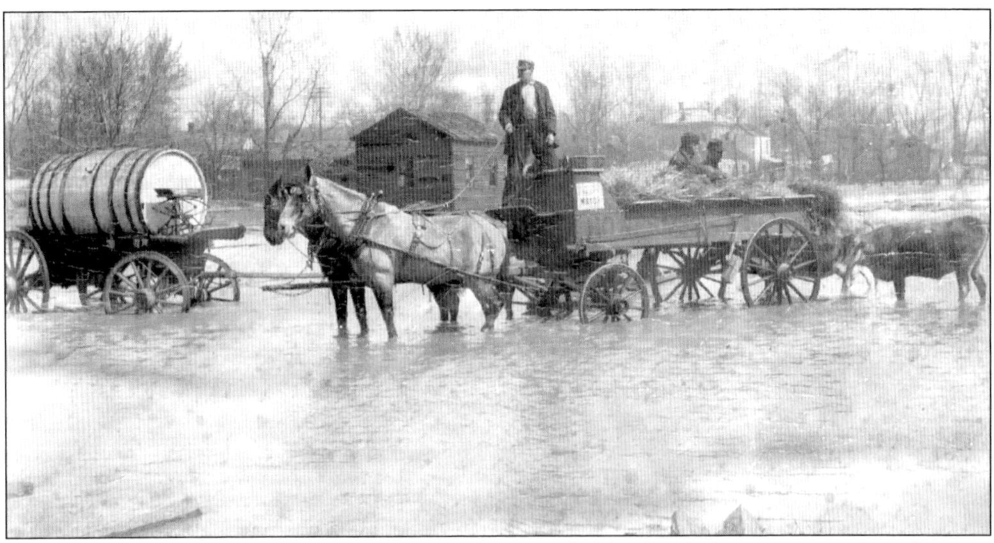

RETURN OF HIGH WATER IN 1913. The river, improbably, flooded twice in 1913, in January and again in March and April, when it crested at 45.21 feet. The water crept more than 60 feet up Spring Street, but again the levee held. A frightening breach in the Pennsylvania Railroad fill opened in Clarksville, which could have resulted in water rushing into Jeffersonville from the west, but inmates from the State Prison worked feverishly and repaired the damage. This photo shows high water at the Howard Works, where long-time Howard worker Steve Miller provides feed and fresh water to the yard's oxen. (Photo: Howard Steamboat Museum)

TRYING TO STEM THE TIDE IN 1937. The rains of winter fell relentlessly for three weeks in January of 1937, pouring 19 inches onto the valley and filling the Ohio River and its tributaries past capacity. Jeffersonville sealed off its sewers from the encroaching flood water, as seen in this photograph, and desperately pumped water back over the levee in several locations. Again Jeffersonville watched the levee nervously. Would it hold? Few imagined that the water would swell over that levee, designed to best the swell of 1884 by two to three feet. (Photo: Jeffersonville Township Public Library)

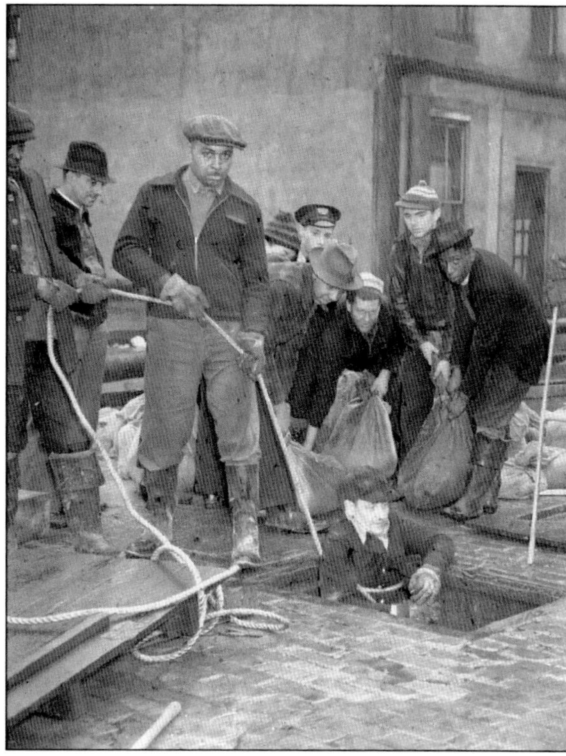

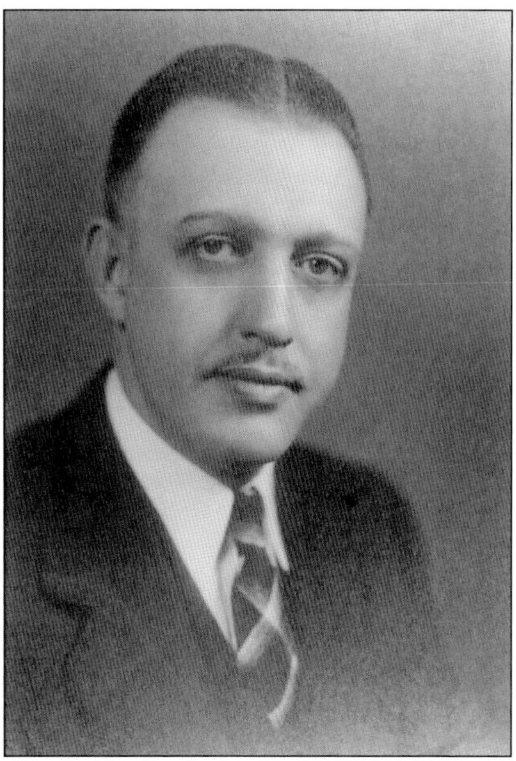

ACTING MAYOR EDWIN M. COOTS II. Mayor Allen W. Jacobs had been in Florida for three months recuperating from an illness when Jeffersonville found itself on the verge of a major disaster. The city council and the Jacobs family requested that county coroner and funeral home owner Edwin M. "Tuck" Coots take charge as acting mayor. Coots issued orders and supervised relief efforts throughout the flood and initiated requests for financial aid from the state of Indiana in its aftermath. (Photo: E.M. Coots' Sons Funeral Home)

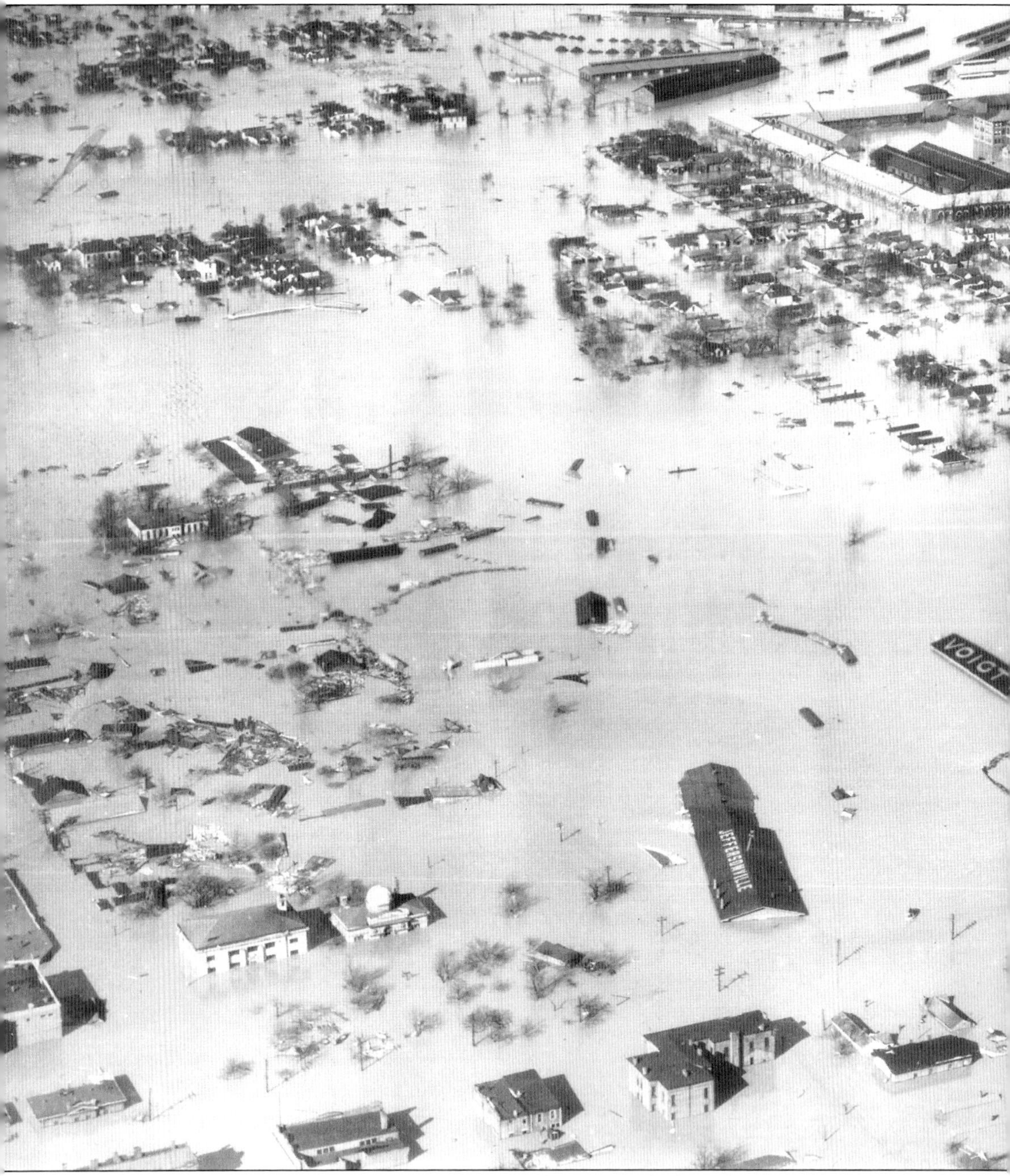

JEFFERSONVILLE SUBMERGED. Jeffersonville quickly succumbed to the worst Ohio River flood in recorded history. Low temperatures added to the city's misery as the thermometer dropped to 16 degrees on January 24. The flood finally crested on January 27, 1937, at a height of 57.1 feet, 40 feet higher than normal and 22 feet over Spring Street. Water covered 90 percent of Jeffersonville, Clarksville, and Claysburg. This aerial panorama shows almost everything except

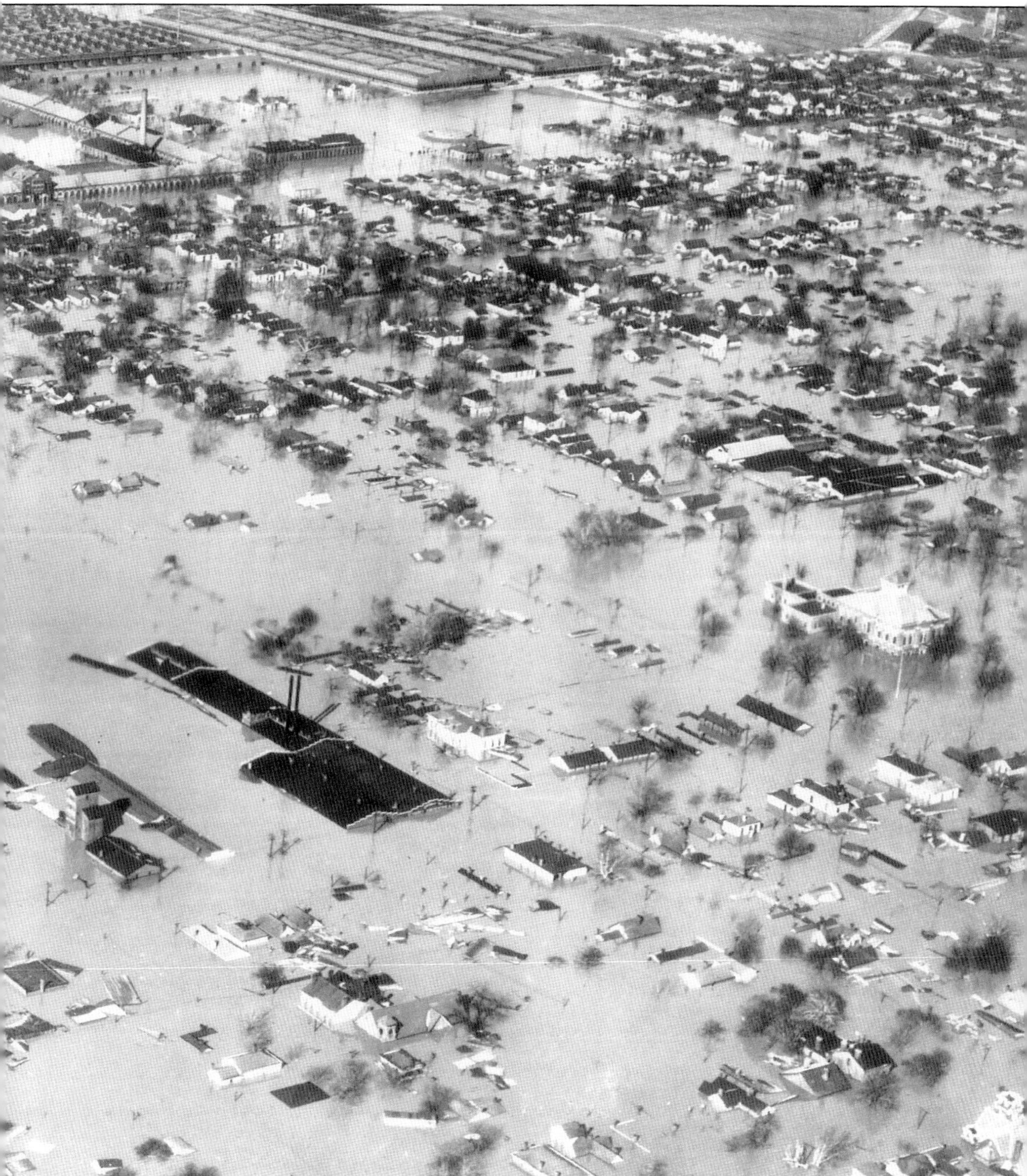

rooftops completely under water. Court Avenue stretches from Warder Park at the lower left of the photo to the Clark County Courthouse at the center right. The Quartermaster Depot, where many sought refuge but which itself surrendered to the water, can be seen at top. Rose Hill School, not visible in this photograph, sat on high ground on the city's west end and served as the city's central relief station. (Photo: Jeffersonville Township Public Library)

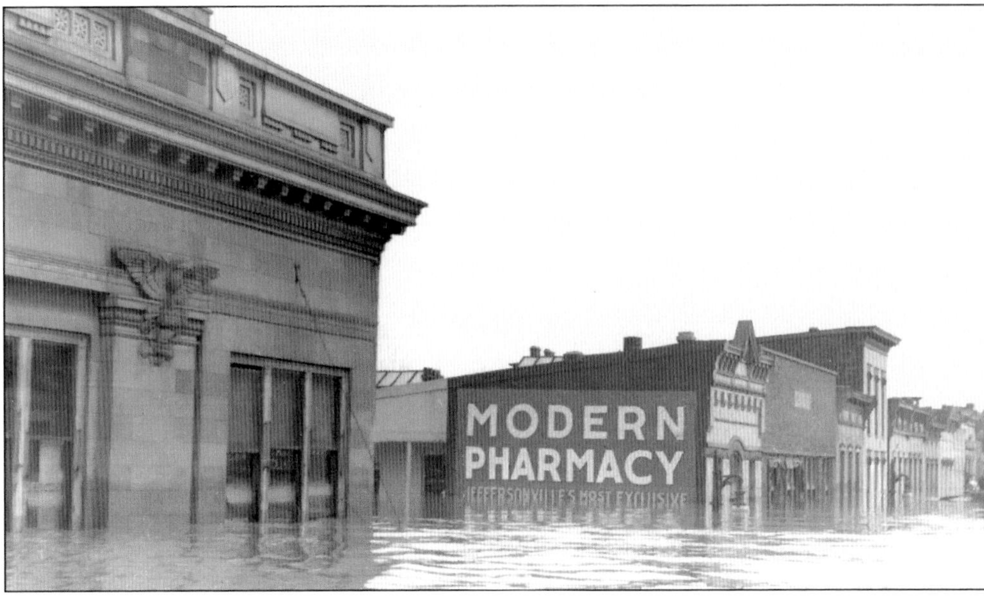

COURT AND SPRING STREETS. This view looking west on Court Avenue at its intersection with Spring Street shows the Citizens Trust building and its former neighbors across the street, including the Modern Pharmacy. The water stain on the wall of the bank building shows that the flood had receded by about two feet at the time of this photo. Citizens had prepared the bank's vault for the flood, but the Louisville company responsible for sealing the vault forgot to seal an air vent, allowing water to surge in. (Photo: Jeffersonville Township Public Library)

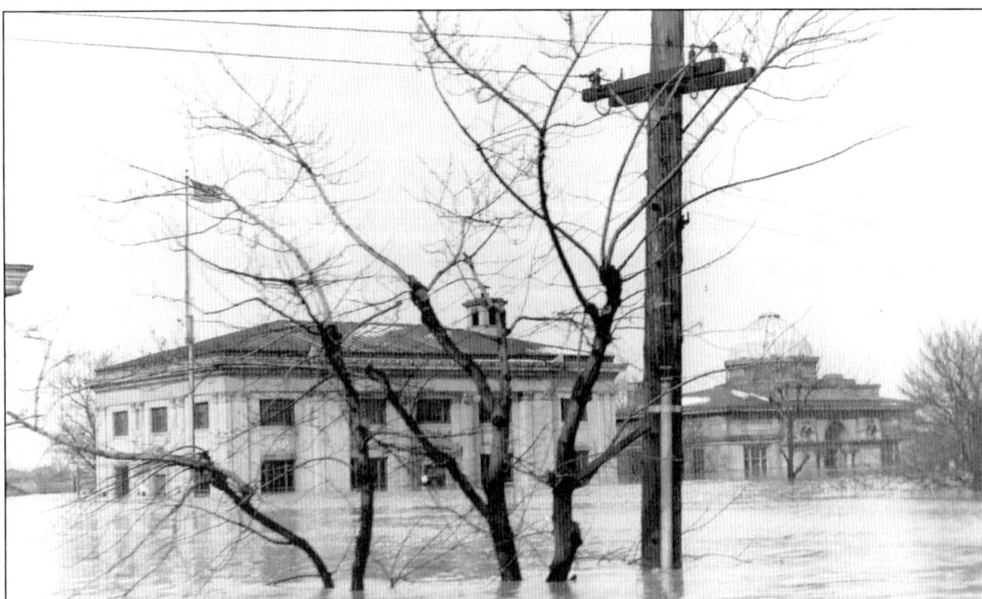

WARDER PARK UNDERWATER. Flood waters inundated the post office (left) and library (right). Cleanup workers later found themselves no choice but to shovel out the library's ruined collection with the rest of the mud and refuse polluting the city. (Photo: Jeffersonville Township Public Library)

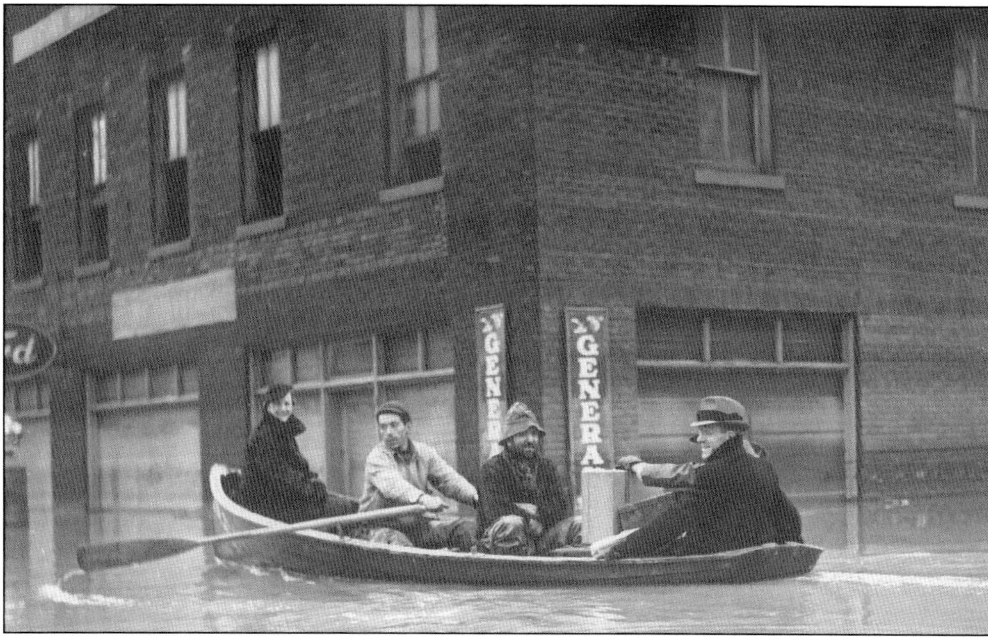

Skiff in front of the Ford Agency. Here, Jeffersonville's bearded and weary police chief, John Hibstenberg, huddles up from the cold for a ride through town with several unidentified companions. At this point, the flood waters had already receded by six feet from the crest. Merchants and officials feared looting, but Mother Nature, with the help of the National Guard and law enforcement agencies, forestalled much dishonesty. (Photo: Jeffersonville Township Public Library)

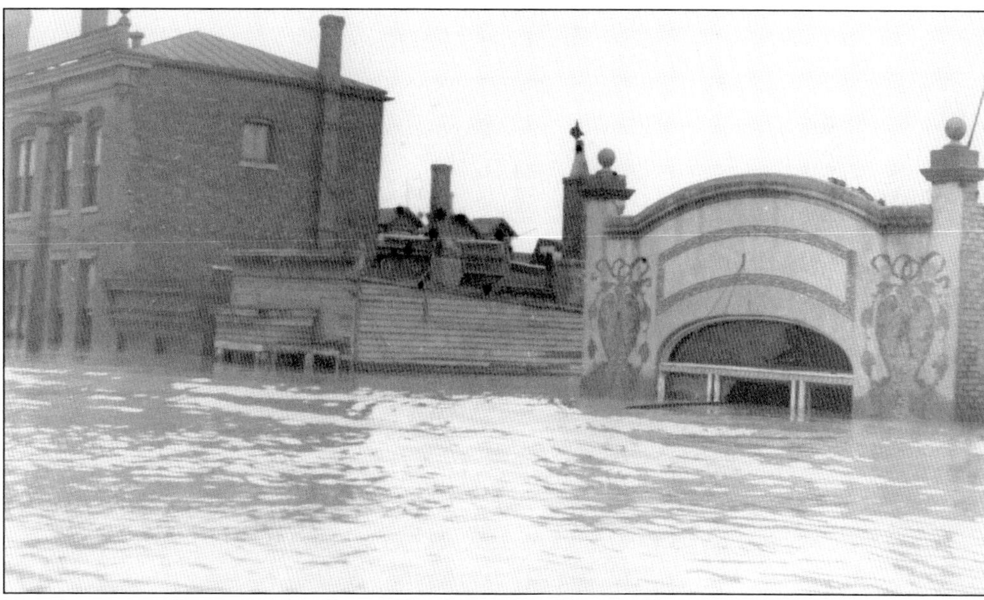

No Gambling Today. The Great Flood struck Jeffersonville in the middle of its "decades of decadence." This photograph captures part of the 100 block of West Court Avenue, where many of Jeffersonville's notorious gambling establishments resided. (Photo: Jeffersonville Township Public Library)

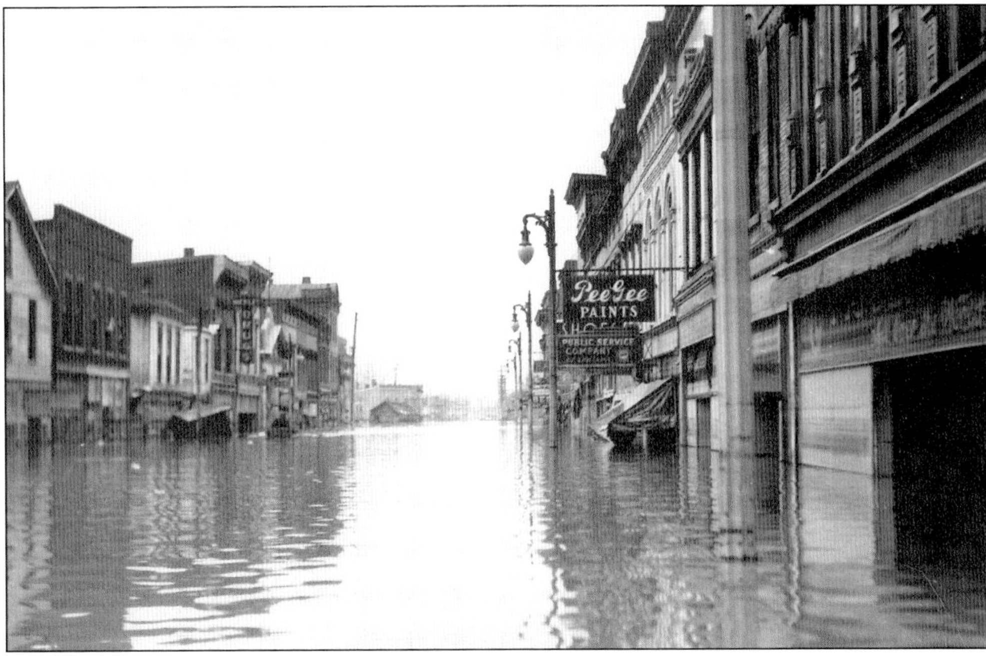

Water Receding on Spring Street. Flood waters drained out of Jeffersonville after the crest on January 27, when it nearly reached the globes of Jeffersonville's street lights. This photograph shows the receding water at the 400 block of Spring Street looking north. (Photo: Jeffersonville Township Public Library)

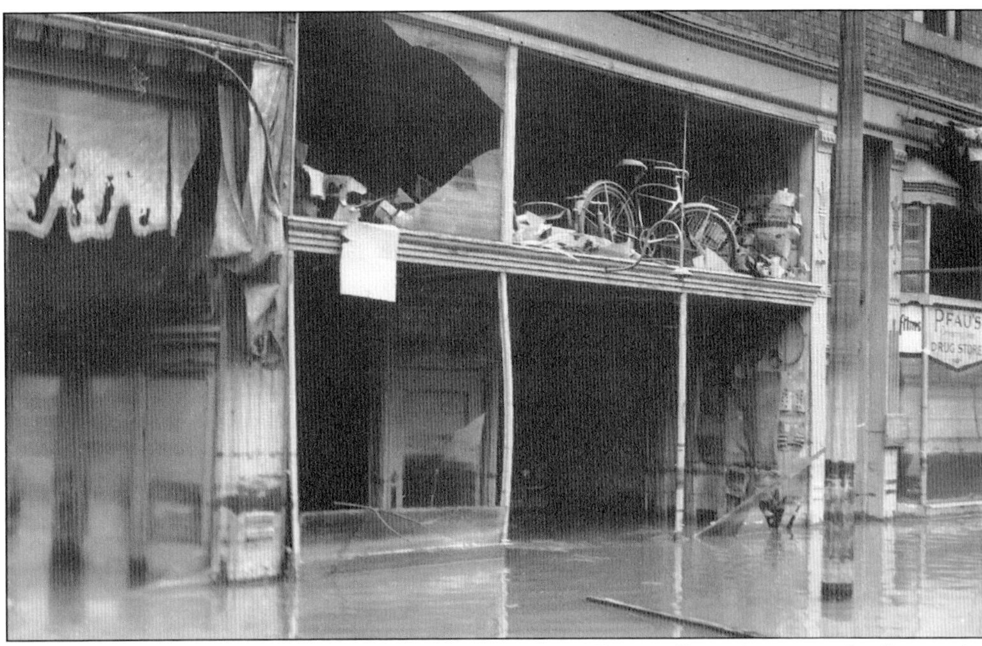

Pfau's Drug Store. Those brave enough to return to Jeffersonville as the waters finally receded witnessed widespread property damage such as this. The current broke out many of the city's windows and soaked, removed, or otherwise destroyed merchants' stocks, such as those in this photograph of Pfau's Drug Store on Spring Street. (Photo: Jeffersonville Township Public Library)

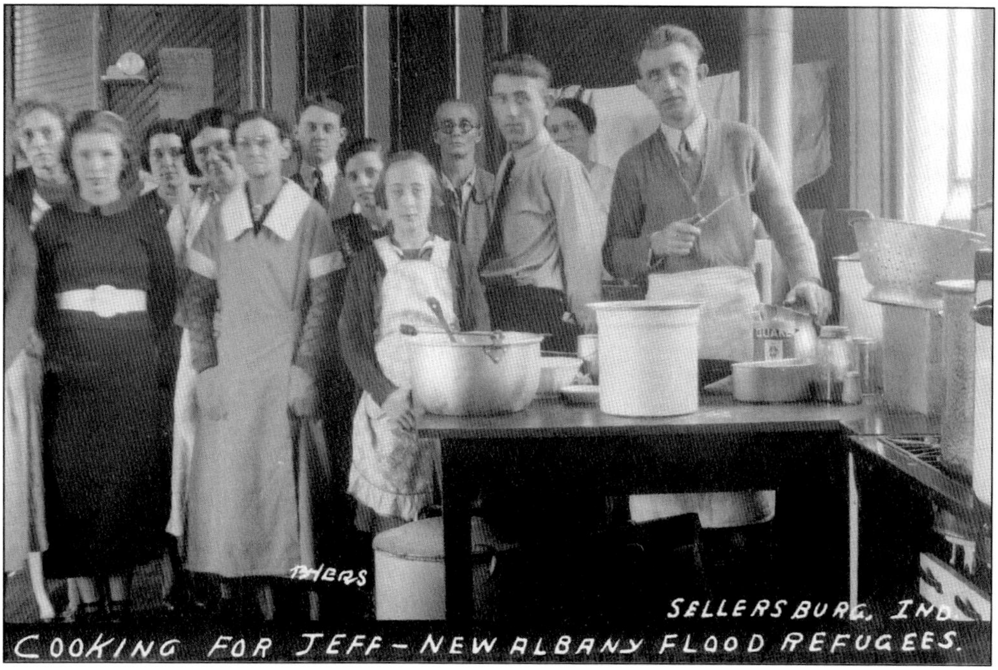

HOSPITALITY FOR FLOOD REFUGEES. Those who escaped the flood waters found gracious hosts in cities and towns that escaped the destruction of those in the Ohio Valley. Some refugees traveled as far as Indianapolis, but a great many found refuge in places like Sellersburg, pictured above, where volunteers prepared meals for the cold and hungry refugees. The Red Cross and the army greatly assisted in the evacuation and relief effort. Officials established a missing persons agency, but many families would have to endure days and even weeks of separation from their loved ones. (Photo: Jeffersonville Township Public Library)

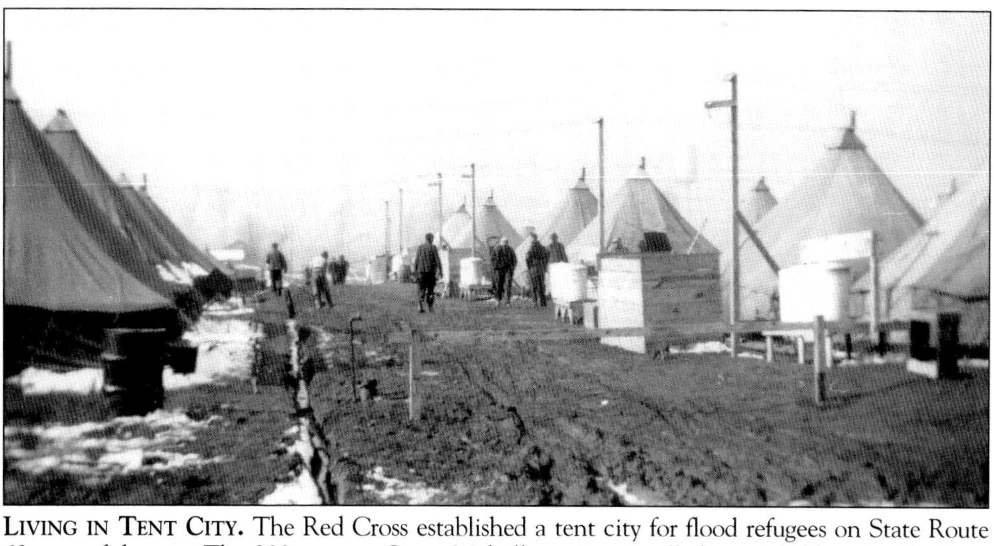

LIVING IN TENT CITY. The Red Cross established a tent city for flood refugees on State Route 62 west of the city. The 200 tents at Camp Melville, as it was called, provided housing for those displaced by flood waters. Tents included cots and bedding, a table and chairs, a stove for cooking and heating, and electricity for lights. Weeks of cleanup and rebuilding followed the high water before families could return to their homes. (Photo: Jeffersonville Township Public Library)

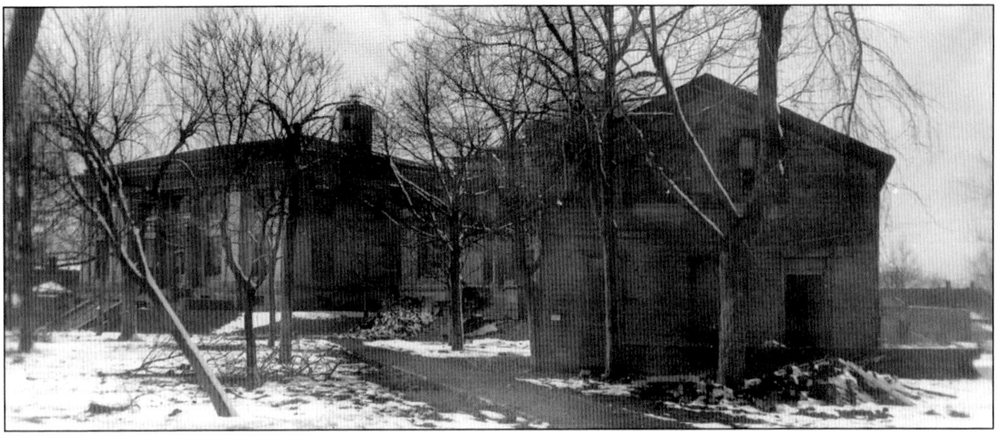

HOUSE RELOCATED TO WARDER PARK BY THE FLOOD WATERS. Warder Park has given the people of Jeffersonville a central gathering place over the years for entertainment, celebrations, and commemoration. In February of 1937, it symbolized the suffering of Jeffersonville's citizens. The flood water lifted many houses off their foundations and deposited them in unlikely locations, such as the one here in Warder Park. Some remain who remember the flood, such as Naomi Mitchell of Jeffersonville, who recalled seeing "everything hanging in the trees in Warder Park: clothes and parts of houses." This photo serves as a stark reminder that the flood struck in wintertime, thus adding to the misery of flood victims. (Photo: Katherine Huddle)

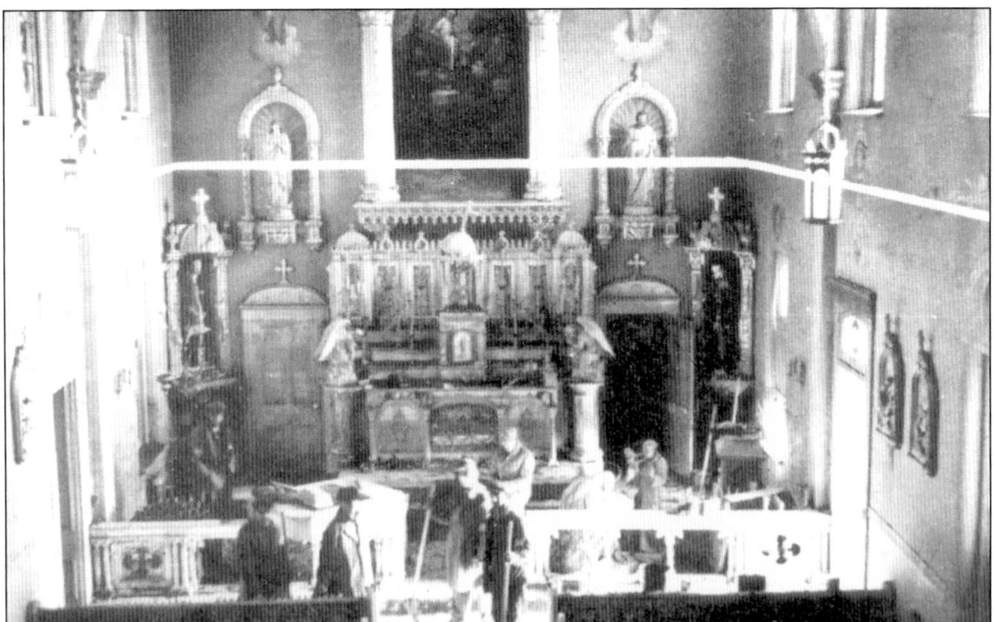

ST. ANTHONY OF PADUA AFTER THE FLOOD. Jeffersonville's downtown churches suffered greatly in the flood. This photo of the interior of St. Anthony of Padua after the flood shows a line demarcating the height reached by flood waters. Seminarians from Mount St. Francis joined parishioners in cleanup operations at the parish on Maple and Wall Streets. Several of Jeffersonville's congregations relate that as the flood water reached into their sanctuaries, the water floated up the lectern or pulpit on which sat the Holy Bible, only to return the Good Book undamaged to its original location after the water receded. (Photo: St. Anthony of Padua)

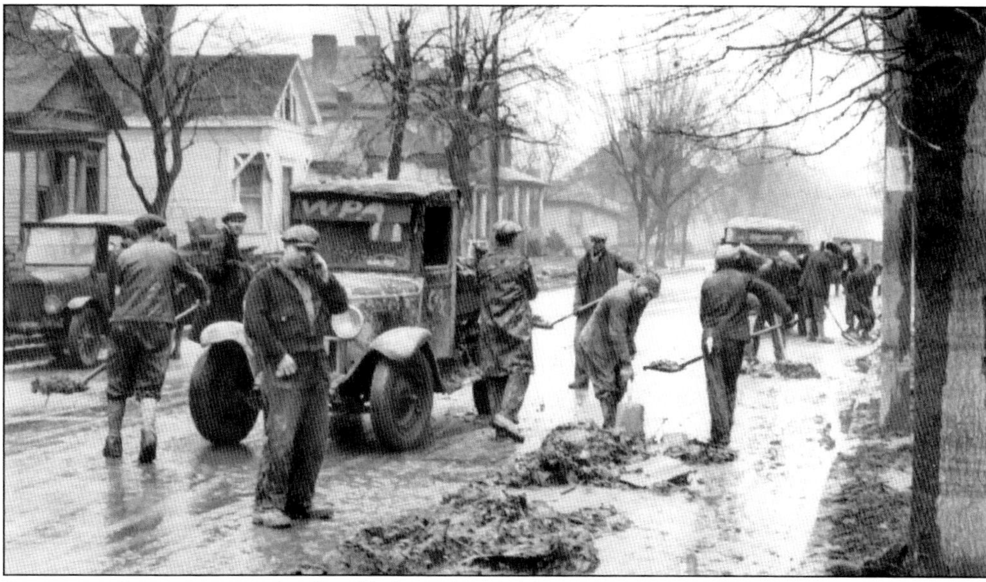

Cleanup Operations. The flood left mud and debris everywhere. Many who have remodeled their homes and businesses years later have reported finding mud hidden inside walls, sometimes many feet above ground level. Many agencies contributed to the flood cleanup, including representatives of the Depression-era Works Progress Administration, seen here shoveling mud off of Maple Street. (Photo: Jeffersonville Township Public Library)

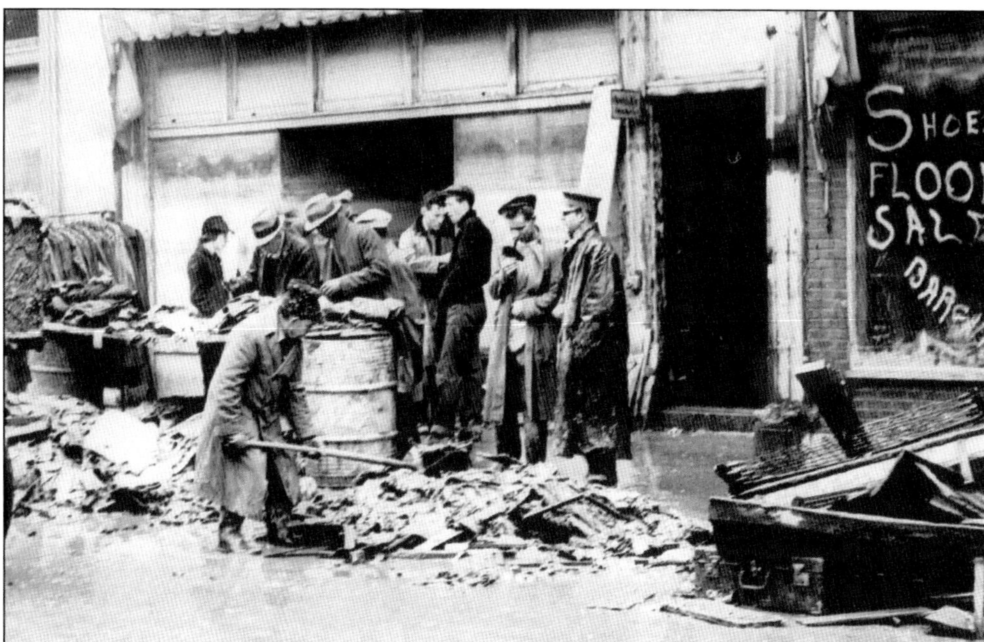

Flood Sale Bargains. Those businesses who could salvage some of their stock offered it at steep discounts in flood sales such as the one above on Spring Street. Most returned to find nothing of value. The time-tested practice of placing goods on high shelves or on a second floor could not compete with the record-setting flood waters. Acting Mayor Coots estimated the city's loss at over $10,000,000. (Photo: Jeffersonville Township Public Library)

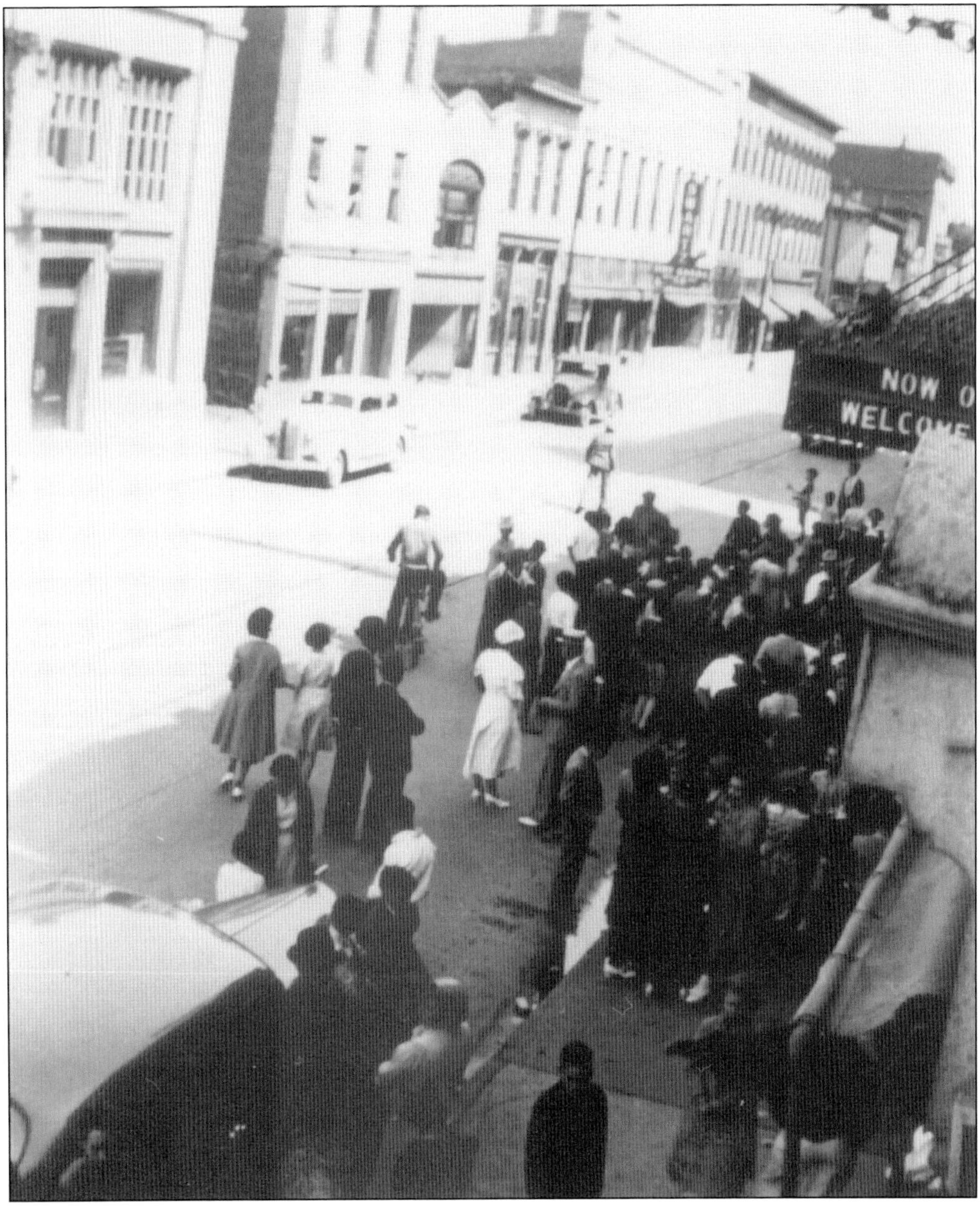

REOPENING OF THE LEROSE THEATER. Eventually the city cleaned itself up, utilities reestablished service, businesses restocked, and homeowners rebuilt. Life had begun to return to normal. The reopening of the LeRose Theater on Spring Street, however, offered the people of Jeffersonville quintessential proof that their suffering was over and they could now have fun again. This photograph, looking down from an upper window at Schimpff's Confectionery, shows a crowd gathering under the LeRose marquee. Just a few weeks before, Warren Volmer, as recounted in *Mud, Sweat and Tears*, had taken a light bulb out of that marquee as a souvenir of his boat ride down flooded Spring Street. But on this day the sign read, "Now Open. Welcome," and the citizens of Jeffersonville could enjoy themselves before World War II, the baby boom, suburban living, shopping malls, and urban renewal would gradually change what many had come to know as Jeffersonville in the pre-flood years. (Photo: Schimpff's Confectionery)

Eight

VANISHING

CHANGED OR GONE FOREVER

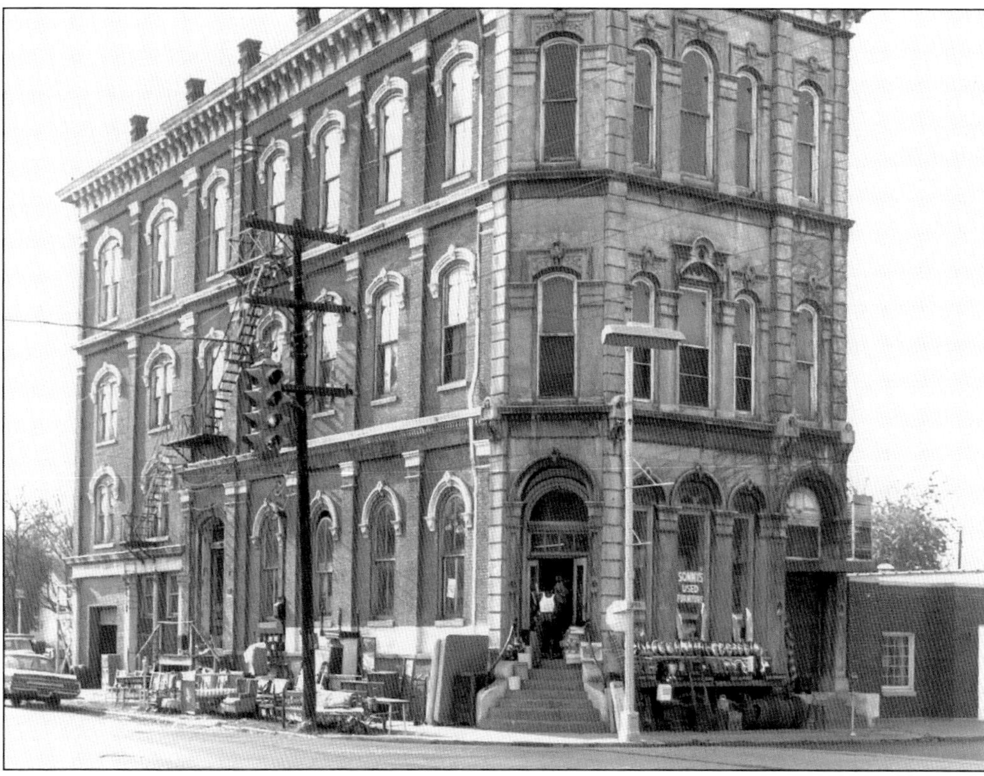

FIRST NATIONAL BANK OF JEFFERSONVILLE. This imposing brick and stone structure stood on the northwest corner of Spring and Market Streets. The First National Bank of Jeffersonville built it in 1870 (see page 74) and occupied it until its merger with Clark County State Bank in 1931. The building was once one of Jeffersonville's tallest buildings but its fortunes declined with much of the rest of downtown in the 1950s and 1960s. It housed a second-hand store in its last years before demolition in October of 1968. (Photo: Terry Stackhouse)

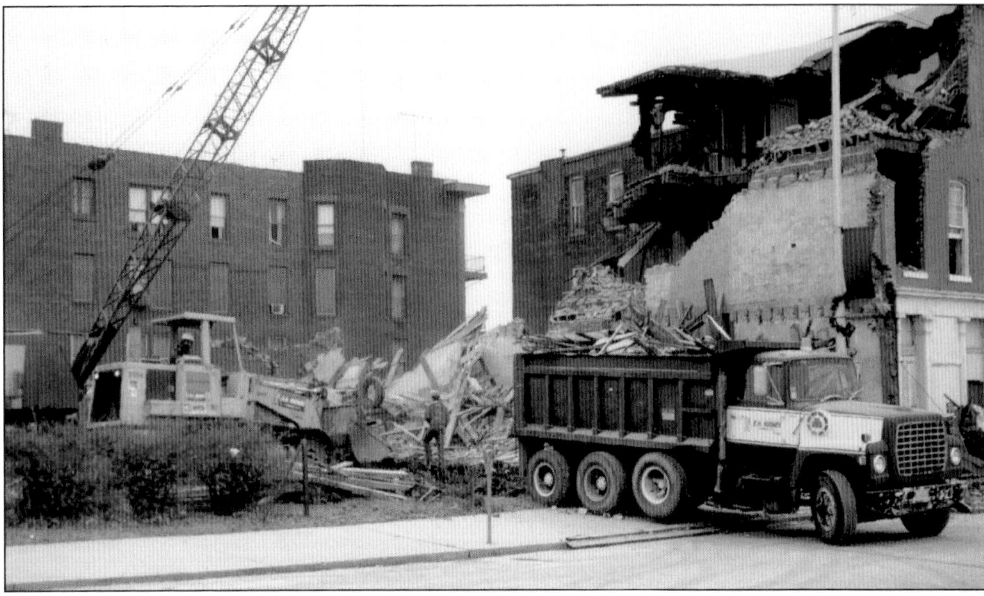

STAUSS HOTEL. The Stauss Hotel, built in 1867, survived the urban renewal era as the Riverview Hotel. Many divorced men, among the other downtrodden, who found refuge there came to know it as "Heartbreak Hotel." Developers renovated the structure and reopened it in 1984 as the Golden Turtle Inn, but the business proved unviable. The building's final owner deemed the structure "unstable" on account of damage from weather and vandals. It met the wrecking ball and bulldozer in fall 1989, 122 years after its construction. (Photo: Tom McCartin)

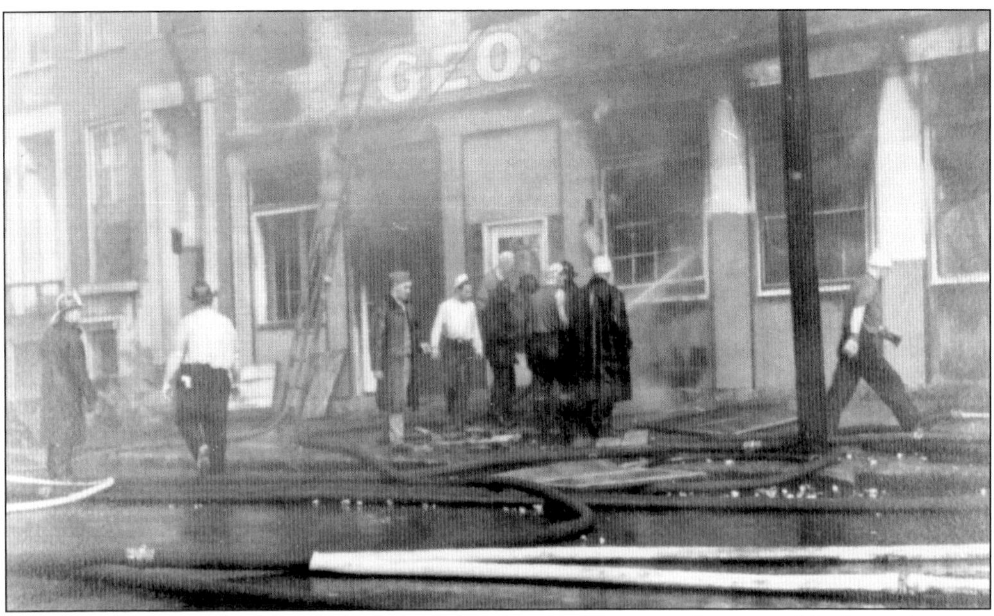

PFAU OIL BUILDING. George Pfau's Sons Oil Company occupied a prime block on the river opposite Spring Street and the Stauss Hotel since the company's founding in 1869. A fire swept through the building in 1944 forcing the company to relocate its business to Wall Street. This photo shows firemen and company workers after the fire has taken its toll. (Photo: George Pfau's Sons Oil Co.)

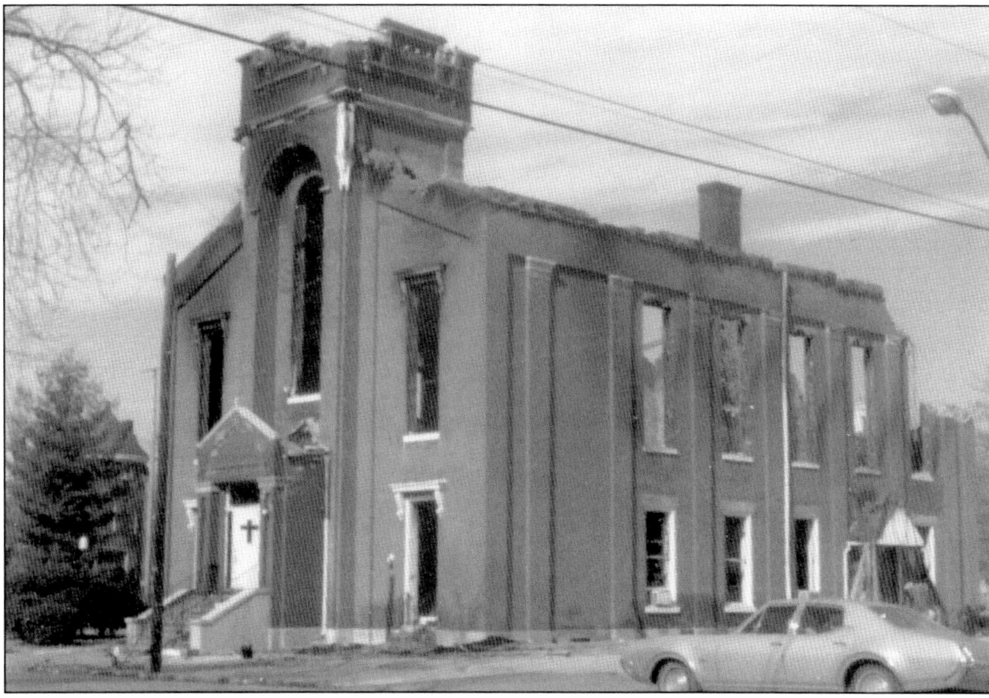

WALL STREET UNITED METHODIST CHURCH. Wall Street Methodist's historic church, built in 1860, burned early in the morning on February 9, 1979. The wind chill factor on that frigid morning hovered at 20 below zero, hampering firefighters' efforts at saving the structure. Historic Wall Street, mother church of many of the area's other Methodist congregations, would end up with one of Jeffersonville's newest church facilities. Fire inspectors would rule it an act of arson. (Photo: Wall Street United Methodist Church)

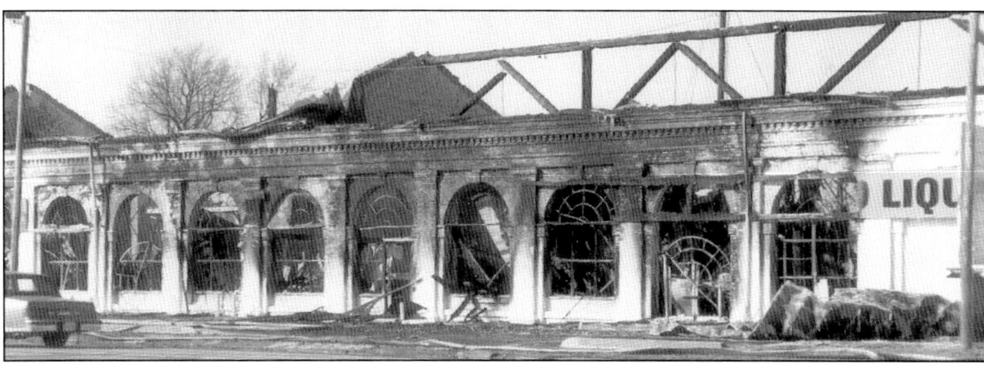

CONFLAGRATION AT THE OLD QUARTERMASTER DEPOT. The U.S. Army deactivated the Quartermaster Depot on June 30, 1958, and parceled out the property to a number of buyers. The army retained a segment of the site for a reserve post, but the U.S. Census Bureau, Kitchen Kompact, and Kessler Distilling procured large portions. The depot's most famous portion, its original quadrangle, was purchased by Joseph H. Conner and converted into a low-rent shopping center. The facility deteriorated over the years and an entire corner of the structure even burned in January of 1992, as shown in the photograph above. The Historic Landmarks Foundation of Indiana placed the old depot on its top-ten most endangered sites in 1996. The city of Jeffersonville purchased the property for adaptive reuse as a commercial and residential development. (Photo: Susan O'Neal)

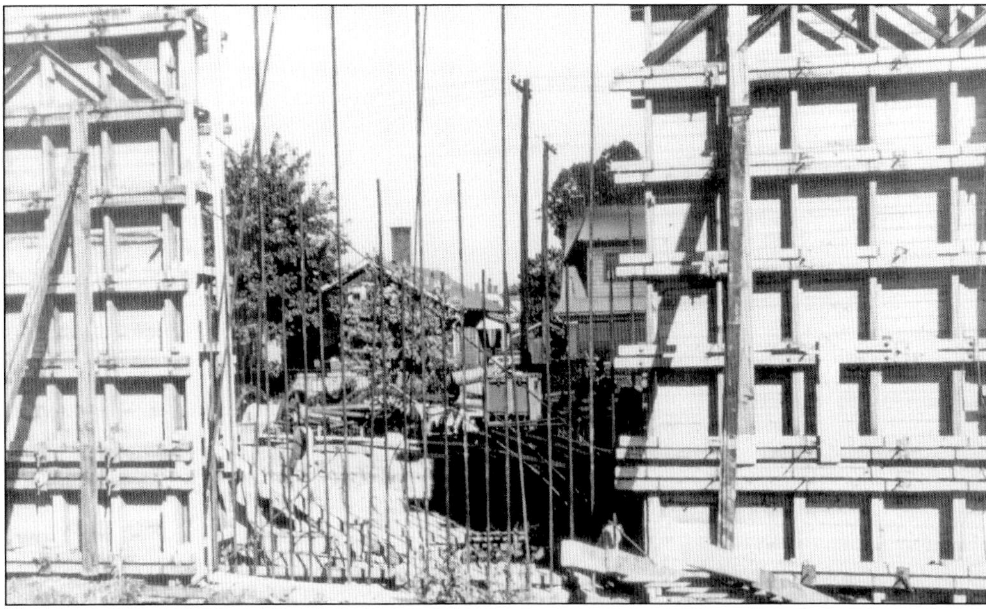

FLOOD WALL AND LEVEE UNDER CONSTRUCTION. The federal government constructed Jeffersonville's old levee shortly after the flood of 1884. The dike protected most of Jeffersonville through the swells of 1907 and 1913, but it proved no match for the Great Flood of 1937. An unnamed Jeffersonville official growled during the 1937 flood, "In this age of motors and good roads there is no reason to build a city on a river subject to floods. . . .The government will probably decline to spend millions upon a levee, preferring to lay out a modern city near Charlestown or on other high ground." Jeffersonville did get its new levee and the Corps of Engineers spent millions to build it between 1940 and 1945. The area lost some historic structures and some homes lost a river view, but floods have not posed a threat since the barrier's completion. (Photo: Dennis and Debbie Duffy)

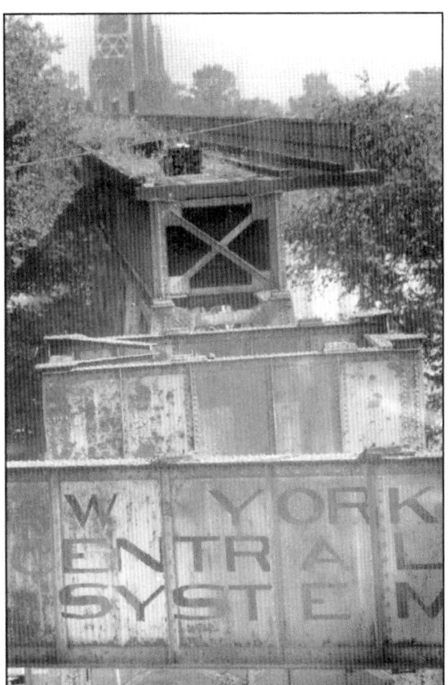

THE BRIDGE TO NOWHERE. The New York Central Railroad (originally the "The Big Four") merged with the Pennsylvania Railroad in 1968 to form Penn-Central. The merged company found itself with two routes across the Ohio, so it closed the Big Four Bridge and redirected all traffic across the Pennsylvania Bridge at Clarksville. The railroad removed the bridge's rusting approaches in 1974, as this photograph of the partially demolished approach on the Indiana side demonstrates. Several groups have proposed creative uses for the old bridge, but the latest plans call for its transformation into a footbridge linking downtown Jeffersonville with Louisville's Waterfront Park. (Photo: *Courier-Journal*)

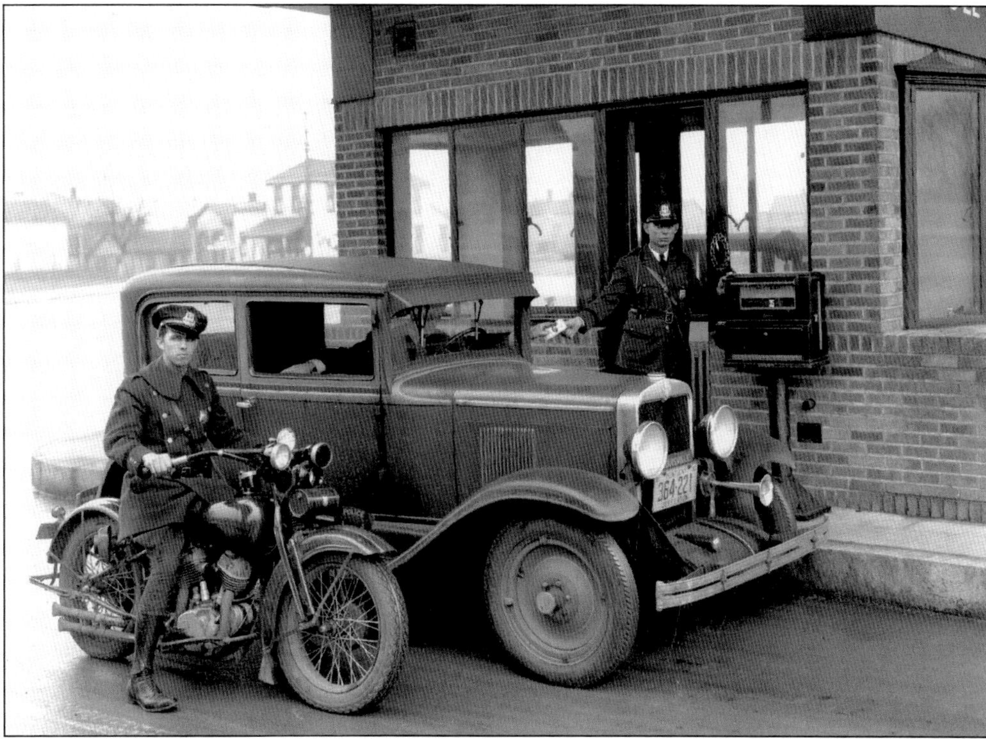

Changes on the Municipal Bridge. The Municipal Bridge collected tolls on traffic until 1946, when sufficient funds had been raised to retire the original construction bonds, thus removing the need for the toll gates and their officers as seen in these images. Many Louisville residents moved to southern Indiana to take advantage of the free route between newly constructed homes in Indiana and jobs in Kentucky. The bridge was renamed the Clark Memorial Bridge three years later for Gen. George Rogers Clark. The bridge commission's art deco-style administration building, just east of the Indiana approach and visible behind the toll gates in the image below, served as offices for the Kentucky Department of Transportation for a number of years. The Clark-Floyd Convention and Tourism Bureau later restored and reopened the building as its headquarters in 1997. (Photos: University of Louisville Photographic Archives)

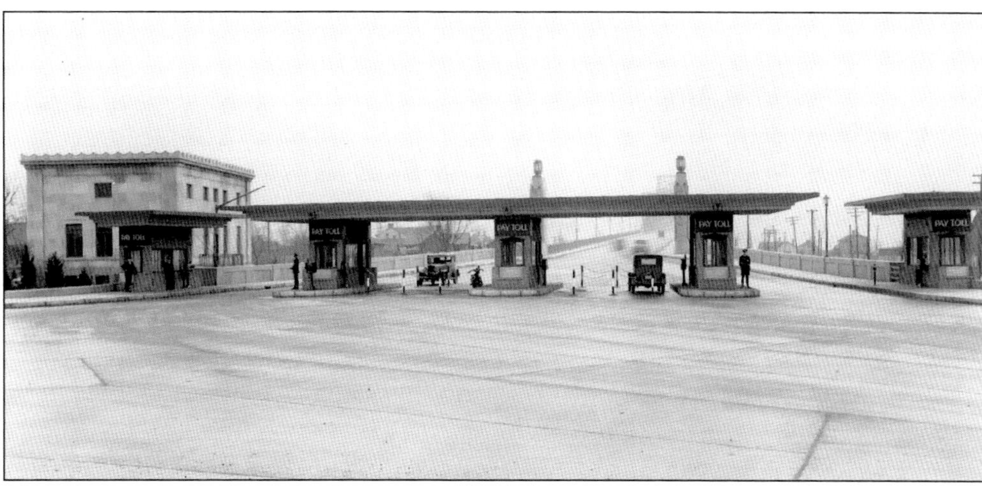

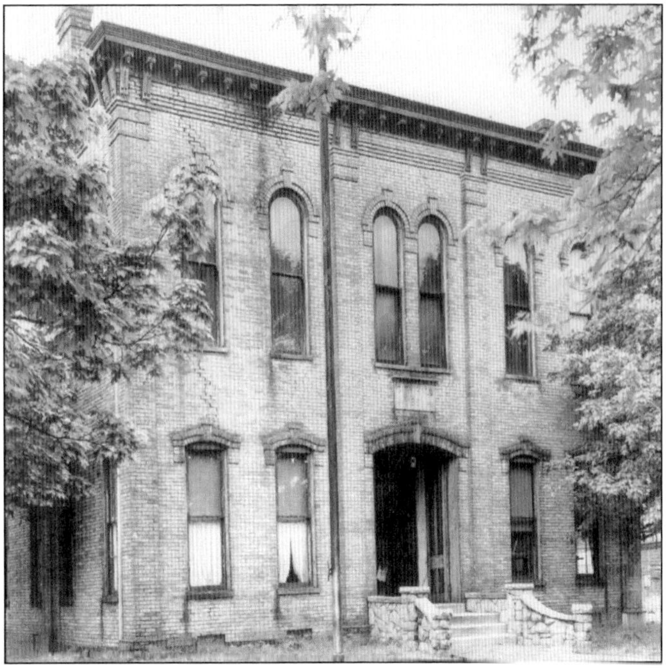

Jeffersonville City Hall. In 1935, the city transferred its offices from Jeffersonville's old city hall, built in 1881, to a newly built annex at the Clark County Courthouse. The old city hall deteriorated to the point that Jeffersonville Mayor Charles Hoodenpyl deemed it a "white elephant" for the city. The building on Market Street west of Spring met its fate in the 1950s during the urban renewal era. Jeff-Clark Preservation saved the city's old Pennsylvania Railroad station and relocated it to this site in 1987. (Photo: *Courier-Journal*)

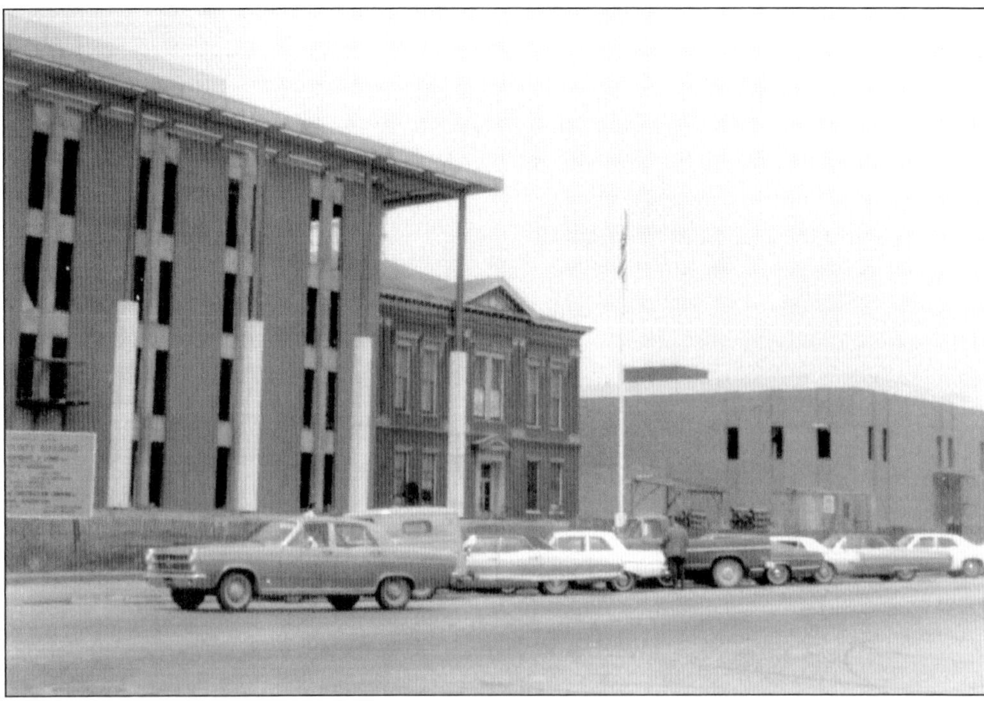

Clark County Courthouse. In 1878, Jeffersonville won back from Charlestown the honor of serving as county seat and the old courthouse stood here for almost 100 years. City and county officials deemed the aging brick structure inadequate and made plans in the late 1960s for a new, more modern-looking structure. The new City-County Building went up around its predecessor, as seen in this photograph, until the final records and furnishings could be transferred. The old building met the wrecking ball in 1970. (Photo: Conrad and Judy Storz)

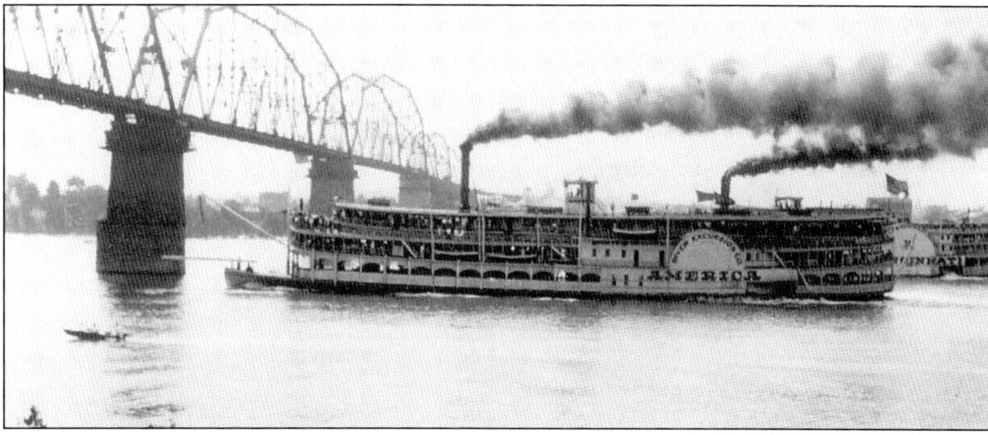

STEAMER *AMERICA*. The side-wheel steamer *America* began life at the Howard Yards in 1890 as the *Indiana*, a packet and mail steamer on the Cincinnati to Louisville route. It began a new life as an excursion steamer in about 1920 and transported many thousands of pleasure-seekers to Rose Island for the next 10 years as the *America*. One of the steamer's most famous episodes took place in August of 1928, when it raced the steamer *Cincinnati* to Rose Island from Louisville. The photograph above captures the boats just beginning the race, which the *Cincinnati* narrowly won. The *America* burned in Jeffersonville shortly after being tied up for the winter, just two blocks, ironically, from its birthplace. (Photo: E.M. Coots' Sons Funeral Home)

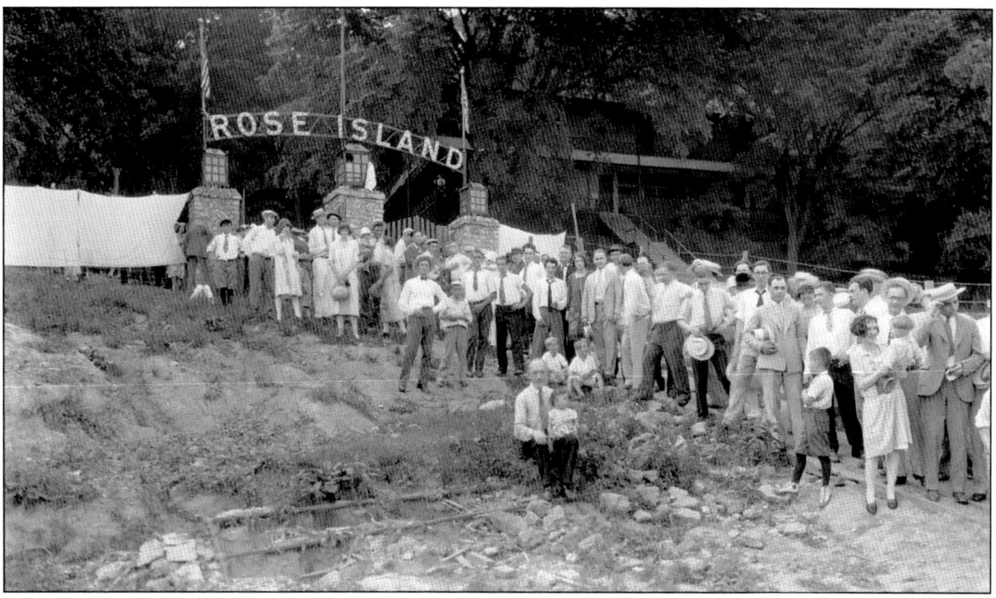

ARRIVING AT ROSE ISLAND. Rose Island, Jeffersonville and its neighbors' popular summer resort, thrived at its grounds near Charlestown in the 1920s. Happy entertainment seekers in their straw hats and summer dresses, as seen in this photograph from about 1925, arrived by the thousands at the park's ferry landing and ascended the hill to its main gate. The Great Depression put an end to the resort's heyday and choked off business. The 1937 flood finally destroyed it. The federal government acquired its land for part of the 10,649-acre Indiana Army Ammunition Plant, on which construction began in 1940. The army deactivated the plant in the 1990s and visitors to the new Charlestown State Park, created on a portion of the property, can still see ruins of the old bridge that served the resort. (Photo: University of Louisville Photographic Archives)

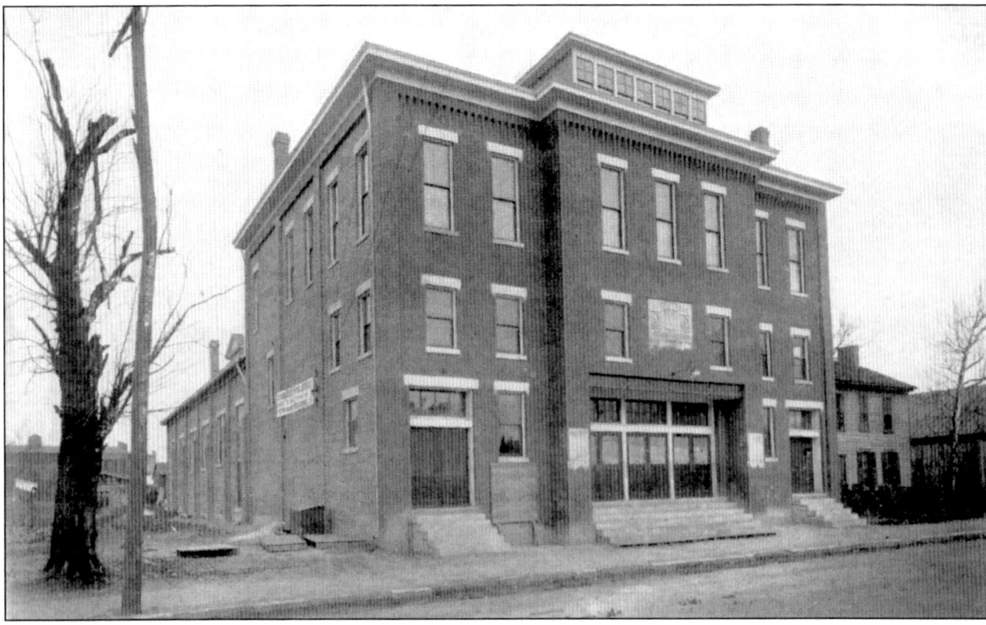

THE ARMORY. In 1908, the Knights of Pythias built a new lodge building and auditorium at 428–430 Pearl Street. It was known as the Armory on account of its construction on the site of the city's old Wigwam Armory. The Knights of Pythias also rented the facility out to other groups and it was at one time Jeffersonville's "largest and best hall." Musicals and plays were often staged in its large auditorium and the Jeffersonville High School basketball team even played there in the 1920s. The 1937 flood damaged the structure, but it reopened as a bowling alley and later as a roller skating rink before fire claimed it sometime after 1960. (Photo: *Souvenir Jeffersonville, Ind.*)

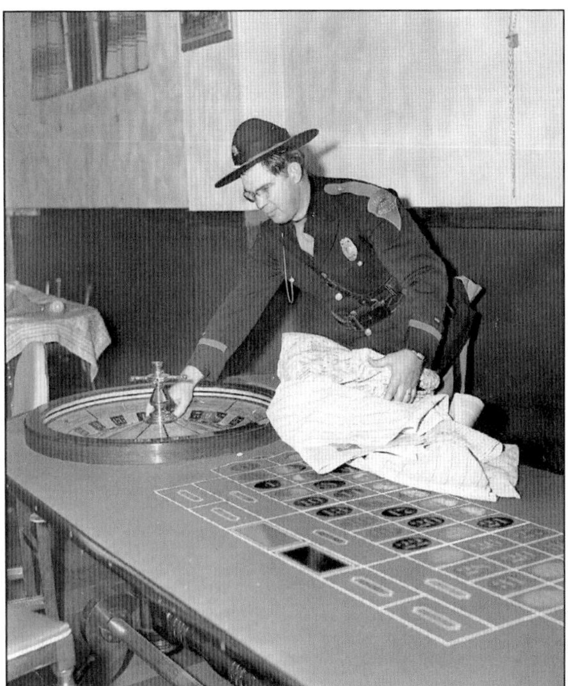

END OF GAMBLING. The mob-style killing of an innocent man at a local casino began changing attitudes toward the gambling parlors and their clientele. Enraged voters in 1938 elected James L. Bottorff as circuit court judge, for the former Clark County prosecutor had promised to close down gambling in the county. Buttorff succeeded in closing down the major clubs, but the illegal establishments reopened after World War II. When investors brashly constructed a large new parlor called Casino X (today's American Legion Hall), Judge Bottorff had enough. Two weeks later, in January of 1948, 75 Indiana State Police troopers raided the Court Avenue gambling parlors, arrested 63 people, and destroyed their gambling equipment. (Photo: *Courier-Journal*)

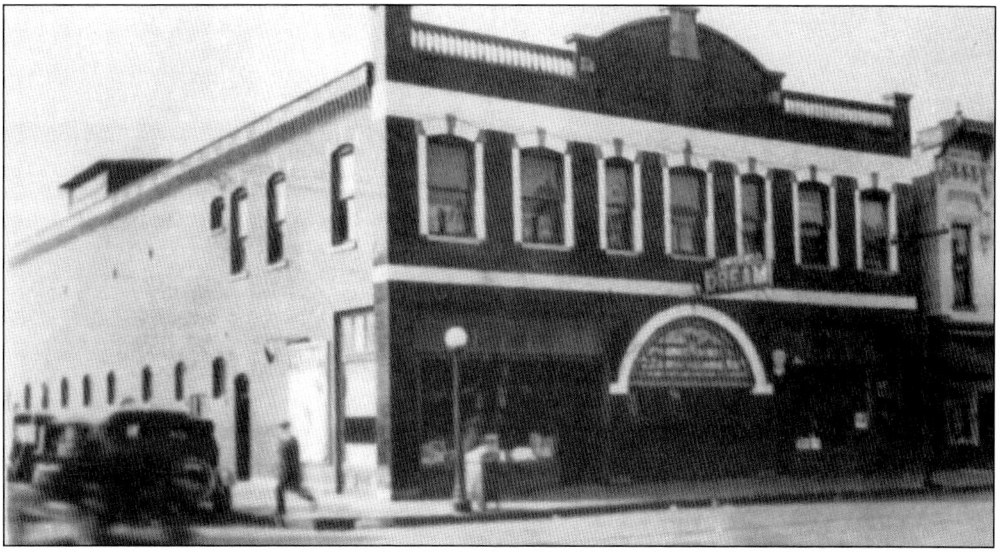

DREAM THEATER. Ice cream manufacturer Michael Switow built the Dream Theater shortly before 1910. The theater featured both movies and stage shows, such as performances during World War I by the Musical Comedy Company. Admission in those days was just 5¢ or 10¢. The Dream closed its doors in about 1950, leaving the LeRose as Jeffersonville's last downtown movie theater. (Photo: Jeffersonville Township Public Library)

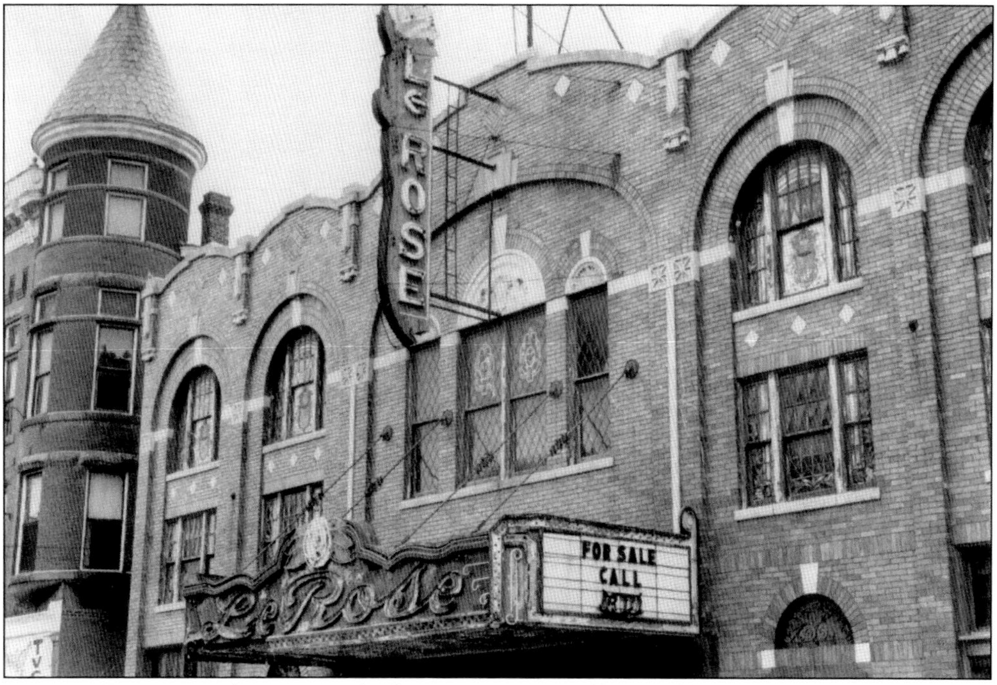

LEROSE THEATER. The LeRose, built in 1920, was Jeffersonville's other great movie palace for many years. Michael Switow's Jeffersonville Amusement Company also originally operated the LeRose. This photo depicts the forlorn theater in 1969, about five years after it had closed. None of the theater's original interior (see page 26) remains today, but developers have restored the exterior and renovated the building into office space. (Photo: *Courier-Journal*)

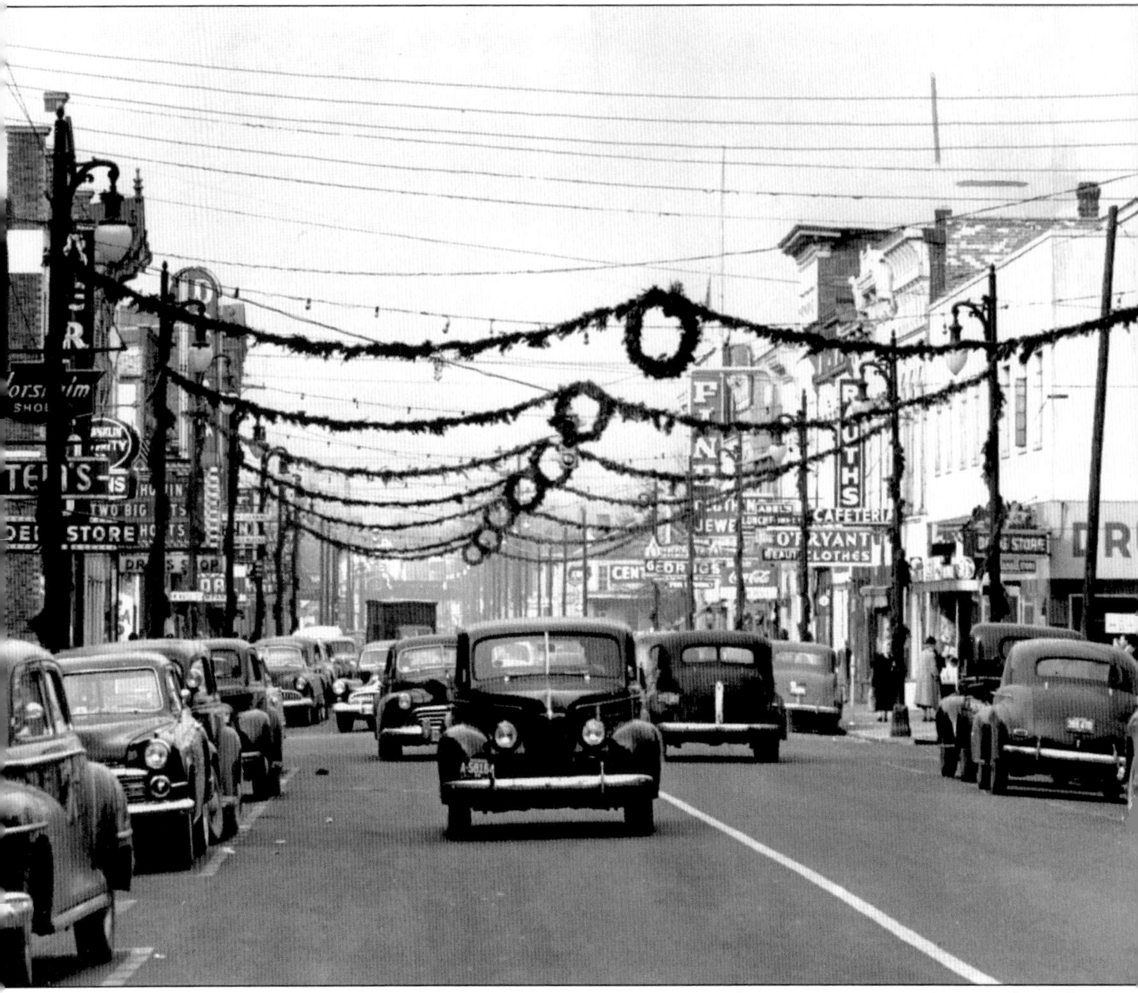

A BYGONE SCENE OF DOWNTOWN JEFFERSONVILLE AT CHRISTMASTIME. Cars jockey for parking in this photograph of Spring Street decked out for the Christmas season in 1949. Cars, in fact, contributed much to the focal shift away from downtown. Plenty of free parking and new roads attracted consumers to suburban shopping centers such as Youngstown and the Green Tree Mall. And owning a car meant people were no longer forced to walk to the store, church, theater, or any number of destinations. In addition, the baby boom and the removal of tolls on the Municipal (now the Clark Memorial) Bridge led to an influx of new residents seeking more space than downtown could offer. Urban renewal, meanwhile, tore fabric from downtown's historic garment. Scenes such as the one above may linger in the memory of those who remember downtown's zenith and intrigue those born too late to experience it, but a great revitalization has begun in recent years. The outstanding work of Jeff-Clark Preservation, Jeffersonville Main Street Inc., the Historic Landmarks Foundation of Indiana, the city of Jeffersonville, and others has made this possible. (Photo: *Courier-Journal*)

Index

Bibliography

American Car and Foundry Company in Khaki. New York: American Car and Foundry Co., 1919.

Baird, Lewis C. *Baird's History of Clark County*. Indianapolis: B.F. Bowen, 1909.

Banta, R.E. *The Ohio*. New York: Rinehart, 1949.

Bates, Alan L., Martin C. Striegel, and Victoria L. Nugent. "Falls Cities Ferries: A Note." *Indiana Magazine of History* 95, no. 3 (1999): 255-283.

Bradley, George K. *Indiana Railroad: The Magic Interurban*. Chicago: Central Railfans' Association, [c. 1991].

Clark County Interim Report. Indianapolis: Historic Landmarks Foundation of Indiana, 1988.

Encyclopedia of Louisville. Edited by John E. Kleber. Lexington, Ky.: Univ. Press of Kentucky, 2001.

Fishbaugh, Charles Preston. *From Paddlewheels to Propellers*. Indianapolis: Indiana Historical Society, 1970.

Fisher, Richard Swainson. *Progress of the Republic. . . .* Edited by J.C.G. Kennedy. Washington, D.C.: W.M. Morrison, 1856.

Haffner, Gerald O. *Citizens Bank and Trust Co., An Informal History (1855-1985)*. Jeffersonville, Ind.: Citizens Bank and Trust Co., 1985.

———. *Informal History of Clark County*. Evansville, Ind.: Whipporwill Publications, 1985.

History of the Ohio Falls Cities and Their Counties, with Illustrations and Biographical Sketches. 2 vols. Cleveland: L.A. Williams, 1882.

Indiana at Vicksburg. Indianapolis: W.B. Burford, 1911.

Johnson, William S. *On Red Devils: A Tribute to Jeffersonville High School Basketball, 1906-1984*. William S. Johnson, 1984.

King, Mike. "Clark County Went to the Dogs, Then to Even Bigger Gambling." *Courier-Journal* (Louisville, Ky.), 2 May 1979, sec. B.

Kramer, Carl E. "Jeffersonville Was Once Wide-Open to Gambling." *Evening News* (Jeffersonville, Ind.), 21 June 1989, sec. 1.

———. *100 Years. . .and Counting: The Jeffersonville Township Public Library, 1900-2000*. Jeffersonville, Ind.: Jeffersonville Township Public Library, 2000.

———. "Supplying the Troops: A History of the Jeffersonville Quartermaster Depot." *Evening News* (Jeffersonville, Ind.), 24 May 2001.

———. *Visionaries, Adventurers, and Builders: Historical Highlights of the Falls of the Ohio*. Jeffersonville, Ind.: Sunnyside Press, 1999.

Lovie, Henri, illus. "Evacuation of Louisville." In *Frank Leslie's Illustrated Newspaper* 12, no. 368 (18 Oct. 1862): 56-57.

Mud, Sweat and Tears: A Community Remembers the Flood. Edited by Bill Bolte et al. Jeffersonville, Ind.: Jeffersonville Township Public Library, [1985?].

Powers, Elvira J. *Hospital Pencillings; Being a Diary While in Jeffersonville General Hospital. . . .* Boston: Edward L. Mitchell, 1866.

Simons, Richard S. and Francis H. Parker. *Railroads of Indiana*. Bloomington, Ind.: Indiana Univ., 1997.

Souvenir, Jeffersonville, Ind.: City of Opportunities. N.p., [c. 1910].

Sweeney, Margaret. *Fact, Fiction and Folklore of Southern Indiana*. New York: Vantage Press, 1967.

Watt, William J. *The Pennsylvania Railroad in Indiana*. Bloomington, Ind.: Indiana Univ., 1999.

Waud, Alfred R., illus. "Jeffersonville, Indiana." In *Picturesque America; or, the Land We Live In. . . .* Edited by William Cullen Bryant. 2 vols. New York: D. Appleton, 1872.